ILLUSTRATED GUIDE TO BETTER FISHING

3RD EDITION

Edited By
Mark Thiffault

DBI BOOKS, INC.

ABOUT THE COVERS

When it comes to rods, reels and the rest of the equipment a fisherman depends upon, there is one name everyone is familiar with — Zebco.

On the covers you will find a good selection of Zebco PROSTAFF rods and reels.

To the far left is a PROSTAFF bait casting reel that features magnetic spool control. That reel is on a Zebco PROSTAFF 5½-foot precision graphite composite rod (medium-heavy action). It's a nifty worming rig. In the center is a rod-reel combination that will look familiar to everyone! The reel is Zebco's PROSTAFF spincast offering as seen on a 5-foot precision graphite composite PROSTAFF rod. This outfit is ideal for jigging or bait fishing.

To the far right is a highly dependable, all-around bass, pike (anything-you-want-to-go-after) fresh water combo. The Zebco PROSTAFF spinning reel is bound on a Zebco PROSTAFF 6-foot, medium-action precision graphite composite rod.

Technical assistance provided by Ed Shirley and Sons Sports, Inc., Palatine, IL. Photo by John Hanusin.

EDITORIAL DIRECTOR
Jack Lewis

PRODUCTION DIRECTOR
Sonya Kaiser

ART DIRECTOR
Gary Duck

ARTISTS
Denise Comiskey
K.T. Bunn

PRODUCTION COORDINATOR
Nadine Symons

COPY EDITOR
David Rodriguez

PHOTO SERVICES
Lori Arsenault

PUBLISHER
Sheldon Factor

Produced by

GALLANT CHARGER

OUTDOOR GROUP

ISBN: 0-87349-100-9   Library of Congress Catalog Card Number: 81-70997

CONTENTS

INTRODUCTION

American anglers are fortunate to have some of the world's finest journalists reporting on the sport. In descriptive prose and wonderful photographs, these journalists show 'n tell fishermen how to be more successful...have more fun...get more enjoyment out of life.

In puzzling over what this book should contain, the editor sought a freshwater companion volume for last year's SALT-WATER FISHERMEN'S DIGEST. This book should contain some saltwater angling, but the bulk should be freshwater fishing, covering all seasons of the year, and for as many different species as possible. Studies say more people catch panfish than any other type, so you've got Jim Dougherty's tips for brawling with "stud" perch and Soc Clay's technique for catching king crappie. Bass fishermen are...well...fanatic in their pursuit of this species, so you'll learn how to take 'em on top in spring, with live bait in summer, and by vertical jigging in cold months. We went out and caught a pair of chapters on walleye and sauger, found hot weather hawg stripers, monster muskies in miserable weather, and a trio of trout chapters. If you ever wanted to know about downrigger fishing or how to troll deep-water reservoirs, Chapter 9 is for you. Don't overlook the catfishin' chapters, or the silver salmon chapter at the end of this book — makes *you*

want to head "North, to Alaska."

The saltwater angler hasn't been ignored. There's Pete Fosselman's diary of a 10-day tuna trip, Hawaiian marlin fishing, barracuda and summertime sand bassin', plus a redfish report. Don't have a boat? How about fishing from one of our nation's numerous piers? Chapter 18 shows you how. Finally, to keep your expensive fishing stuff in top shape, you get a full chapter on rod, reel and line maintenance.

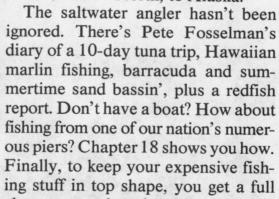

What you have here are 24 chapters full of fishing information, written by the best in the business. Enjoy them — and the greater success you will realize on the water!

Mark Thiffault
Capistrano Beach, California

CHAPTER 1

STICKING STUD PERCH

The Best Fishing You Can Find —
And Find Everywhere! — Is The Search
For Perch. Try It!

Some of the best perch spots are overlooked and ignored by anglers seeking more glamorous fish, but matched with light tackle, perch are big game. This three photo sequence shows soft presentation (top) start of retrieve (center), desired result (bottom). Bigger fish are normally found deeper.

Author (opposite page) took these husky bluegill on fast-sinking line and Woolly Booger flies. Fish had suspended at 20 feet in 30 feet of water. Author "counted 'em down."

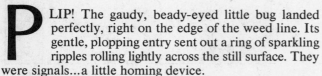

By Jim Dougherty

PLIP! The gaudy, beady-eyed little bug landed perfectly, right on the edge of the weed line. Its gentle, plopping entry sent out a ring of sparkling ripples rolling lightly across the still surface. They were signals...a little homing device.

Picking up slack in the four weight flyline, I turned the bug's nose in my direction with a quick twitch. Blup! Pause...blup! Digging its nose into the water, kicking, rubber legs jiggling frantically. More signals...blup!

It was time. I could see it coming. Beneath the lure, a subsurface boil, the vortex created by an upward spiraling fish skidding to a halt — contemplation — he's thinking about it.

Twitch! Sploosh! The four weight swoops up, not too hard, just let the needle-sharp hook meet the aggressive strike. The rod arcs in a thrumming bow as the fish surges in the circling, stacatto fight typical of a husky perch, a good one. I can feel myself grinning as the circles narrow.

It's a brilliant, chunky male, round as a dinner plate, almost three fingers thick through the shoulders; a sunfish, actually, but everyone calls them "perch." I think this one

was a hybrid, crossed between a green sunfish, *Lepomis cyanellus,* and a bluegill, *Lepomis macrochirus.* At least, that was my best guesstimate of the creature's parentage. These fish are often mistaken for bluegill, but close observation of the mouth shows it's significantly larger, matching his more-aggressive temperament. Distinguishing between a pure sunfish and a hybrid by checking the gill cover lobe (ear) or the coloration of the two is not reliable. Here in Oklahoma, they often are referred to as "black perch."

It seems that all sunfish, purebred or otherwise, carry a hodge-podge of colloquial names. I have fly-fished for perch throughout the country, in any type of water I could find with free time to sneak off. I have caught them in Florida, with angling legend Homer Circle. Those fish, in a pond near his home, were a strain of big bream called "copperheads" locally. On a golf course in Wisconsin, I caught fine, big flashy perch my club member host called "stumpknockers," and in Georgia, the apparent same fish was called a "shellcracker." Throughout the West, in backwater swamps of Louisiana, on the outskirts of Chicago, and the oxbows of the Mississippi River in Arkansas, I

When wind comes up, a longer rod and heavier line overcome casting problems, as author demonstrates on mottled water surface of Oklahoma farm pond (left). The big popper was slurped (center) by broad-shouldered perch, which promptly headed for the center of the pond (bottom). He came to the stringer after a whoopingly good battle, author says.

have found an abundance of pugnacious perch. They come in all sizes and colors, carrying a variety of local names. What they are called doesn't matter, so long as they are there!

Once, I took a pair of International Game Fish Association (IGFA) flyrod world record bluegill out of a — I won't tell you where it is — reservoir in Idaho. There, surprisingly, the locals called them bluegill.

Flyfishing for the sunfish species has been one of my favorite pursuits for a long, long time. An entry in an old notebook bears testimony; *"June 21, 1952. 10 bluegill, 5 crappie on my flies. Red & yellow bug-eyes. Crappie averaged 2 lbs."* If I had a dime for every perch I've caught since, I would be a very wealthy fellow, but I wouldn't take the money for all the enjoyment they have provided.

Unless you're looking for IGFA record fish, nicknames or purity of perch species is unimportant. With the high incidence of hybridization among some sunfish, determining what you have caught can be a task.

The IGFA recognizes the following fish most often considered in the perch or sunfish family: Bluegill, Crappie (white and black), White Perch, Yellow Perch, Green Sunfish, Redbreast Sunfish, Redear Sunfish, and Warmouth. It takes a minimum weight of one pound to qualify in tippet classes of 2-, 4-, 8-, 12-, and 16-pound. Discounting crappie, which regularly attain that weight and size, it takes a helluva perch to weigh over one pound.

The true importance of this subject is the pure, simplistic pleasure in flyfishing for husky sunfish. Properly matched to the tackle, they are great sport. The old line that goes: "Pound for pound, nothing fights better than a bluegill," has merit. Not much eats better, either.

I am a strong supporter of catch and release, but I will kill the occassional batch of trout for the table, or keep the odd bass now and then. I have no such qualms about sacking up a pile of perch. Invariably, their numbers are excessive and harvesting is good for them. I happily string up gobs of succulent perch every year, trotting them off to a meeting with my fillet knife. In my book, it's tough to beat a plateful

You can't be certain what you'll attract when casting for panfish, since bass and other big predators occupy the same habitat. Wading angler (above) is about to lip lock a chunky black bass. (Right) Don't worry about keeping all of the perch you catch — it's good for the species. Few meals are better than fresh perch panfried to a crisp!

Unless you're interested in International Game Fish Association records, you needn't be concerned with genetic purity of panfish you put on stringer. They cross-breed readily and are known by many local names.

Notice the heavy competition the author has while lifting slack out of four-weight flyline. Such emptiness is usual and welcome for those tired of battling boaters, crowds.

Let's try a cast to the deepest part of this pond, and let the sinking flyline take the wet fly down to Lunkerville. Author will fish various depths until locating stud perch.

Wham! Rod arcs in pleasant bow as something solid takes hold and attempts to escape. In a second, wading author will move farther into pond, following fish's acrobatics.

Exhausted, broad-backed sunfish is exposed for camera and is headed for future main course. You don't need much finesse with these brawling fish, author says.

of fresh, crispy perch fillets. Top notch!

My friend, George Bennett, and I were enjoying ourselves completely this sunny, spring afternoon. Wading quietly with slow, careful steps we flicked soft, short 20-foot casts on the pond. The action was typical of spring — fast! Almost every cast was bringing a strike from one sort or other of tough, bug-sucking perch. About every fifth fish was a heavy-shouldered stud, the rod-doubling sort that makes you grin and shout.

There was a pattern in fishing this pond that seems typical everywhere mixed sunfish species coexist. Very close-to-shore casts, tight to rocks, logs and brush, produced instant strikes from green sunfish, a tenacious critter that seems to survive and thrive anywhere. If you miss a greenie, cast back again quickly. Greedy and aggressive, the are not easily spooked into backing off. If they weighed five pounds, it wouldn't be safe to go in the water!

The good bluegill lie farther offshore, mostly outside the weed line. They hit with a neat little "slurp" after a bit of topwater coaxing. Less suicidal than the greens, you can't miss a big one more than twice.

The bigger perch invariably hang on the outside perimeter of your fishing area, charging up from deeper water and often boiling under the bait before the final strike. Crappie come along frequently, as well as black bass that regularly take the size 8, 10, and 12 topwater bugs or wet flies. These generally are small fish, eight to 13 inches, but three- to five-pounders happen along often enough to spice things up — or ruin your day, depending on your perspective! There's more than a few of my perch flies swimming around Oklahoma ponds stuck in the lips of bruiser bass.

When the fish are really on, 'most any type of small top-water bug will generate action. On still, flat days with no surface clutter from wind, my preference is for simple,

The black stripe down the side of this stumpy bug eater denotes black bass. You'll frequently take smaller bass, and occasionally a bruiser will inhale your fly/popper/bug and leave.

On a typical outing, author's fishing buddies release your average half-pounders, to grow into stud perch!

Call it what you will, this is a huge sunfish and a good match for light tackle. Peak fishing time for all sizes is during spawn in the spring.

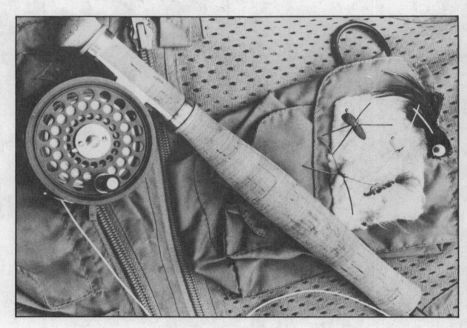

Few fish are so ideal to flycaster as is panfish. Bigger, wiser perch will require more finesse in presentation, but that's half of fishing challenge.

rubber-bodied spiders with four or six legs that twitch and wiggle in a spasmodic action that drives perch silly. If the wind is up, selecting a bigger-bodied popper that blurps audibly while producing more thrashing on the surface seems best.

Colors on top seem to be only marginally important. Long, light leaders and a gentle landing of the fly are sometimes called for in clearwater ponds where above-average-sized perch lurk. Older, they are a bit wiser. But, all in all, the myriad of subtleties most often associated with flyfishing are lost on the sporty sunfish.

Seasonally speaking, anytime from May through October is right on topwater bugs. Where waters warm quicker, the action starts sooner. The peak periods for fast action that fills stringers takes place when the fish are on the spawning beds. In Oklahoma, we get after them as soon as we've caught our breath from chasing spring turkeys. By mid-May the action's hot, running strong through the first of July. During the heat of summer, surface bites are best in the early or late hours of the day.

Topwater bugs aren't the only way, either. In fact, wet flies fished deep — down to 15 feet — are deadly producers. Oftentimes, even with good topwater action taking place, a sinker fished outside the area of surface-hitting fish

Author's wife, Sue Dougherty, enjoys a day on the water and is no slouch at handling long rod either. Panfish provide top sport for the whole family, and usually are found in close proximity to the house.

One of the more spectacular sights in nature is a fish blasting a topwater offering, in this case a rubbery-legged popper being ferociously attacked by the three-pound bass on the opposite page. Good fight!

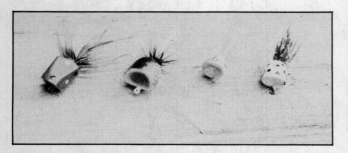

When wind picks up, a hollow-nosed popper that chugs and slurps in addition to presenting visual appeal is the key to perch performance (above). On an invisible leader, the popper awaits attention from fat, hungry sunfish (right).

is the key to nailing the true studs of perchdom. In the hot summer months, deep, slowly twitched flies like the Woolly Booger are pure killers.

When conditions call for deep stuff, my selection is a six- or seven-weight rod with a fast sink line, and a Johnboat or float tube to get farther offshore. The heavier rods allow longer casts that gets the fly down, and through, the depth where fish are holding.

I use a line with a sink rate of 4½ to 6 inches per second, so a count to 20 puts me in the 10-foot depth range. I can adjust up or down until fish are located. This is the way to catch the big boys. Midsummer days can be stiff-wind breezy, and the heavier combination is a real wind beater, too.

Deep fishing often produces other rewards. Perch are not the only takers. Good bass are often stuck. On larger impoundments, creeks or rivers, the catch on perch-sized

flies has yielded channel catfish, walleye, white bass, drum, and stripers, to name a few. It makes the game more interesting!

Overall, days such as that one George and I spent, with the fish eagerly busting bugs on top, are my favorite. A four-weight rod is plenty of stick, a two even more enjoyable if heavy brush or whipping wind is not a serious problem. The sweet "Twos" are great fun, matching up perfectly with a stumpknocker that wants to brawl.

But you know, the best part about perch is that there are so darn many of them, in so doggone many places: Places close to home; peaceful, ignored backwaters; overlooked sloughs; meandering creeks at the edge of town; city lakes in tidy, green parks; big, man-made reservoirs; and a zillion farm ponds. They are easy to find, inexpensive to get to, and they can brighten your days for a lifetime.

Author practices catch and release, especially with larger bass that aren't as toothsome as smaller ones. This gal provided great action and photographic record of relaxing day's trip.

CHAPTER 2

TOM MANN'S TOPWATER TWITCH

There's No Style More Exciting In The Angling World, And This Legend Shares His Secrets!

By Chris Altman

When fish meet steel on the silvery surface, anything can happen! This brawling seven-pounder is just about ready for a lip lock after lengthy battle. Try topwater baits anytime.

Tom Mann says you can fish topwater baits even in mid-day, but throw small stick baits into the shady patches. You could likely be rewarded with an explosive strike!

Heddon's Zara Spook has put more lunkers into livewell than perhaps any other topwater lure. It's effective on bass as deep as 20 feet when impoundment is clear.

T'S A SILVERY, shimmering dinner plate, one made of an ethereal china and flecked with glimmers of pure golden sunlight. The surface also is a boundary separating the air breathers from the gill-equipped, a boundary which often serves as a common meeting ground. For here the fish find food, from insects to frogs, mice to baby ducks, and anglers find a thrill unlike any other in the world of sportfishing.

Trout sip daintily at floating insects and bluegill pop 'most anything falling onto the water's surface, but it is those species of fish which we refer to as bass that smash helpless swimming creatures (or reasonable facsimiles!) in explosions of fins and foam and cause our hearts to skip and stutter. Pound for pound, black bass, striped bass, and white/striped bass hybrids provide more topwater entertainment than all other freshwater species combined. If you need a quick burst of energy, there's nothing like the eruption of an eight-pound bucketmouth on a Zara Spook, or a 30-pound striper violently engulfing a RedFin, to get the adrenalin surging.

"Topwater plugs are one of the best lures in existence for catching big fish. But even if that were not true," says angling legend Tom Mann, "topwater fishing would still be the most enjoyable way in the world to catch fish!"

Tom Mann, one of the greatest bass fishermen of all time, ranks topwater fishing among his list of favorite techniques. Hailing from Eufaula, Alabama, Mann was not only a founding father of modern-day bass fishing, but a leader in the angling industry as well. Under his guidance, Mann's Bait Company and Humminbird became household names — in fishing households, anyway — and the Fish World Company, Tom's most-recent undertaking, is a rapidly growing tackle manufacturer.

Topwater fishing, more so than any other form, is a learned art. From choosing the plugs to knowing when, where, and how to work them, no other angling technique is so seemingly simple yet so covertly complicated.

"The key to topwater fishing," says Tom Mann, "is knowing when to fish different types of plugs. Basically, I use minnow-type twitchers in calm water next to shallow cover, poppers and chuggers when the water is choppy, and stick baits when I'm fishing open water or relatively clear and deep water. A prop bait is kind of a catch-all topwater plug in that you can use it in place of any of the other three lure types. You just have to experiment to see what the fish prefer. And buzz baits are great lures to use when

Poppers like Rebel's Pop-R shown here are superb in choppy or dingy water. For years this noisy plug was called the "secret weapon" of pro bassers, but it was dropped from Rebel lineup until demand from anglers brought it back into the product line.

Fishing legend Tom Mann nailed this nice hawg bass using one of his firm's Fish World Pogo Minnow. He says you should forget about color — fish respond to the shape and action of the lure on the surface.

the fish are hitting topwater baits but are scattered, because you can quickly cover a tremendous amount of water with a buzzer."

Mann says most anglers believe that topwater baits should only be fished in the morning and evening. "That is a grave mistake, for topwaters are often productive throughout the day. In my opinion, the key to using topwater plugs in the middle of the day is fishing them in shade next to cover."

The tall, easy-smiling angler notes that all topwater plugs are worked with movements of your wrist. "To be a successful topwater fisherman, you need to learn the proper technique to fish each type of lure," he drawls.

"When fishing for black bass, you should concentrate on shallow water structures if the water is at all dingy. In clear water, switch to a stick bait and work it over the top of deeper structures in open water. Also, you should always use long casts in clear water and decrease the size of your line. For all-around use, 10-pound-test is ideal for topwater plugs, but you should increase the line size when fishing around heavy cover.

"The color of the plug is the last thing you should worry about," Mann states emphatically. "Fish are hitting the bait's silhouette and its movement. Those pretty colors are to catch the fisherman and his wallet."

For the most part, the same topwater lures are effective for black bass, hybrids and stripers, but they should be fished in different areas. Black bass are basically shallow-

A buzz bait worked under brushy overhang brought a topwater strike from this largemouth. It's good to use any time of day during the summer. See text.

water creatures which inhabit thick, cover-rich environments. Stripers and hybrids, on the other hand, are openwater fish which prefer a cool water temperature and therefore tend to remain most often in deeper water than the black bass. Topwater plugs for these striped fish are most effective in the spring when the cool water temperatures allow the stripers and hybrids to remain in the shallows. Too, they are also extremely effective whenever the fish are busting schools of shad on the lake's surface. Black bass and hybrids prefer lures of about the same size, while it takes a giant plug to attract the attention of a giant striper.

MINNOW-TYPE TWITCH BAITS

Typical black bass baits of this sort include the original Rapala, Storm's Thunderstick, Bomber's Long-A, Bagley's Bang-O-Lure, Mann's Stretch 1-Minus, and Fish World's Pogo Minnow.

For the most part, these four- to six-inch, pencil-like lures are the first topwater baits used in early spring. Cool water means inactive fish, and that calls for a bait with a slow, quiet retrieve...a bait that can be worked at a productive crawl over the top of a likely looking spot. When the surface temperature breaks the 50-degree mark, knowledgeable anglers begin working these lures over hard-bottomed spawning banks, focusing primarily on individual pieces of

Buzz baits enable anglers to cover a lot of water in a short time, but they're effective only on the largemouth bass. Or is it because we don't sling them at stripers, hybrids? Find out for yourself.

Tom Mann says that topwater baits shouldn't be relegated to the tackle box when the sun rises in the sky. Rather, use the right bait in the right situation and stand by.

structure such as stumps and brushpiles. The basic technique here is to cast the minnow imitation past the structure, let it sit for a moment, twitch it ever so softly, and then repeat this sequence until the lure is well beyond the structure. As the water warms, the presentation is accelerated. When the fish are aggressive, some anglers will "slosh" the bait over the surface, sometimes moving it three or four feet at a time.

In the spring, these baits are tremendously effective on largemouths, smallmouths, and hybrids when worked over expansive, shallow-water gravel flats.

Minnow imitations are superb striper baits as well, though larger lures like seven-inch Cordell RedFins, Storm's Shallow-Mac, Mann's Super Stretch 1-Minus, and seven-inch Rebel minnows are typically used. These gargantuan pieces of plastic are most effective when retrieved slowly and steadily just under the surface so that they leave a V-shaped wake like a fleeing shad. Likely areas include points dumping into the old river channel, shallow flats which are near deep water and crawling with schools of baitfish, and over the top of underwater humps.

Though topwater striper fishing is most often considered a spring sport, these big linesides can often be found busting acre-sized patches of shad on the surface during the summer and fall months.

Because bass often short-strike a buzz bait, it's wise to add a trailer or stinger hook to these baits. When used in open water, position hook so the point rides upward.

While there's no argument that topwater baits perform outstandingly well early in morning and late in afternoon, they can take fish during other times — especially at night. If you spot a school busting shad on surface, go and get 'em!

Most knowledgeable anglers agree that topwater lures are most effective when worked around aquatic vegetation. A weed bed that hasn't yet grown to the surface is prime topwater territory, as bass hide in cover and watch overhead.

Prop baits can be readily substituted for the other types of topwater lures, their sputtering and buzzing calling attention to them over a large area. Work all topwater baits with your wrists to maximize action and improve results.

STICK BAITS

Typical baits of this type include Heddon's ever-popular Zara Spook, Ozark Mountain's Woodwalker, Mann's Bait Company's Mann-Dancer, and Poe's Jackpot.

These lures are traditionally worked in a side-to-side manner known as "walking the dog." Although difficult to learn, the technique is well worth the effort. After the cast, leave about six inches of slack in your line, point your rod tip down toward the water's surface, and start snapping the rod downward in short, quick jerks while reeling at the same time. The key is establishing a cadence which swims the lure from side to side while bringing it back to you rather slowly. Experienced dog-walkers can work the bait back and forth over the same spot without moving it forward, and true experts can actually make the lure back up!

Stick baits are extraordinarily effective clear-water lures. Their sloshing dog-walk creates a tremendous surface action which attracts the attention of the predators lurking below, sometimes calling fish to the dinner table from 20

feet of water or deeper. Spooks and their kin are tremendous big bass baits, especially on deep, clear lakes.

For the most part, the same stick baits used for bass are also used when hunting stripers. Cordell's Pencil Popper, a six- or seven-inch plug which dances and splashes over the surface when worked with jerks of the rod tip, is one stick bait used principally for stripers. Stick baits are exceptional topwater baits to use for stripers on a clearwater impoundment as their loud surface display will attract the attention of even submarined stripers.

POPPERS AND CHUGGERS

Good representatives of these lures include Rebel's Pop-R, Poe's Blurpee, Heddon's Lucky 13, Storm's Chug Bug, and Arbogast's classic dynamic duo, the Jitterbug and the Hula Popper.

Easily recognized by their concave faces, these lures produce an audible "bloop" with each snap of the rod tip. The harder you pop the rod, the louder the "bloop" will be. When you want the lure to create a lot of surface commo-

A Cordell RedFin presented to a school of spring stripers resulted in a 46-pound trophy coming to the net. Huge!

When you spot any school of bass tearing up the shad on top, speed is important. Hurry over and throw a topwater.

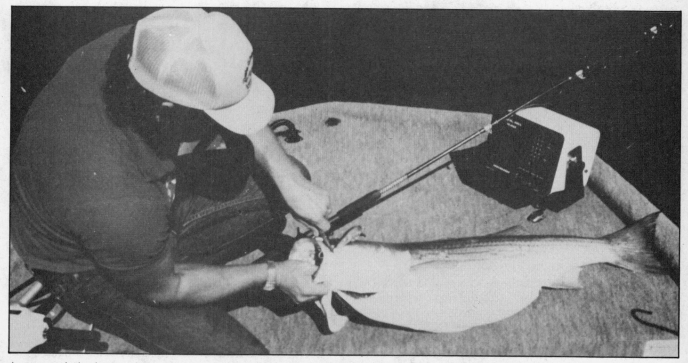

In general, the larger the species sought, the larger your bait should be. Huge plastic worms and seven-inch topwater lures are needed for the big bruisers like this striper. The presentation technique varies with situation.

Some topwater enthusiasts feel you must go big when after trophy fish, and this seven-pound, post-spawn largemouth nailed a seven-inch Cordell RedFin. Would she have hit smaller topwater if presented at same time?

tion yet remain in generally the same spot, a popper or chugger is your best bet. And when the situation demands fishing a topwater plug in choppy or stained water, pick a popper.

Poppers and chuggers are basically the only topwater lures which are truly productive at night. When you can hear fish chasing baitfish in the shallows, a black popper blooped in the vicinity will often bring a near instantaneous explosion of fins, foam, and spray. And a black Jitterbug

worked over shallow, submerged stump rows or weedbeds and producing an almost hypnotizing blip-blip-blip is often a deadly moonlighting technique.

PROP BAITS

Poe's "Ace in the Hole," Heddon's Dying Flutter, Smithwick's Devil's Horse, and Strike King's Prop Scout are typical lures of this type.

Prop baits are easily recognized by a set of small pro-

Hybrids in the four- to eight-pound range are often taken by black bass anglers slinging topwater baits over spawning flats in springtime (right).

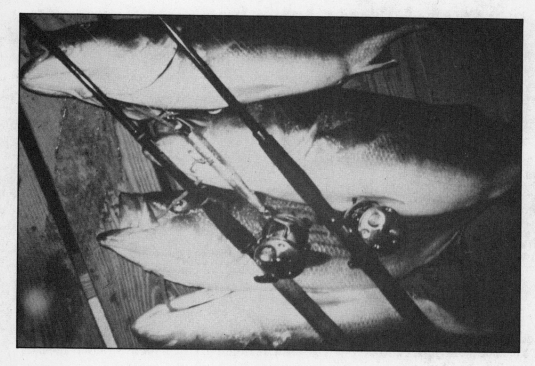

Limits of giant stripers, like these taken on the RedFin, are not uncommon for anglers who know the ways of using topwaters.

pellers located on the front and rear of the plug. These lures are usually worked with sweeps of the rod tip, which causes the lure to buzz and sputter over the surface, followed by a pause. Prop baits are a good topwater pick when the surface is relatively choppy or when you want to cover a lot of water quickly but the fish aren't aggressive enough to hit a buzz bait.

Giant prop baits like Ozark Mountain's BigGame Wood-Chopper are wonderfully effective striper baits when the fish are relatively shallow. In the hot months of summer, stripers will vacate the deepwater impoundments and run upstream into the cooler rivers. And here, over the shallow riffles of a sandbar, a giant prop bait will often provoke strikes from fish so large that they often strike fear into the hearts of anglers — no joke!

BUZZ BAITS

These double-wire baits resemble spinnerbaits but are

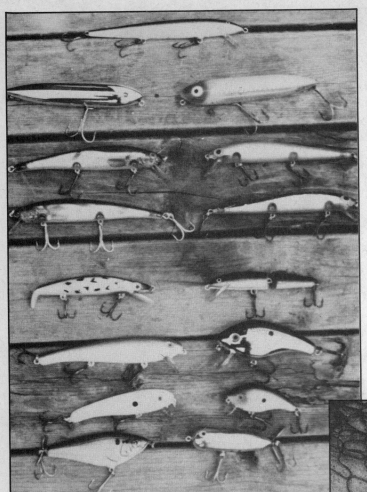

Some of the all-time classic topwater baits are shown at left. They are (top) original Rapala in black and silver, (left row, from top) Heddon's Zara Spook in chrome, Bomber Long-A in gold, Bomber Long-A in black, silver and orange, Fish World's Pogo Minnow in white with black spots, Mann's Stretch 1-Minus in blue and white, Mann's Baby Stretch 1-Minus in chartreuse, and Bagley's Spin 'R Shad in a shad finish. (Right row, from top): Heddon Zara Spook in a yellow finish, Storm's Thunderstick in chartreuse/orange and again in blue, silver and orange, Jointed Rapala in silver and black, Mann's 1-Minus in chrome and blue, Mann's Baby 1-Minus in green and white, and Heddon's Tiny Torpedo in chrome. Author won't leave home without them!

Okay, so if you couldn't take the whole tackle box with you, which topwater baits would you prefer on really huge predators? You can argue, but these are what the author chose: At top is Heddon's Zara Spook in chrome, second row left is Mann's Super Stretch 1-Minus in white and red, second row right is Mann's 1-Minus in chrome and blue, Cordell RedFin in seven-inch size with blue and chrome, and Rebel's seven-inch Minnow in black and chrome.

equipped with a blade or blades designed to lift the bait to the surface. Typical buzz baits include the original Lunker Lure, Zorro's Aggravator Buzz Bait, and Strike King's Cackle Buzz.

Of all topwater lures, buzz baits are fished most rapidly. Their design is such that the lure must be retrieved fairly quickly in order for the bait to ride the surface, which it does with a buzzing, sputtering spray of water. Too, buzz baits are one of the only topwater baits which are effective throughout a summer's day. A relatively weedless lure, buzz baits are most productive when retrieved over shallow, submerged cover or actually against structures protruding from the surface (timber, blow-downs, boat houses, docks, etc.). Short strikes are common when using buzz baits, so

the addition of a trailer or stinger hook is well advised.

For some reason, buzz baits are typically black bass baits. Unfortunately, stripers and hybrids pay little attention to these lures, though that may be because no one tosses buzz baits over open water structures inhabited by the linesides. It might be well worth your time to throw a big-bladed buzz bait over a few points next spring when the stripers are surface-oriented.

Topwater fishing is not a sport for the faint of heart. But if you happen to be fearless and Pacemaker free, the sport is undeniably the most exciting in the angling world. For when fish and steel meet on a silvery surface, anything might happen!

TOM MANN'S TEN TOPWATER TIPS

1. Learn to select the correct topwater type for the angling conditions. I use minnow-type twitchers in shallow water near cover, poppers and chuggers in choppy water, and stick baits in clear or open water. Prop baits may often be used successfully in place of the other baits.

2. Learn the proper technique for working each type of topwater plug, but don't ever hesitate to experiment from the accepted standard.

3. While 10-pound line is ideal for most topwater situations, use a heavier line when fishing around thick cover and switch to a lighter one when fishing clear, open water.

4. Most topwater plugs work best when you keep about six inches of slack in your line.

5. Make long casts in clear water.

6. Pay close attention to your first topwater strike of the day. That can tell you a great deal about the type of presentation demanded by the fish.

7. Don't limit your topwater fishing to mornings and evenings. Topwaters are also good throughout the day, even in the heat of summer. During the day, concentrate on shady areas adjacent to cover, or fish a stick bait over deep structures in clear water.

8. Don't worry too much about the color of your topwater plugs. The fish are striking at the bait's silhouette and movement, and cannot actually see the color of the plug.

9. When black bass fishing, concentrate on shallow water structures if the water is at all dingy. In clear water, switch to a stick bait and work it over deep-water holding areas.

10. Work topwater plugs with movements of your wrist.

CHAPTER 3

TROUTIN' LITTLE LAKES & SKINNY STREAMS

When The Cutts, 'Bows & Browns are 12-Inch Natives, You'll Have Top Sport On Matched Tackle!

By Russ Thurman

Russ and Debbie Thurman savor the moment of triumph — seven native rainbows on ultralight tackle. But as important to them was chance to spend time outdoors with nature.

A 12-inch rainbow can be a real trophy when taken from tiny stream. You should first study terrain, determine holding and feeding stations, then approach carefully.

Author advises fishing the shoreline areas of small lakes before casting into deeper water, as big 'uns might be close by. Fish need cover for access to food sources.

FISHING SMALL LAKES and skinny streams for aggressive native trout is a special adventure. In the midst of isolated rushing water and post-card scenic beauty, the challenge isn't high-tech angling. Rather, it's patience, skill and savvy. Fooling a 10-inch rainbow can be as thrilling as landing a 10-pound largemouth bass.

Many of us grew up fishing small streams and lakes — ponds, really — for trout. Tackle often consisted of a willow pole, a hank of line and crooked hook: Not fancy, but oh! The exhilaration of yanking a frisky brown out of a swirling stream hooked us on fishing.

The excitement awaits still. The challenge and occasional frustration are undiminished. But, by mastering a few techniques, you can enhance your enjoyment of this special outdoor adventure...and catch more fish!

There are several species of trout in North America, varying in mature length from less than six inches to nearly four feet. The trout family is classified with salmon, smelt and whitefish. The most familiar trout are the rainbow, steelhead, sea trout, golden, cutthroat, lake trout, Dolly Varden and brook trout. While all provide excellent fishing and eating, we're concerned with the ones darting through shallow rapids or holding under a log in a small lake.

The rainbow may be the favorite trout gamefish because of its fighting nature. It's a "flyer" or "leaper," leaving the water when hooked and putting on a breathtaking display with its crimson stripe. It greedily boils up for flies, and 'bows measuring 12 inches in small lakes and streams are trophy size. A West Coast native, the rainbow has been easily introduced throughout North America.

The golden trout rivals the rainbow in fighting spirit and surpasses its close relative in sheer beauty. Its yellow/gold belly is tinged with red and creamy white, contrasting with its emerald back and black speckles. Inch-for-inch, it may be the fightingest gamefish in North America. Goldens are another West Coast original.

The cutthroat, also a close kin of the rainbow, may only reach five to six inches in small streams, though it grows much larger in big impoundments. It, too, is a fighter, distinguished by a red slash along the gill plate and below the jaw. Found initially in mountain waters from California to Alaska, cutthroat are now taken throughout North America.

The brown trout is a European import. Often called the German brown, this trout averages six to eight inches in

While fish normally feed heaviest in morning and late in afternoon, a midday outing still can provide results — and permit you to sleep in! Debbie Thurman waits for hit.

small waters. They are a golden brown with black or brown and red or orange speckles. An excellent fighter, the brown also is a favorite table fish.

The brook trout originated in the Northeast, but now can be found throughout North America. Also called the speckled trout, brookies are a lovely dark green with wavy yellowish lines on its back, bright red spots highlighted by a bluish aureole, scarlet belly and fins tinged with black, and yellow speckles. A small-water brook trout of more than 12 inches is quite a catch.

Trout are, by nature, extremely skittish. They spend their lives hiding and running from predators. Combine this wary nature with the tiny fishing areas of small streams and little lakes and you have a real fishing challenge.

But that's what makes catching these trout such a thrill. Remember, we're not after the three-pound rainbow. A trout of more than 10 inches pulled from a five-inch-deep "pool" below a swirling "rapid" is braggin' size!

The trout's habitat is characterized by cool, clear water with a high oxygen content. The rainbow, however, adapts well to water less-aerated, and up to 70 degrees in temperature. Trout locate where they can feed and find protection from predators. In streams they also seek protection from the current.

Undercut banks, submerged logs, rocks, weed beds and sunken brush are excellent sheltering lies for trout. These are primarily protection areas for trout that also provide access to food. For the most part, trout will hold in a sheltering lie and move to a feeding lie when food appears.

Both of these areas are relatively easy to spot, even in a small stream or lake. But getting to the spot, and making a hook presentation without spooking your quarry — ah, that's the challenge!

Trout feed on insects, larvae, worms, freshwater shrimp, slugs, snails and smaller fish. They pick their food primarily by sight, with taste and smell used as secondary senses in the selection of food. The bottoms of lakes and streams supply most of the trout's food. But some of the most exciting fishing occurs when a winged insect hatch is on.

Because of their spooky nature, trout don't spend much time examining food. Their survival depends on quick decisions. They usually feed quickly and return to a sheltering lie. This again adds to the excitment of catching trout.

In extremely cold weather, trout normally feed in the

If it takes more than two hops to cross, then it's not a "skinny stream" in author's mind. He studies topography of stream with an eye to fish behavior, then begins to seek fish in identified locations.

There's a bruiser worth braggin' over in this stringer, taken with the ultralight equipment and terminal tackle discussed in text. Good work!

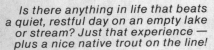

Is there anything in life that beats a quiet, restful day on an empty lake or stream? Just that experience — plus a nice native trout on the line!

afternoon when the water is warmer. When the temperature is high, they feed during the cooler morning hours. However, don't shy away from casting your line at other times. While fishing a small lake in early July, my wife and I caught a good batch of rainbows between 11 a.m. and 2 p.m. Still, trout take most of their food when the light is dim, especially when insect activity peaks.

The tackle I use for small-water fishing isn't much different from the willow pole I used as a kid, although it's significantly more sophisticated. As a kid hopping trout streams in Colorado, I always cut a very limber willow pole about five feet long. The flexible willow provided great action, even when the trout were six inches long. That action is reproduced in today's ultralight fishing rods.

In addition to the light action, I prefer rods I can carry in a backpack or fannypack. Zebco's UL3 and UL4 Classic Ultralight Travel Paks are perfect for little lakes and skinny streams. Both Paks have 4-foot 6-inch telescopic rods that reduce to 13½ inches. The UL4 has a TriggerSpin reel that gives you the touch of spinning with the advantages of a spin-cast. The UL3 has a FeatherTouch cast control system.

The Tackle Tote by Zebco also is an ideal ultralight outfit. It has a five-foot sectional rod and a Pro Staff 2010 Ultralight Reel, all nicely fitted into a multipurpose case which has compartments for lures.

Shimano's two-piece Bull Whip Super Ultralight Rods have excellent action and are easily tucked into the trunk of a car. The MK-2450 is 4½ feet long and the MK-2500 is a five-footer. Both are designed for the Mark-ULS spinning

After fishing empty shoreline, Debbie Thurman lets fly with cast to deeper waters. Overhand casting often is impossible on small lakes and streams due to brush and tree cover found.

Regardless of its size, any fish seeks protective cover to keep it from being eaten by a larger fish! While hiding, it waits to ambush smaller fish or insects, grubs, worms.

reel, which has an extraordinarily smooth mechanism.

While it's debatable, I consider ultralight monofilament to be four-pound test and under. Anything heavier reduces the challenge and the excitement. You also want a thin line that's difficult for the trout to see. (This will, of course, make it difficult for *you* to see, so a pair of polarized glasses will reduce glare and aid in locating your line.) If you're up to an added challenge, use a two-pound leader with your rig.

You need to handle ultralight line differently than you do 10-pound mono. Knots should be tightened with a steady pull instead of a snap. I favor the Palomar knot for all my fishing tie-ups. The double strand through the eye of hooks, swivels and lures is especially useful with ultralight line.

The line should be inspected often for abrasions, since it is going to be hitting a lot of limbs, rocks and other structure when fishing small, brushy streams and lakes.

Think small when putting together an assortment of hooks, lures and swivels. Size #10 Eagle Claw hooks and size #12, even #14, South Bend snap swivels are the largest I use for small lake and stream trout. I don't use treble hooks here. BB-sized split-shot sinkers are all the weight you'll need for streams and close-to-the-bank fishing in lakes. For those "long" casts on small lakes, use quarter-ounce bell sinkers.

I use three line setups for ultralight trouting. First I attach a size #12 snap swivel to the end of four-pound mono. To this I can attach "bulkier" lures for lake fishing, or attach my three setups. For my first version, I tie a loop

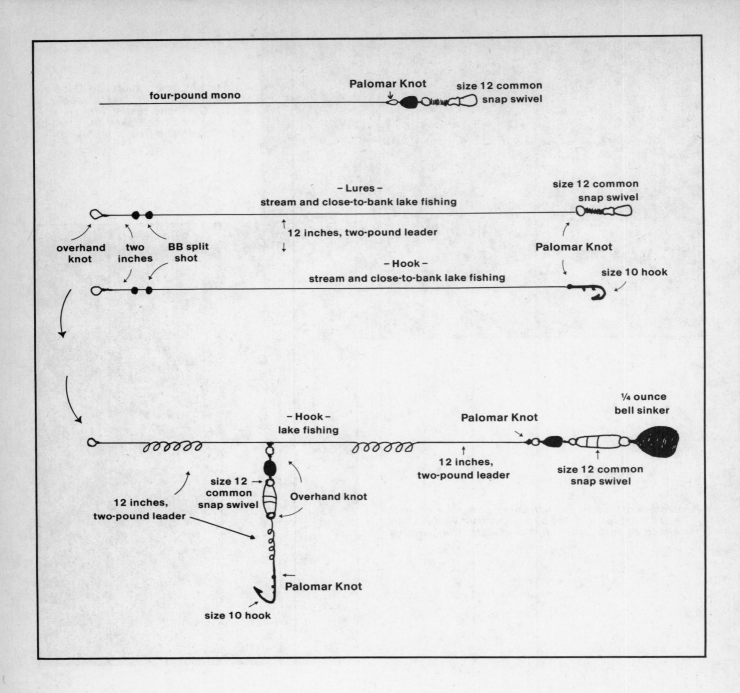

four-pound mono   **Palomar Knot**   size 12 common
snap swivel

– Lures –
stream and close-to-bank lake fishing   size 12 common
snap swivel

overhand knot   **two inches**   **BB split shot**

12 inches, two-pound leader

Palomar Knot

– Hook –
stream and close-to-bank lake fishing   size 10 hook

– Hook –
lake fishing   **Palomar Knot**   ¼ ounce
bell sinker

size 12 → **common snap swivel**   **Overhand knot**

12 inches, two-pound leader

12 inches, two-pound leader   size 12 common snap swivel

← **Palomar Knot**

size 10 hook

at the end of two-pound leader, then attach two BB split-shot two inches from the loop. Twelve inches from the weight I attach another size #12 snap swivel. To this I can attach and change lightweight lures.

My second setup is exactly the same, except I attach a size #10 hook to the end of the leader. With these two setups I can quickly change from lures to hook and back again for both stream and close-to-bank fishing on small lakes.

For bait fishing the deeper parts of lakes where I need a longer cast, I have a third setup. Starting with a loop on the end of two-pound leader, I measure off 12 inches and tie a midline loop to which I attach a size #12 snap swivel. I know there are three-way swivels designed for this, but that's another piece of hardware I don't want to handle. To

use a three-way swivel you need to cut your line and then tie two knots — seems a lot of work. To the midline swivel I attach my hook setup. For it I use two-pound leader. After tying a loop at one end using an overhand knot, I measure off 12 inches and attach a size #10 hook with a Palomar knot. Twelve inches from the midline loop I attach another size #12 snap swivel that holds my quarter-ounce bell sinker. This setup keeps my bait off the lake's bottom and between me and the heavier sinker, so I can feel the slightest strike.

Picking the right lures can be a chore, since there are so many on the market. Start, as always, by thinking small. Lures should be no larger than one-eighth ounce; I prefer 1/16-ounce. As trout find food by sight, the color and action of a lure is important. But don't select only brightly colored lures; On clear, bright days, you should use dull-

When first approaching water's edge, get down as Debbie Thurman shows. It could prevent spooking fish keeping up close to the shoreline. See text.

How's your back-hand casting? Might have need for it on a brush-choked bank, where forehand casting is impossible. And don't forget the bug juice — mosquitos can get thick!

finish lures and on overcast days or when the water isn't clear, shiny lures are best.

Some of the favorite lures in my arsenal include a Shoff's Triple Teazer, which is extremely effective in the shallow rapids of a small stream; Jake's Spin-A-Lure Super Duper — never fails on small lakes; Eppinger red and white Lil' Devle for both lakes and streams; and Panther Martin Ladybug that has a special way of calling trout away from small lake weed beds.

There are, of course, other baits. Nightcrawlers were my favorite trout bait as a kid, and still can be depended on to attract a suspicious trout. Pautzke's Green Label Balls O' Fire salmon eggs stimulate a trout's sight and smell.

There also are a number of trout attractants on the market. The best from my experience is Berkeley's Power Trout Bait. My wife and I became sold on the bait while fishing a small mountain lake in eastern Utah. We'd thrown everything — bait, lure and skill — at some very picky trout without even a hint of a strike. I then dug out a jar of the Berkeley bait. For the next hour it was cast, strike and battle a brawling rainbow. The bait is a yellow dough that's recommended for use on a treble hook. However, the bait clings quite well to a snelled hook.

Then there's the world of flyfishing for trout, which author Roger Combs describes as the ultimate challenge and the most exciting way to catch trout in another chapter of this book. On most of the small streams I've visited, fly-fishing would almost be impossible because of the low over-hanging trees and brush. On small lakes it would be excellent; review Roger Combs' words and pictures for more info.

What a lovely spot to chase trout! Author figures there's a couple of biggies holding in the cover provided by overhanging tree limbs to left. The natural eddy will serve food right to noses.

On to some techniques for little lakes and skinny streams. A small stream to me is no wider than a two-hopper, meaning if it takes more than two steps to get across then it's too big. If you have to wear waders, it's too big. If you feel you need a boat on the lake, it's too big.

Many small lakes and especially small streams are often overlooked as desirable fishing waters; they just don't look exciting. For those of us who enjoy this type of fishing, such attitudes mean we're not likely to bump into a large crowd. You may have passed such a trout stream or lake without considering its real potential. Give it a try.

The number one thing to remember in trout fishing small bodies of water is how you appear to the trout. Or, better yet, how you *don't* appear to the trout. You easily can be seen, heard and felt by a trout that's primed to bolt at the slightest indication of a predator. I call it stalk-fishing — moving undetected, making a gentle, unannounced presentation of a 1/16-ounce lure, reeling in steadily, primed for the strike.

When approaching a small stream, don't just walk up to it and start popping in your line. Stay back a bit, moving slowly to a spot where you can observe a section of the stream. Sit or crouch so you blend in with the brush.

What do you see? We've talked already of where trout are most likely holding. You see those small rapids where the stream narrows to just a couple of feet? Look just upstream to the left and right a few feet, especially to the right where the brush is overhanging the water. Trout will hold there, taking advantage of the shelter of the overhang and at the same time be in a position to capture food being channeled into the narrows. Make sense? A small lure placed upstream just above the lie and worked this way would pass right over the trout.

Now, look just below the rapids. See that moss-covered rock about two feet from the opposite bank? That's an ideal feeding lie for trout. Food is rushed through the rapids into calmer waters and is caught in the eddy that swirls toward the bank, looping food behind that rock. Trout there are protected from the current and are served their food on an eddy platter. Getting into a casting position could be tough, though. I'll probably crawl right behind that brush to the left and "flick cast" some Powerbait into the rapids and let it be carried on the current.

That small riffle just in front of us is forcing the stream to channel to this side of the bank, probably causing an under-cut. I'll save fishing it until I move downstream a few feet.

Author scopes out likely areas below falls on the Utah stream. No doubt plenty of food will be washed over the falls into the pools below, where fish wait.

But just below the riffle, see where the water is bubbly? Trout are having a late afternoon snack. A lure cast just upstream a bit and pulled over the riffle, diagonally through the bubbling water, will probably attract a strike.

Downstream just beyond that fallen branch is a perfect feeding and sheltering lie. It even looks like there may be a bit of a pond — see how the water is a bit darker? There's also a seam, right there where the faster water meets the slower water. Trout hold right on these seams. With the shadows, fallen branch, deeper water and the seam, that may be the best spot so far for a trophy trout.

By taking a little time and studying a section of a stream, it will become obvious where trout are holding. Getting a hook to them is by far the difficult task. It's vital that you move quietly, crawling if you have to, to keep from being seen.

Should you fish upstream or down? I don't think it makes a difference. I usually work upstream first, stopping at a turnaround point to enjoy the quiet, and then fish back downstream.

Presentations aren't really casts, they're flips, pitches, flicks and plops, but they need to be done in such a way as not to disturb the water. I usually spend a lot of time at the first section of the stream I fish, mostly practicing my cast, getting my "gentle wrist" back. This is especially important if you've recently been yanking on bass.

When you do hook into a small-stream trout, don't yank or jerk; it only takes a soft lifting of the rod to set the hook, and then enjoy the moment. As a kid I remember flinging trout into the trees...now I savor the catch. It can take a lot of time and a good dose of skill to get a wary stream trout on a hook, so let the fish run, putting on its display.

Try an overhead cast in thick scrub like this and you'll ruin your whole day! You might need to strip line and plop it into likely spot — not pretty, but effective.

Debbie Thurman enjoys the final splashes of a beaten Utah rainbow. Author used to "put fish in trees" with teenage hookset, but now prefers to enjoy tussle with new "cane pole."

Fishing small lakes for trout isn't as arduous as fishing streams. While you do have to be quiet and cautious, the larger body of water allows you to move about a bit more freely.

When arriving at a small lake, as with a stream, take time to study it. If possible, observe it from a higher point, noting the likely spots where trout can be found. Again, it's not that difficult. If the shores are crowded with brush and trees, you may only be able to study the open water of the lake, but that's important, also. You'll want to know where the deepest part of the lake is and the location of any structure that may not be visible when you're fishing from the bank.

Reading a body of water is easy. See where the water color looks greenish along the short stretch between that tall tree and fallen log? As you move your line of sight away from the bank, the water turns a light blue and then dark blue, almost black? That's a gradual slope and probably won't hold trout. However, look right there where the light blue water meets the green. That looks like a weed bed. That would be worth fishing. Just to the right is where we'll start. The shore is a bit crowded with brush, but notice how blue the water is right up to the brush overhang: shadows + deeper water + shelter = trout.

Approach a small lake as you would a small stream: quietly, with a low profile. *Always* fish the shoreline first,

Many of the best troutin' spots are overlooked by big-fish fanciers or high-tech anglers. That's okay with author and other ultralighters who prefer solitude and foot-long trophies.

then fish farther out. Just because the entire center of the lake is covered with rings where trout are feeding on insects doesn't mean Mr. Trophy isn't holding a few feet from the shore. Take your time. Fish the shoreline much the way you would a small pool on a stream. Once done, fish your way out as far as you can cast.

Casting any real distance from a brush-crowded shoreline can be a challenge. That's where the short, ultralight rods show their real value. In thick, overhanging brush I cast with the rod tip pointing down and my right hand held even with my right shoulder. With a sharp flick I send the

quarter-ounce sinker to its target. It takes practice, but it works.

Fishing small lakes and streams for trout is not high-tech and it's not crowded. In addition to hooking and landing aggressive trout, there's the quiet touch of nature: The batch of baby frogs tumbling over each other in the water grass at my feet; the doe staring at me 35 feet away, protecting a spotted fawn; the talkative squirrel, upset about my intrusion, finally settling to watch my efforts.

It's a special adventure...and a heckuva lot of fun!

CHAPTER 4

CARING FOR YOUR FISHING TACKLE

Rods, Reels & Line Will Serve Better and Longer With A Minimum Amount Of Preventive Maintenance!

By Pete Fosselman

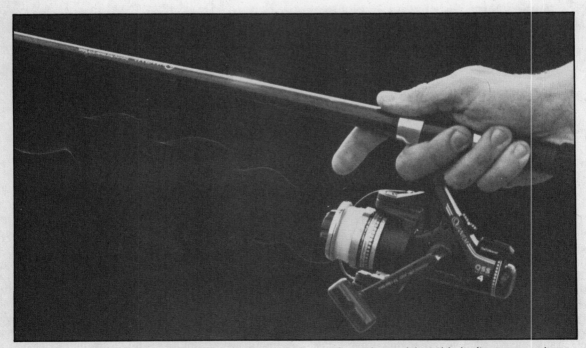

Line memory will cause the "slinky" effect when cast from the reel, but this isn't permanent. Text gives information on how to remove it, plus other tips on making tackle last and last.

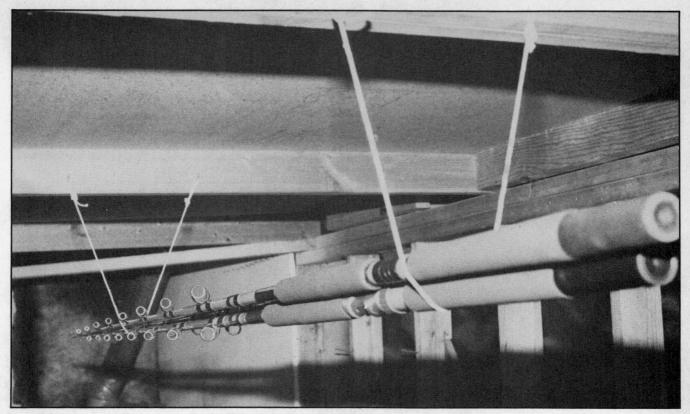

One of the best ways to store your valuable fishing rods is demonstrated in author's garage. Short ropes are looped around nails hammered into rafters. Two ropes suffice and prevent rods from disfigurement.

WHEN OUR angling predecessors used their hands to catch fish, a technique known as "guddling," it wasn't "sportfishing" at all; it was "survival-fishing." The patient hours spent learning to move your hands close to a passing or resting fish hardly would classify as a sport. If you weren't a good "guddler," you went hungry!

After frigid fingers came spears, nets, traps and even hooks with lines. No one knows when the rod and reel first saw service. As far back as the Fifteenth Century, specialty books advised in detail how to make a rod and use it in conjunction with a hook and line. Early rods were no more than a stick or a reed. Lines were made from braided horsehair, usually three strands thick. Hooks were fashioned from bone.

Today's angler is blessed with the latest in technology and state-of-the-art equipment. Yet, without proper maintenance and care, it becomes as ineffectual as bone hooks and horsehair lines. What follows is the advice of some real fishing industry experts. Most advice that is freely given is rarely taken. I hope this information proves the exception.

RODS

Toyo Shimano, Shimano's top research and marketing executive, says the most-recent developments in fishing rods involve materials. New technology has centered around refinements, not breakthroughs; the last breakthrough was the introduction of graphite into fishing rods.

Some rod manufacturers began by using graphite alone, while others blended it with fiberglass. One claimed his rod was stronger, the other that his rod was more flexible. A compromise was needed, and most reached that happy medium either by blending or using the two separately in construction.

This brief technological background doesn't concern rod maintenance, but it does give a little insight with respect to today's revolving dilemma on rod manufacturing. Some pluses have been designed into the modern equipment that can be construed as minuses in the long run.

First and foremost with the new graphite composite rods, remember that they are brittle. You don't have to baby them because the rod itself is tough, but treat them with care. While their fishing characteristics for pulling fish are greatly enhanced, some of their overall durability may have been lost.

If you drop or step on a rod, examine it carefully. They can and will fracture, and now is the time to locate any cracks or signs of stress fatigue. Car doors are notorious for breaking off the tips of rods. Newly designed rods with solid tips are intended to stop some of this breakage, but I imagine a car door or misplaced step still will break a few.

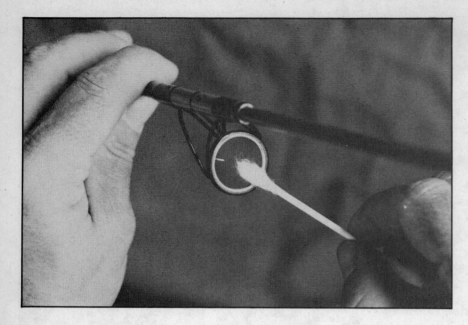

A cotton swab is helpful in showing rough spots in line guides, even on ceramic ones. Any nicks that could cause line abrasion will snag some of the loose cotton. Replace them.

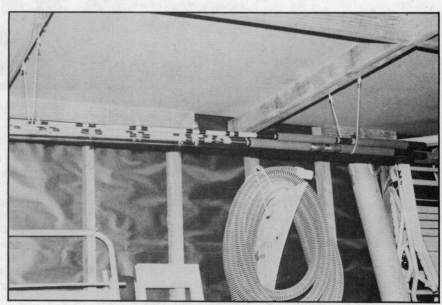

Another look at author's rod storage system — up and out of the way, yet easy to access and protective, too.

After each fishing trip, or even during a multi-day trip, clean your rods with a mild detergent and warm water. While fresh water won't hurt a freshwater outfit, salt water will destroy ocean-fishing gear if you don't remove the salt-water residue. Once the rods have been washed and rinsed, dry them carefully with a clean towel. The rod's finish is sufficient to protect it from the elements.

Make sure the reel seats are clean and dry. I like to put a light coat of oil on the reel seats and metal guides; a light oil like reel lube or gun oil. Stay away from the all-purpose spray lubricants: Some of the additives might adversely affect the rod's finish or the fishing line.

Waxing rods is not advisable. Most waxes are designed for cars, floors or furniture. While their ingredients may be swell on the floor, you risk harming the finish or your line as with spray lubricants.

While the addition of modern-day rubber protectors might make the Hypalon or cork grips look pretty, they normally have an adverse reaction when they get wet — they become very slippery! Clean these grips with the same detergent and warm water solution. A very soft brush can be used for some light scrubbing if needed. Hard scrubbing will remove some grip material.

Once your rod has been cleaned, take the time to inspect it. Look at the guides and reel seats to ensure they're in good shape. I use a Q-Tip to check the insides of guides and rod tips for abrasions. Wipe the inside of the guide and tip with the cotton swab. If there are any nicks or scrapes, they will snag the cotton swab, indicating needed repair. If you don't fix it, the line will be weakened by the sawing action, and there goes your IGFA record!

Store rods appropriately. Keep them out of direct sun-

Brushing your reels with light oil is preventive maintenance that keeps tackle young — and functioning. Text has myriad other suggestions.

Cotton swab is coated with light reel grease to keep surfaces friction free and operating smoothly. You'll be glad your reel is functioning in midst of battle with wallhanger.

light and away from high heat. Don't use rod holders to stand them in a corner. This may establish a bend in the memory that's not in proper alignment with a natural fish-fighting arch. The rod still might work, but you will have an added dimension working against the intended design. The memory bend might correct itself, and then it might not. Don't take this chance and ruin a good — and expensive — rod. Use rod holders to store them against a flat surface. If a flat surface of adequate length isn't available, build a suspension hanger in the garage. Rope or wood suspended from the ceiling or rafters at proper spacing intervals will support the rods and keep them from bending in the middle or at the tip.

REELS

Reel maintenance is the most important subject when it comes to tackle care. With minimal care, your rod and other tackle will work pretty much to their optimum. A fishing reel, no matter how simple its design, requires occasional owner attention for it to work correctly.

Internal care and cleaning of an expensive saltwater reel is best done at a service center. By talking to your friends, or a local tackle store, you should be able to find a reputable repair and cleaning center. Once you've located a service center, check it out like you would a good auto mechanic. Find out if the person doing the service is trained and experienced, able to recognize fatigue and worn-out parts. Can he answer questions about your reels? You wouldn't want a body and fender man adjusting the valves on your foreign sports car, and the same principle applies to reel maintenance.

You can service and clean many reels by yourself, if you have a little Yankee ingenuity or mechanical savvy. There

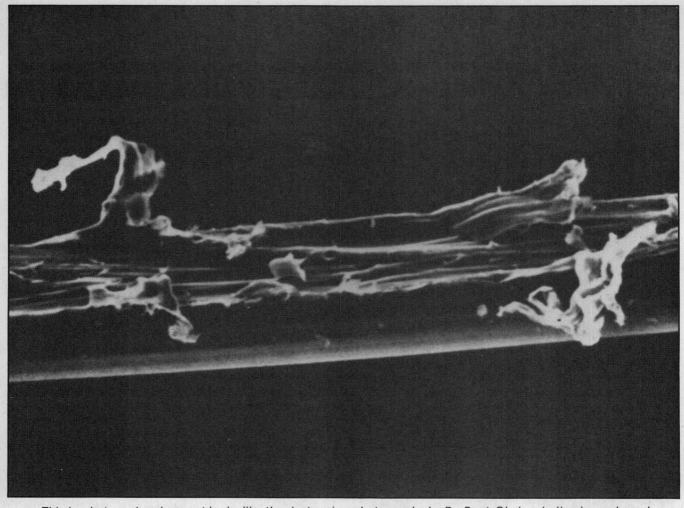

This is what an abrasion spot looks like thanks to microphotography by Du Pont. Obviously, line is weakened at this spot and could break if stressed. Rough spots are felt with fingers as line is rewound on the spool.

are some things the do-it-yourselfer should know, and there's no better authority than Ray Lemme, better-known to West Coast anglers as "The Reel Man." Reel maintenance is a subject dear to Lemme. Before retiring a year or so ago, reel maintenance was his livelihood for nearly 20 years. His past customers read like a *Who's Who* in big game ocean fishing: Ralph Mikklesen, Dick Cresswell, Gil Onaka, Frank Lo Preste, and Tommy Rothery, to name just a few.

Lemme started in business after purchasing a new reel that didn't work quite right out of the box. "Having been a tinkerer most of my life, I wasn't afraid to disassemble the reel and find out what made it tick," he explained.

He was shocked by what he found: leather drag washers. "This meant that water was really a hazard to fishing reels!" Lemme stressed in astonishment. "I found this hard to believe, since fishing and fishing reels usually have *some* type of contact with water. The leather washers would soak up water and really cause havoc."

To prevent this, Lemme invented a small water seal to help keep the drag washers dry. "Today's drag washers are made of different materials, so this isn't the problem it used to be," Lemme said. "There isn't a need for the water seal anymore. That was 15 or so years ago."

Soon after Lemme opened up that first reel, his career as "The Reel Man" began. He performed custom tune-ups, in addition to regular cleaning and servicing. His reputation developed through his work with Penn International big game reels. When anglers began overworking the Internationals, he found ways of increasing their braking capabilities and giving them a fine overall tune-up. It was through this 20-year relationship with reels that Lemme learned how to make them last; things the average angler could do to protect his substantial investment. Following are "The Reel Man's" tips:

Keep water away from those reels: "So many times, I see people return from a fishing trip and they have their

Ray Lemme is known as "The Reel Man" to serious Southern California saltwater anglers. He built a living from reworking and reconditioning expensive reels. His advice on reel maintenance may just surpise you!

rods and reels all bunched up in the front yard. Next thing they do is grab the garden hose and wash down everything. This does absolutely nothing for the reel. It doesn't wash a thing. It only adds more water to the inside of the reel, where it doesn't belong. So don't hose down or submerge your reels."

Wipe down your reels: "To clean the outside of a reel, remove it from the rod. Take a wet towel and wipe it off thoroughly. Don't neglect in and around the reel base, handle and sideplates. Wipe the whole thing down and dry it. If you've been using the reel in salt water, this will help remove the saltwater deposits that'll lead to corrosion."

Clean the inside of the reel: If you disassemble the reel for internal cleaning and lubrication, Lemme stresses the need to reassemble it exactly correct. "It sounds simple, but I've seen hundreds of reels put together by the do-it-yourselfer that are missing some important shim or other

part. Use the schematic or draw yourself pictures to assure the exact reassembly.

"It also is very important to put metal, fiber and brake washers back in the same fashion they came out," Lemme continued. "Same sides and surfaces against the same sides and surfaces that they were against when the reel was originally assembled. You wouldn't switch your car's brakes from side to side, so don't do it with your reel brakes."

Disassembly procedures: As you disassemble the reel, lay all the parts on an old newspaper or a paper towel. "This absorbs any grease, oil or water that drips out," Lemme stated. "One by one, hand-clean each greasy or dirty part, with the exception of the ball bearings, in solvent. The ball bearings are sealed and don't require cleaning. If you get solvent in them, it will wash out the oil and ruin them. If this happens, replace them."

Keep in mind the requirement of matching sides and surfaces of washers. "If you hand-clean the reel, you should

When Lemme reconditioned reels, he would disassemble them first, in this case a Penn International, for thorough inspection.

be able to lay it back down on the table in an order to match an exact reassembly. Obviously, if you throw all the parts into a can of solvent, you won't be able to do this," he said.

An old toothbrush is good for scrubbing gears or those parts that require some extra muscle. "Use a Q-Tip or cotton swab to clean the shoulders, inside crevices, and openings on the sideplates or spool shroud. Once everything is clean, inspect the parts for signs of wear and fatigue. Make sure that none of the gears have any burrs or broken teeth, which can happen when throwing a revolving-spool reel into gear on a running fish. Be sure to check the bail spring on spinning reels. If it doesn't look or work right, replace it now."

Reassemble and lubricate: Once everything is clean and inspected, you're ready to reassemble. "All surfaces and parts on the inside should be coated with blue grease," Lemme said. "I use a paste brush to apply a thin coat to everything on the inside, except the ball bearings and brake surfaces. Blue grease is waterproof and won't melt or run. If water does get inside, the grease won't be affected and it will help protect any metal parts from corrosion."

Don't put blue grease around the ball bearings. It's a little gummy and will cause friction in lieu of lubrication. Sealed bearings are lubricated during their assembly and can't be lubricated from the outside. If they feel a little rough or sticky, replace them.

"If the reel does not have ball bearings, then a fine grease, similar to gun grease or reel lube, should be used to lubricate the bearing cups," Lemme instructed. "This same fine grease should be used on the gears themselves. Even though blue grease is a lubricant, it's too heavy and gummy for use on the gears."

Each part should be carefully inspected, and any showing signs of wear should be replaced. Now is the time to find flaws, not when you've hung a 100-pound tuna! See text.

Hand-cleaning each part with old toothbrush and solvent is required before applying fresh coat of grease.

Once the reel is completely reassembled, Lemme suggests that the entire reel be coated with a thin film of fine oil; nothing gummy or sticky, but wipe it down like you would a firearm. A shaving brush is helpful here. Put a few drops of oil on the bristles and brush the external surfaces until they're coated evenly.

Another helpful tool to maintain your reel is a syringe type of grease or oil applicator. Since oil or grease must be forced into some of the external oil ports, a syringe applicator comes in handy and can accomplish this task.

When everything is back together, check it for proper function. "Check the brake system and make sure it's smooth and working properly," Lemme said. "Now's the time to find out if it doesn't work, not when you're fighting that keeper fish!"

Cleaning and servicing your reel may be cheaper, but keep in mind you must know what you're doing. Today's tackle makers spend thousands of dollars on test equipment and the training of service personnel. Yet, it can be done at home, and done well if you're careful. Just look at "The Reel Man." He started tinkering in his garage and built a reputation worldwide. If you have the ability and knowledge, have at it. If not, take it to a reputable service center.

FISHING LINE

Questions about line deterioration and replacement are the ones most commonly asked by fishermen. How often should I change the line? Does the line have a shelf life? What types of substances damage monofilament line?

Answering these questions is the job of Mark Thomas, Public Relations Director for the Du Pont Company. Du Pont makes Stren and the new High Impact monofilament fishing line.

Chuck the reel parts into a can of solvent and you'll never get the right surfaces mated back together. Follow "The Reel Man's" advice when it comes to disassembly and you'll be fine.

Lemme recommends using blue grease applied with a paste brush. Fresh grease not only lubricates surfaces, it repels highly corrosive saltwater.

Today's fishing line attempts to deliver the best possible overall balance of properties, balance being good knot strength, good abrasion strength, good shock strength, and tensile strength. The line also needs proper limpness, controlled stretch, and a good visibility. "All these things must be targeted to develop a good line," Thomas explained. "Sometimes it is easy to improve one property that greatly hurts another. As you can see, millions of dollars go into the development and research of fishing lines. When a new line hits the market, it isn't just someone's hare-brained idea. It is backed by megabucks in laboratory tests and on-the-water developments."

Line replacement depends on how often you use the line, not necessarily the age of the line. This subject causes many arguments among anglers of any circle. Some say line gets stale and old, others say it doesn't. According to Thomas, today's nylon monofilament fishing line is virtually ageless. "By being virtually ageless, you could store a spool of line in its original package for years and it would be just as good as the day you bought it — if it was properly stored," Thomas added.

How much a line has been fished is the key to replacement. The less-frequent fisherman might need to replace his line only once a year, while the avid bass fisherman who gets out on the water every chance he gets should re-spool his reel at least once a week.

The type of fishing is another guide. Fishing in deep, unobstructed water can call for line replacement once a year. Surf-casting subjects the line to more punishment, more abrasions, so the line ought to be replaced once a month. Fishing around rocks in a stream bed or near trees in a reservoir might call for line replacement every trip. As you can see, there is no "pat" answer. Each angler must evaluate the circumstances, check his line, and act accordingly.

One thing that will cause nylon line to deteriorate is prolonged exposure to the ultraviolet rays of sunlight. "Day-to-day fishing under bright sun has negligible effect, but continuous exposure for several months may weaken the line," Thomas explained. "Consequently, when your reel and/or spool of spare line are not being used, they *should be stored in a dark place,* such as a closet shelf, or in the basement. Remember to keep it away from sunlight or even artificial light just to be on the safe side. Wrapping a large spool of line in foil is a good way to help seal it from light."

Besides ultraviolet light, nylon monofilament appears to have only one other enemy: Battery acid. The sulfuric acid

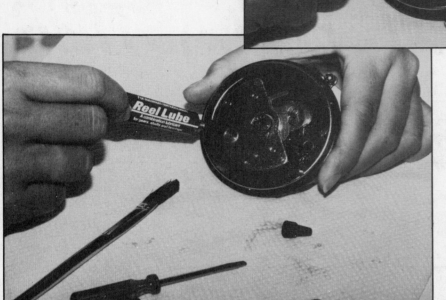

Cotton swabs come in handy when you clean crevices of a Penn reel. Take your time and do a thorough cleaning.

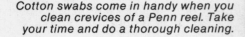

A light grease is preferred on gears, which prevents them from gumming up.

found in most batteries will destroy nylon.

Laboratory tests at Du Pont have shown that nylon line is not damaged by salt water, gasoline, motor oil, insect repellent, sunscreen lotion, detergents, rust inhibitors or lubricants. However, you wouldn't want to subject your line to these chemicals because their odor could have an effect on fooling the fish.

Fishing line "memory" is another characteristic of nylon line that often puzzles the fisherman. "It is the nature of nylon to take a set or remember a position it has been in for a period of time," Thomas explained. "This set or memory is directly related to the amount of moisture in the line and the amount of tension on the line. Nylon is hydroscopic, and it absorbs water. Line with absorbed moisture increases in both diameter and length.

"When line is stored on a reel for several days or weeks after being used, the absorbed moisture evaporates and the line shrinks back to its original length and size. This causes tension and forces it to set to the curvature of the reel. It doesn't harm the line, but your first cast the next time you use it will look like a 'slinky' as it fluffs off the reel.

"Line curl is not a permanent problem," Thomas added. "It is easily solved by returning the moisture that has evaporated. This can be done by soaking the spool (not the reel) in water or trailing the line through the boat's wake for a few minutes. Once the line has absorbed the proper amount of moisture, line curl will disappear and you'll be back in business."

SUMMARY

Extensive research has helped the avid angler in many ways. Graphite rods give us that extra feel and power demanded by the world's top fishermen, but they require care. Our reels today are very much performance-oriented. They are the only "mechanical" aspect to the rod, reel, and line combination. Like any mechanical item, it must be serviced periodically and done so properly. This can be done by the angler if he has the ability, or a reputable serviceman like Ray "The Reel Man" Lemme. Fishing line changes about as frequently as the seasons. The designs of the new cofilament lines versus monofilament lines may someday be the big breakthrough. Time will tell.

Meantime, remember these tips for rod, reel and line care. It will save your equipment and give you more bucks to spend on fishing trips. That's the name of the game!

CHAPTER 5

BEGINNING FLYCASTING

The First, Essential Ingredient For Flyfishing Is Learning To Cast — Getting Started Is Easy

By Roger Combs

The goal of flyfishing is to catch fish. After the correct equipment has been selected, and the technique of casting an artificial fly into the water is mastered, one in the net is the object.

Fishing guide/flycasting instructor Fred Rowe, of Mammoth Lakes, California, holds class for novices on Hot Creek, a stream managed for barbless hooks, catch-and-release only. Rowe, the professional, makes it look easy.

CASTING AN ARTIFICIAL fly is the essence of successful flyfishing. To do so, you must have correctly balanced equipment — rod, reel, line, leaders and flies. It also is necessary to develop the physical ability to place the artificial lure where it should be to catch fish. Flycasting takes hand and eye coordination, physical strength, good instruction and practice, practice, practice! Even the most successful flyfishermen with years behind them continue to practice on or off the water.

Flyfishing and its basic skill, flycasting, must be learned and practiced to become successful. It is not the easiest of physical skills to learn and is double difficult if the correct equipment is not selected and matched. The correct equipment for one person, or one type of fishing, may not be correct for all.

Trout probably is the most common fish sought by flyfishermen. But panfish, bass and Atlantic salmon are among others susceptible to a carefully cast fly. Other species of salmon, shad, steelhead, bonefish, bonito, tarpon and even sailfish are taken by flyfishermen using specialized tackle and heavy, sinking lines.

Whatever your quarry, the right equipment is essential, especially for the rookie flycaster. The beginner will do well with a low- or medium-price fiberglass or graphite rod eight to 8½-feet long. You may pay less than a hundred or up to several hundred dollars. The rod may break down into two pieces for general use, or into three or four sections for easy backpacking. Today's technology makes the four-piece rod as good as the two-piece.

Consider the rod's designated action: What weight flyline does it handle best? Flylines — and rods — are designed to best handle one or two weights of line. The rod and the line must be matched; modern rods and line packages are marked by the manufacturers. Line weights range from Number 1 to 15, based on the weight in grains of the first 30 feet of the line, exclusive of a tapered tip and as agreed upon by the American Fishing Tackle Manufacturers Association (AFTMA). When a rodmaker marks it as designed for a certain weight of line, the angler can then purchase flylines of any manufacturer. A seven-weight from Orvis will work as well as one from 3M or AirCel.

Which comes first, the line or the rod? Both must be considered, since they must be balanced. Many experts recommend selecting the line first, based upon the type of fish sought. A good balanced selection for trout and for learning to cast is a Number 7 line matched with a rod marked Number 6-7. An untapered Number 7 line is a good one for the learner. You will need 60 to 100 yards of flyline, plus an additional 150 yards or so of braided backing.

The reel is important, but should not be viewed as overly complicated. It is merely a storage device for the line. In an

Instructor Fred Rowe demonstrates the correct casting for novice Jean Combs. Practice area should be open and free of obstructions which may tangle line or distract student.

As the student begins to get the feel of a correct forward and back cast, action of the flyrod and line can be felt. Beginners must learn how to maintain the desired loop in the flyline, to front and rear, as confidence builds.

emergency, you could flyfish without a reel by letting the loose line coil at your feet.

You want a strong precision-made reel that will be ready at all times. It must have the capacity to hold the line and backing mentioned. It must release and recover line with little friction and should be made of modern, non-corrosive materials if intended for saltwater use. Most modern reels feature rim control which allows the angler to control a hooked fish by rubbing his palm against the outer rim of the reel.

The reel needs an adjustable drag for fighting larger fish, too.

Interchangeable spools are now almost universal on reels. You can carry one or two spare spools with different

weights of line and change without removing the reel from the rod. Extra spools cost less than buying a second or third reel.

Many sporting good stores and most flyfishing specialty stores have beginners' kits on display at reasonable prices. These provide all the basics; rod, reel, line, leaders and instructions to get you started without spending too much money while learning. Mail-order catalogs are another good source of equipment at reasonable prices. Two companies which are reliable and reasonable are Cabela's and Bass Pro Shops.

To learn basic flycasting, we need not concern ourselves with leaders, knots and artificial flies. Casting techniques should be learned first starting with the overhead roll cast

Jean Combs shows the relaxed and correct casting arm position as the fly drops onto the target. Both hands are at waist level.

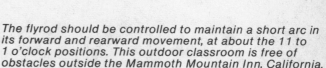

The flyrod should be controlled to maintain a short arc in its forward and rearward movement, at about the 11 to 1 o'clock positions. This outdoor classroom is free of obstacles outside the Mammoth Mountain Inn, California.

that can cast a fly 40 to 45 feet away. For most of us, two or three hours of basic skill development will get us out on the water with some degree of competency.

For those who have fished with spinners or heavy lures, a certain amount of "unlearning" may be necessary. In flycasting, the weighted flyline is what you're casting, not the tiny fly. The rod simply guides the line while conveying the power from your hand and arm to the line. The line is cast forward and back in a looping or unrolling motion by the movement of the rod. The angle formed by the rod determines the size of the loop, while the speed of the rod movement determines the distance the lure is cast.

Your grip on the rod handle is a matter of choice. Start with your hand near the top end of the cork, farthest away from the reel. Your fingers should not touch the rod itself. This location may be modified with time and experience. Some casters prefer to have their thumb on top of the handle as a way to control backcast motion of the rod. Others have a better feel for the rod's action if it is allowed to ride lightly between thumb and forefinger.

The rod should be held so that it is an extension of your forearm. The rod butt should almost touch your forearm throughout your cast.

Without stripping any line from the reel, move the rod overhead, back and forth in a single plane, from about 11 o'clock in front of the body to about 1 o'clock to the rear. Feet should be beneath the shoulder and you should be facing the direction in which you're casting. Whip the rod gen-

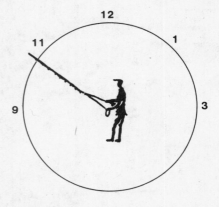

Bass Pro Shops' White River Classic flyrod, above, is suited to the beginner as well as the professional. Instructors expressed their approval of the rod's action and construction.

After a few hours of classroom work, the intrepid flycaster is ready for her first efforts on the water. A medium-priced Browning 2100 Series flyreel is well suited to the Number 7 rod. A flyfishing vest, such as the Bass Pro Shops model at left, is essential.

tly, then vigorously, above your head from the 11 to one position, feeling the action of the rod as it "loads up" with energy near end of each arc.

As the rod reaches 1 o'clock the rod butt will drift away from the forearm a bit. As it moves toward 11 o'clock, the butt closes the gap until it will be touching the wrist. Don't let the wrist bend away from the rod butt at the beginning or the backstroke. The forearm must move first, before the rod starts to swing in either direction.

As the forward cast is made, try to feel the forearm pushing ahead, not down, with the rod handle in nearly a straight line. The motion is not so much an overhand stroke as it is a push forward. Try to maintain the relative positions of the rod and forearm on the backcast in the same manner.

Breaking your wrist during the stroke will tend to put a much large angle to the rod tip. Some beginners swing the

rod from 9 to 3 o'clock; even farther at times. Don't control the rod and save wear and tear on your arm and wrist.

Now strip about 10 yards of line off the reel and let it fall at your feet. Instead of tying a lure to the end of the line, tie on about six feet of leader material with a short piece of brightly colored yarn for easy visibility while learning.

Lift the rod up from in front and bring it back smoothly to the 1 o'clock position. The rod halts abruptly, lifting the line off the ground and moving it backward. Inertia keep the line moving backward as it rolls out into a loop. Watch the line and as it flattens to a horizontal position, the rod is moved smartly forward and stopped in the 11 o'clock position. Again watch the line as it rolls forward until nearly straight out. The rearward motion is repeated, the line rolling to the rear as before and the forward cast is begun.

The loops won't be perfect at first; it may take consider-

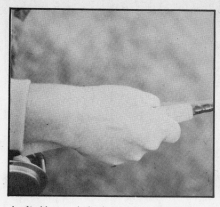

Left: Here, right hand is gripping rod handle improperly, more like club than lightweight fishing pole. The thumb should be on top of grip to better control action. Center: Another incorrect grip with hand too far forward, fingers touching the rod in front of grip. Rod action will be dampened with this grip. Grip at right is correct; rod butt close to forearm.

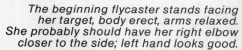
The beginning flycaster stands facing her target, body erect, arms relaxed. She probably should have her right elbow closer to the side; left hand looks good.

able practice to achieve the necessary coordination and rhythm. Allowing the rod to exceed the 11 o'clock to 1 o'clock arc will widen the loop too much; it cannot be controlled. Keep the rod within a 30-degree arc. Stop it suddenly at the 11 and 1 o'clock locations or the proper loop won't develop. Too large a loop reduces the distance of the cast. If the forward cast is started too soon — before the line has had a chance to roll almost all the way out to the rear — the line may crack like a whip and break the fly or the leader off completely. That movement is called "the $1.25 cast," since most commercially tied flies retail for about $1.25. Too many such snaps and your flycasting career becomes expensive before catching any fish!

As the line begins to pick up the motion and rhythm of the rod, casting becomes easier. The added weight and momentum of the weighted flyline will bend and move the rod tip as you stop the motion in your hand. Some find that more line stripped from the reel actually makes a smooth cast easier.

After a time, you begin to get a feel for what the line is doing without watching the loops. But do not hesitate to observe the line whenever you wish. Move the forearm forward and back in a push-pull motion, rather than an arcing-back-and-forth motion. Keep the rod in a single plane front to rear, not allowing the tip to fall off in either direction. Practice 15 or 20 minutes and take a rest before beginning again.

The left hand (if casting right-handed) holds the flyline lightly. The off-hand does not have to follow the motion of the casting hand and rod. Carry it near the waist in a comfortable position. Use it to strip more line from the reel and when we get to the fishing part, the off-hand grips the line as

Two photos above demonstrate correct rearward and forward flyrod movement which should result in a good loop cast. Novice flycaster must remember to let rod's action and line do their work, resisting the temptation to "muscle" the lure into desired location. With minimum practice, using a well-matched set of equipment, casting skills are quick to learn.

the hook is set in the fish's mouth.

A smooth-cut lawn, the local park or unoccupied golf courses in the early morning are good places to practice casting. Just remember to cut the grass short — too long and you'll be catching those grass-trout!

If you haven't located a professional casting instructor, have a knowledgeable friend observe your efforts. Make sure your friend knows something about casting, however. Bad habits developed early in the learning curve are difficult to unlearn. Try for a smooth, open loop as the line moves forward and back. It won't be perfect each cast. Proficiency takes considerable practice and patience.

Remember, not even big league ballplayers hit homers each time at bat.

The more common mistake is in the forward stroke, moving the hand in an arc as if wielding a hammer or throwing a ball. The hand is pushed forward, rather than being swung down in an arc. Many beginners develop a nice loop cast, only to try to smash the line down on the final cast of the lure to the water. The fly ends up only a short distance away with much of the line folding into the water and you have no control.

One of the better methods of learning flycasting is with the help of a professional instructor. An experienced pro

Some instructors consider polarized glasses, above, essential equipment. The glasses enable angler to see well beneath water's surface, easily spotting fish. Fishing guide, below, extends reach, placing artificial fly on opposite bank. In this case, student Jean Combs had attempted for three hours to lure a trout. It took instructor three casts to hook up.

Author Combs has learned that once on the water, the floating artificial fly must be watched constantly for any movement or possible strike from fish.

Many flyfishermen enjoy the feeling of isolation and self-sufficiency gained by carrying virtually everything needed in vest pockets. The waters of Hot Creek, near Mammoth Lakes, California, are ideal for the beginning flycaster.

has the skills and can teach them quickly and easily. One such teacher is Fred Rowe of Mammoth Lakes, California. Mammoth Lakes is in the Eastern Sierras of California, about six hours drive from Los Angeles, and is a Mecca for flyfishermen. Tens of thousand of anglers fish for millions of trout in the high mountain streams and lakes of the area each year.

Rowe operates his own Sierra Bright Dot (P.O. Box 9013, Mammoth Lakes, CA 93526) specialty shop, as well as guiding and teaching flyfishermen in three-day flyfishing courses in association with Mammoth Adventure Connection (P.O. Box 353, Mammoth Lakes, CA 93546). Included lodging is at the comfortable Mammoth Inn.

For the beginner with no equipment who wishes to start off right, Rowe furnishes rods, reels and other supplies. Learning is an easy experience in the beautiful mountain setting. Rooms are inexpensive in the summer months at the 9,000-foot Mammoth Inn, a popular ski destination in the wintertime.

Fred Rowe starts his course with a three-hour classroom introduction which includes the balanced flyfishing concept. The information on proper equipment will save the cost of the course.

Next, the students proceed outside to practice casting. Rowe and his assistant offer individual instruction as students put into practice what they have learned in the

Fred Rowe is typical of the many young, professional fishing instructors offering classes in fly techniques. He explains that in today's world, many of the fish in Hot Creek are caught and released several times over spring, summer season.

Men and women, young and old, may learn the pleasures of flyfishing. they know that correct casts take practice.

classroom. Most start out rough, but soon are getting smooth, even loops.

Learning the art of flycasting, says Rowe, requires considerable practice. There are those who pick up the technique rapidly and others who need more practice. Some don't do well on the grass, but when they get to water, are able to concentrate on fishing and unconsciously produce beautiful casts.

There is no substitution for plenty of casting practice. Fred Rowe has been a professional fishing guide and teacher for years and still finds time to practice before and after fishing season, as well as with his students. Once you get the feel for the flyline pulling on the rod tip, loading the pole with energy, better loops become easier to cast.

In time, the beginner will learn that the casting motion may be sidearm as well as overhand. It may even be to the opposite side of your body, as long as the movement remains always in the same plane. This additional skill comes in handy when fishing in waters with obstacles nearby.

Flycasting is not a matter of strength. It is developed timing and coordination — and practice. The movement should be smooth and graceful, with no jerks, stops and starts. The rhythm comes with practice and improves with time. Enjoyment follows.

CHAPTER 6

DIARY OF A TUNA TRIP

A 10-Day Run To Exotic Places Is Recounted In Detail That'll Prepare You For Going!

By Pete Fosselman

It takes two days of running hard out of San Diego to reach the famed Alijos Rocks off Baja California, where outstanding fishing on large tuna is the norm...providing King Neptune cooperates with anglers!

Author (right) shows off nice 60-pound-plus yellowfin tuna he caught on a rod made by Custom Rod & Marine, saddled with Shimano TLD 15 spooled with 25-pound pink Ande line. His largest tuna was over 80 pounds, but jackpot winner scaled 106 pounds. (Below) Mike Marino earned the title of Mr. Hard Core — and respect of fishing peers — for his ability and perseverence on trip. Here, he has bow and starboard side of boat to himself as he battles huge yellowfin. He's using "handy strap" over his shoulder to assist in the fight, which lasted better part of an hour.

A NOVICE fisherman, at age 13 I was introduced to long-range fishing on a two-day albacore trip out of San Diego, California. I didn't catch a single fish. But from that day forward, I was hooked. I knew I would return.

In the following 25 years, I've made many multi-day fishing trips. Some had all the excitement you dream about, some with empty sacks. Some have produced huge yellowfin tuna, yellowtail, black sea bass and others. Each trip was a good time: As they say, the worst day of fishing is better than a good day at work!

What follows, then, is a primer on long-range fishing — what you'll catch and when, what to take, what to expect.

The waters off Mexico are full of fish. The type and size are unpredictable, but here are a few hints as to what you should encounter: The summer months are usually geared towards catching albacore, if they come within range. If not, in recent years, long-range trips target yellowtail,

yellowfin tuna, black sea bass, dorado and wahoo. The fall months cater to the same species, plus pargo, grouper, and many types of bottom fish. Winter and spring usually are for 10- to 23-day trips after monster yellowfin tuna, wahoo, and an occasional billfish.

Plan your trip as far ahead as possible. In recent years, long-range trips have begun to fill up up to a year in advance. If you're interested in a specific species of fish, contact a landing for the best advice on when to schedule a trip. But remember, there are no guarantees! Landings can only control the food, crew, and 100 percent effort. The bait, sea conditions, weather, luck, and the bite are up to King Neptune!

Start preparing for your trip by contacting several landings and requesting free literature describing their trips.

San Diego has four primary landings that offer multi-day long-range fishing trips: Fisherman's Landing, H&M Landing, Point Loma Sportfishing and Seaforth Sportfish-

This was the task that awaited American Angler *fishermen upon return to San Diego berth — unloading tons of tuna. They're put on numbered areas of sidewalk that correspond to gill plate tags affixed when fish were caught.*

ing San Pedro, about 100 miles north, has one long-range boat that operates out of LA Harbor Sportfishing.

You'll receive a list of available trips, along with the prices and the number of anglers each trip will allow. Study this material. Decide which trip will suit your needs and make a commitment. This is done in the form of a deposit to guarantee your reservation. "Check's in the mail" won't cut it.

Each landing caters to different needs. Costs for a long-range trip vary, but you can figure on spending about $150 per day, depending on the angler load. Some trips with fewer anglers per boat will run higher.

I selected January for a recent 10-day trip. Work at the office was slow and it would be easy for me to get away. It's usually dreary in Southern California in January, so why not head south for some good fishing?

I checked at these landings, sent for their information, then selected the *American Angler* out of the Point Loma Sportfishing. Their reputation on recent trips was outstanding, so I went with them.

Yellowfin tuna in the 100-pound range would be the main target, but who knows when you venture into the fertile waters off the Baja coast? We'd also have great chances of catching bluefin tuna, black sea bass, grouper, pargo, dolphin, wahoo, yellowtail, and other miscellaneous fish. A 10-day trip normally checks the fishing spots at Alijos Rocks, Magdalena Bay, Thetis Bank, Hippolito, and Uncle Sam Bank.

As to recommended tackle, the best suggestion I can give, in addition to the basics, is to try to use the tackle you have. It might not be exactly what a landing suggests, but if it fits the pocketbook and you're familiar with it, take it.

Refrigerated fish holds on long-range boats freeze catch like author's yellowfin solid as a rock. You can then ice them down for transport home, or trade for canned tuna.

Nick Coleman displays a 10-pound "space fish" — largest ever seen by Capt. Chris Flores or deckhands on American Angler. *Author says it's ugliest fish he's ever seen!*

Lists from the landings are only suggestions; you should get by with some flexibility on the listed tackle.

Also remember that there are no tackle stores 300 miles southwest of the landing. The *American Angler,* like other boats, keeps a good stock of gear on board for last-minute changes, but they just might be out of the item you need. Give your tackle selection some thought, and use my suggested tackle list that appears elsewhere in this chapter as a starting place.

All suggested rods and reels can be rented at the landings if needed. This is particularly attractive to those flying in from across the country, whose means of transporting rods, reel and tackle are difficult. If you plan to rent tackle, notify the landing early so it will be ready when you arrive. Rental tackle for a 10-day trip will run around $140 for the basic assortment of rods and reels, and rod belt and harness. Terminal tackle like hooks, sinkers, jigs, etc., must be bought or brought.

Personal gear on a long-range trip is easier to discuss. I've seen folks use the same pair of fishing pants for five to six days straight. This is no place for dress-up clothes. Your basic yardwork variety will be fine. Pack your clothes and extras in a duffel bag. These are easier to handle on the boat and store nicely next to your bunk or in the closet.

Don't forget to throw in a light rain jacket or parka. It will come in handy for those unexpected rainstorms that creep up off the Mexican coast.

The *American Angler,* like most boats, supplies linen, pillows and blankets. You must, however, bring personal toiletries, suntan lotion, hat, bath towels, etc.

What follows now is a daily diary of my 10-day trip on the *American Angler.*

Ed Pearson is all smiles as he holds onto a yellowfin tuna that has the best of him — for the time being! The need for a rod belt is clearly demonstrated — unless you want to "farm" every fish you hook on trip!

DAY ONE

Thursday, departure day, finally arrived. With my suggested tackle loaded into the car a hundred times over, I headed toward San Diego, where I found the beautiful *American Angler* waiting at the dock. Several other anglers had already arrived, put their gear on board, and made themselves at home. It was nearly 3 p.m. and we weren't scheduled to leave until 6 p.m.

I placed my gear aboard and began to get familiar with the boat. She is one of the newest and finest long-range sportfishing boats in the San Diego fleet, 90 feet long and sporting a beam 26 feet wide. That's a lot of room for fishing in the stern. To get to the fishing grounds fast, the *Angler* is powered by twin GMC V-12-92 turbo engines. Thirteen carpeted staterooms with closets and sinks are divided among the passengers. There are four freshwater showers and heads, and a water maker to replenish the 1,600 gallons of fresh water taken on board before departure. I found four specially built bait receivers above and below the deck, to assure the best possible bait for our trip.

Around 4 p.m., Judy Collins, secretary for the *American Angler,* came on board to collect any money due for required Mexican permits, and to sign up those interested parties for the biggest-fish jackpot.

At 5 p.m., things started popping around the boat. The skipper and crew arrived and the boat was given a last-minute once-over. I knew the importance of this — once we left, it would be difficult to obtain something left behind!

At 6 p.m. sharp, we pulled away from the dock and headed to the bait receiver in the harbor. It was a 20-minute ride before anchovies started bouncing in the bait tanks. I tried to count the scoops, but the crew was working so hard and fast that I lost count. I was past 70 when I gave up. I knew we had the capacity.

As we left the bait receiver, Skipper Chris Flores came over the PA system and announced that we had a two-day

Galley aboard American Angler featured modern equipment so Donna Moss and Gary Koca could prepare sumptuous daily fare.

Breakfast of eggs to order, bacon, crisp hashed browns and toast, as prepared by "Koko" here, was served in two shifts so everyone could chow down. Forget any food if a hot bite was on, however! At such times, "Koko" was busy gaffing fish!

ride ahead of us. Formal introductions and a class full of instructions for the fishing we would encounter would be held in the galley the following morning. With that in mind, I adjourned to the galley for a soda and some reading. I turned into my bunk around 10.

DAY TWO

My first night's sleep was a little uneasy. The bunk was surely comfortable enough, but getting used to the hum of the engines often takes a day. First call for breakfast was around 8 a.m. Breakfast and dinner are served in two sittings, while lunch is served only once because this meal is a little more flexible. No meals will be served in the middle of a hot bite. Bacon and eggs to order, hashed brown potatoes, toast and jelly, along with fresh fruit, rounded out breakfast. I could see there would be no starving on this trip!

At 10 a.m., Skipper Chris Flores announced that an introduction of personnel and an instruction class would be held in the galley. We all gathered around while Chris introduced himself and the crew.

Chris is a native Southern Californian, having grown up around Santa Fe Springs. He spent four summers working around various boats, graduating through the "pinhead" ranks to full deckhand. In 1978, he received his skipper's license and began running sportfishing boats. His list of credits includes the *Bold Contender, Royal Polaris* and *Pacific Star*. He now skippers the *American Angler* pretty much full-time.

Our experienced crew was led by Dain Balle. Dain has worked in the fishing world for 25 years, several on commercial boats. There wasn't anything he didn't know. Dain's two assistants on the deck were John Kay and Mike Brown.

The galley was tended by two of the finest ocean-going cooks, Gary "Koko" Koca and Donna Moss. Donna was the lone female on the trip, but she loved every minute. I had been on previous trips with Koko and knew we were in for some real treats. This guy can really cook and he's not

Among the hundreds of miscellaneous fish that were caught as boat was heading home was this nice four-pound sand bass, which deckhand John Kay readies for the fish box. They were wide-open on jigs and made for light-tackle fun.

Many of the flag grouper taken on the trip were destined for "Koko's" fillet knife and skillet aboard American Angler. When coupled with peas and spuds, fresh fillets made delectable fare for famished fishermen who ate well.

fish rarely bite when the water is below 64 degrees. We still were running hard toward Alijos Rocks in search of warmer water and yellowfin tuna.

The rest of the afternoon was spent lounging and readying gear. I brought nine outfits and decided to rig up four of them, one each with 25-, 30-, and 40-pound line, along with a trolling rig with 80-pound monofilament.

The day ended with many anglers in the galley still working on the new knots they had learned. Some were preparing wire leaders in case some wahoo were located. Card playing and reading were popular, as well as the swapping of fish tales. By 9:30, I was ready to call it a day.

DAY THREE

Day Three started with the first call for breakfast at around 7 a.m. On up through the noon meal, it was some more R&R and getting ready for that first opportunity to wet a line.

At noon, still some six to seven hours from Alijos Rocks, the water temperature was only 61.4 degrees. Chris decided to put out a few trolling lines — you never know what might be swimming around out there!

While the trolling lines were out, I gave my gear a second look. It wasn't my turn in the trolling rotation, but I was ready. I moved one of my light and heavy setups closer to the stern so I wouldn't have to track 'em down in a panic.

bad with a gaff, either, when action requires a second or third gaffer!

After the introductions, Dain put on an excellent class on the expected fishing. Hook size, sinker size, and how to rig for yellowfin tuna and yellowtail were the main subjects. Dain talked intimately about the situations we might encounter, and a good portion of the lecture was devoted to knot tying. This was "hands-on" instruction and all the other deck hands pitched in to help out. Anglers were introduced to the Spider Hitch, a somewhat fast answer to the Bimini Twist, and a knot that Dain calls the "San Diego." The pros and cons of each knot for various line weights were discussed. It was informative and well-received.

Water temperatures all the way from San Diego had been real cold for fishing. The crew explained that these

Part of the suggested tackle you should take is shown in this photo: heavy-duty Penn and Shimano reels attached to short, beefy sticks for use on really big exotics.

Salad/fruit bar in galley was stocked 24 hours a day for that anytime snack or case of the munchies. When waves and water were rough, fruit eased stomach.

A blind jig strike could turn into a good bait bite and then it's time for fishing for fish, not your gear!

Around 1:30 that afternoon, the boat was stopped with the first jig strike. It was a stray yellowfin tuna of the 18-pound variety that hit an orange albacore feather. With no other fish hitting baited lines, we changed the trolling rotation. It was my turn so I put out a D-8 size "Pink Lady" Doornob lure. Right behind the lure was a 7/0 Lip-Latch trolling rig from Area Rule Engineering in Laguna Niguel, California. This lure is quite a bit larger than your standard albacore feather; but I wasn't trolling for albacore — I was looking for large tuna!

Around 3:10 p.m., we were still about 20 miles from Alijos Rocks and could make them out with binoculars. Suddenly, there was a hit on the trolled lure belonging to Jimmy McWilliams. I started to wind in when I got hit. Jimmy was using the same type of lure and the stop produced six fish caught on bait, in addition to our two trolled fish. All were in the 20- to 25-pound class.

We arrived at the Rocks around 6 p.m., but didn't find the 64-degree water we wanted. There were two more jig stops along the way for a total of four more fish; two on the troll and two from fly-lined anchovies. These fish also were around 25 pounds.

Skipper Flores took the *Angler* to the Alijos Banks, 10 miles west of the Rocks themselves, still looking for war-mer water. We anchored there for the night, and night fishing was available for those interested. Since everyone had a case of the "itches," we all gave it a try for awhile. The bottom was 55 fathoms below us and several methods were tried to hook a yellowtail or whatever. Cut bait and anchovies started producing a variety of bottom fish. Handy Dandy's were tried for mackerel bait, to no avail. At 8:30, with a half-dozen bottom fish to my credit, I called it a night. I had no trouble falling asleep while a few diehards hung out at the rail, soaking anchovies and cut bait.

Few sights are prettier than the setting sun while far out to sea. Such are the memories you take home — plus the huge world record that got away, of course!

Penn has put two-speed gearing into its new 30-wide International lever-drag reel, now termed the 30SW. When in high gear, reel delivers 3.8:1 retrieve ratio and goes to 1.8:1 in low for cranking on those big 'uns. Author forgot the two-speed feature on his first big tuna.

DAY FOUR

Day Four did not start with the usual first call for breakfast. I was roused around 2:30 a.m. by the sound of furious tails beating on the upper deck. I had never heard bottom fish sound like that before.

I couldn't get dressed quickly enough to search out this noise. As I scampered out of the galley to the stern, I found several 40-pound yellowfin tuna lying about. The lone deckhand, John Kay, had drawn first watch that night and was working his tail off gaffing fish.

The secret was to use a Handy Dandy and catch a mackerel for bait. Then put the mackerel on a heavy rig and cast off. Hold on!

Making mackerel was not an easy process. I lost two or three to the scavenging tuna before I was able to get a single bait back aboard. The tuna were thick under the boat, but they would only hit a mackerel. I finally succeeded and

hooked the elusive bait on a new, two-speed Shimano 4/0 reel. The reel was affixed to a matched rod that had been made for me by Custom Rod and Marine in Florida.

The mackerel was lip-hooked with a 2/0 bait hook. It swam about 15 feet before it was inhaled by an awaiting tuna. After setting the hook, a good 75 yards of line was peeled off before the drag began to tire the fish. I pumped and pumped as the fish came closer to the boat. Then the fish sounded and I continued to hold on, fighting the fish in high gear. This was my first experience with a two-speed reel and I completely forgot about the low gear! I popped that sucker into low and what I thought had been a reel became a winch. In less than four minutes, John Kay sank the gaff into a good 50-pounder. These two-speed reels were...well...reel impressive!

It took me the better part of a couple hours to make another two mackerel, one I farmed while casting that

Back at the dock, Carlos Monzon displays a hefty yellowfin that broke the century mark. It wasn't quite big enough to take jackpot purse, though. That's still lots of meat!

It took more than three hours to unload the holds of the American Angler. Then fishermen like Ed Pearson had to spend 1½ hours hauling fish to the dock. This is the biggie, a 100-pounder that tested the big man's endurance.

instantly became easy pickings for the tuna. The second one came right at daybreak and I managed to get it into the water with my hook and line attached. About the same instant that my mackerel hit the water, Mike Brown came on deck and started chumming anchovies. The bite exploded on anchovies, while I sat there soaking my mackerel. Couldn't get bit for nothing! Seeing 10 to 15 hookups going at once convinced me to switch bait. I set the mackerel free and hooked on a 'chovie. Instant hook up.

Right through breakfast we fished. Several tuna were on board in the 80- to 100-pound range. You could get bit on any line, with 40- and 50-pound being the most popular. I preferred to fish with 25 to 30 and have fun. I fought the fish for a longer time, and even lost a few, but that didn't draw any tears. The boat wasn't going anywhere.

We remained throughout the day. The fish were fairly constant, and we called it a day with over 200 tuna. A cou-ple would tip the scales at the century mark, but the largest for me was around 80 pounds. I was happy because I had whipped it on a medium-weight rod and Shimano TLD-15 spooled with 25-pound pink Ande line. It took about an hour, but I was having the time of my life. This was one of those days you normally only hear about.

By 6 p.m., everyone was tired and it was time to clean ourselves and the boat. The three refrigerated holds on the *Angler* will hold about 15 tons of fish. The starboard hold was already 90 percent full and the port hold was at 30 percent capacity. Another day like today and we'd have to call it quits with no room left in the holds!

Skipper Flores told everyone to relax and enjoy dinner — prime rib with all the fixings was on tap, including wine. The hungry anglers made short order of the meal. The aroma of Ben-Gay was present here and there. These tough fish had created a few sore muscles!

Head deckhand Dain Balle gives informative class on how to rig for and catch the huge tuna and yellowtail anglers would hopefully find upon arrival at the fishing grounds. Most anglers hadn't been on multi-day trip previously, which made classes invaluable. By Day Four, there were no novices aboard.

Ocean-going craft like the American Angler are fitted with state-of-the art navigational, communications equipment.

Fish-finders and depth-finders are standard equipment in the wheelhouse. When no fish showed on the multi-colored graph, Capt. Chris Flores headed elsewhere. Temperature was the key to finding cooperative fish on this adventure.

After dinner, a few of us tried to catch mackerel for bait, but struck out. It was off to the bunks for a well-deserved night's sleep.

DAY FIVE

Our well-deserved night of sleep was interrupted by high waves and winds. Our vessel felt like a 90-foot cork bobbing in boiling water. Most of the fishermen were up around 5 a.m. and back at the rail. Winds had cooled the surface temperature. Everyone was trying hard to catch some mackerel for bait, but the pickings were slim. Several white fish and rock fish came over the railing, enticed by the Handy Dandy bait-catching rigs.

By 6 a.m., most everyone was fishing with anchovies and the tuna began to show sporadically. Everyone managed breakfast until the bite broke wide open around 9 a.m. At times I counted 15 guys hooked up.

The bite was constant until lunch, then tapered off. I wasn't surprised to find that Koko had turned the galley into a Mexican Cantina serving a delicious tostada lunch. We'd caught a total of 127 tuna that morning.

After lunch, it took awhile for fresh hookups, so Skipper Chris moved the boat to check out the bank. We trolled back and forth for a good hour, up and down the bank about 12 miles from Alijos Rocks. A jig strike for Mike Marino on a Zucchini feather brought the GMC turbos to a halt and Ed Pearson followed the stop with an instant hit on bait. Another bait hit...then another — we were atop a hungry school! Once again it was wide open. Ed Pearson managed to pull six fish off this one stop. Ed was an aggressive, but polite, fisherman. Ringeye hooks were his secret and deadly weapon.

By 5 p.m., nearly 400 tuna stacked the holds of the American Angler. The tuna had been hungry at this stop, not discriminating between anchovies or mackerel.

Six o'clock brought first call for a chicken dinner, capped

During a trolling rotation, anglers check their lines for crisscrossing, as a crossed line will easily cut another when fish is on. Smart anglers keep rod belts and harnesses on at all times, ready for that big strike!

by strawberry sundaes for dessert. My day ended shortly thereafter, as I called it quits for some much-needed zzzs. I had managed to pull in nine tuna each weighing over 45 pounds. Coupled with the non-stop action the day before, I was beat.

DAY SIX

Today started pretty much a carbon copy of Day Five. Rough seas and cold wind caused the water temperature to drop two degrees during the night, to 61.7 degrees. With the drop in water temperature, the fishing also slackened. We noticed a few jumpers around the boat now and then, but there was no interest in our bait. Mike, Dain, and John rotated throughout the morning tossing chum, but the tuna wouldn't react.

The rough water caused a few of us to feel squeamish, and we skipped breakfast. The fresh fruit and bananas that always are available earned a nibble around 10:30.

We made several moves that morning, but nothing much was brought over the rails. The skipper headed toward the Rocks in search of warmer water. Just prior to our destination, a stray jig strike stopped the boat. Only one 18-pound tuna was added to the count.

Skipper Chris Flores anchored near Alijos Rocks and everyone began throwing iron in all shapes and sizes. "Top Gun" fisherman Ed Pearson managed to hook the only yellowtail on a blue and white Salas 6X jig. The rest of us loaded up on flag grouper that would be cleaned and prepared for dinner. These grouper weren't picky — now was the time to try that favorite lure or jig that had never before caught a fish!

We made one more move and metered a ton of tuna. A chum line created instant boils everywhere around the boat. Action got fast and furious. I landed two 35-plus-pound tuna quickly, hooked a third but got cut off by a deck hand who cut the wrong line. The fourth hookup came and left about as fast, as I got sawed-off in a corner tangle with

Rod racks up and down the port and starboard sides of the *American Angler* are ample for storage and provide room to fish. Out-of-towners can rent rods and reels from landing, but terminal tackle must be purchased or brought aboard.

A shot from the top deck of the *American Angler, looking down on one of the tackle stations. Note the easy access from three sides — critical when action gets hot 'n heavy!*

four to five other lines. By the time I got back in the water, the bite had shut down.

This was to be the last tuna we'd see for the remainder of the trip. The count stood at more than 430 yellowfin tuna by 4 p.m. on Day Six.

Dinner was the delicious grouper we had caught earlier in the day, complemented with rice, peas, and fresh biscuits. Dessert was a specialty anywhere, let alone at sea — coconut cream pie!

DAY SEVEN

The sound of the *Angler*'s engines startled most sleepers at around 5 a.m. Capt. Flores had a blank meter and decided to head back out onto Alijos Banks to find some hungry fish. The 12-mile journey took about an hour and

not a single trolled line was bumped en route. At the Banks, the meter lit up like the Las Vegas Strip on a moonless night. Chris and Dain both estimated the school beneath the boat at close to 10 tons! Tuna were clearing the water all around the boat, their acrobatics putting on quite a show. You'd think the bite would explode, but these fish weren't hungry. Everyone pulled out the stops and gave any idea a try, but still no luck.

With several tuna jumping a hundred yards or so from the boat, I had a thought. I tied a small balloon approximately eight feet from the hook and slipped on a 'chovie. I used the wind and current to drift the bait a hundred yards or so from the boat. The red balloon bobbed out there for half an hour while disinterested tuna jumped all around it. Probably was a good thing: It would have been utter chaos

Gary "Koko" Koca shows he's handy with a rod, bringing a pair of sand bass over the rail simultaneously. At times when big tuna weren't cooperating, you could always go deep for bottom fish and fill your slow hours.

Tackle boxes varied from author's custom creation in center to milk crates and Fenwick or Plano boxes. Author has listed tackle recommendations at the end of chapter.

"Top Gun" Ed Pearson pumps sand bass to surface during a lull in tuna bite. Varied action is what you hope to find.

on the boat for my few remaining balloons!

We stayed at the outer banks until after a delicious hamburger lunch with potato salad and chips. With the tuna being uncooperative, the captain started the engines and headed toward Uncle Sam Bank some 158 miles away. Travel time was estimated at 16 hours and that would put us there for a good morning bite if fish were to be found. Water temperature was 61.4 degrees here with little likelihood it would warm up soon.

As we trolled past the Rocks, Capt. Flores took the boat inside for one last try — strictly an iron stop to see what we could entice. No matter what we threw into the 60-foot depths, you caught something: rock fish, sheephead, flag grouper, and the ugliest fish I ever saw. Nick Coleman called it a "space fish," a type of bottom fish with red, blue, yellow, white, and a touch of fluorescent green.

That night, turkey was the main course at the dinner table, with all the appropriate side dishes. Once dinner was

Deckhands were kept busy assisting anglers during wide-open sand bass bite. Jigs of all descriptions did job.

Ed Pearson has just about boated a hefty sand bass, as his sinker is just visible below the rail. While he didn't wear rod belt here, what'd happen if he got bit by a big gamefish lurking below the school? Be prepared! (Right) This shirt says it best — especially when hooked up!

out of the way, most of the folks settled down to watch "Platoon" on the VCR before calling it a night. The seas were calm and the swells were mild.

DAY EIGHT

We had been running all night. At 6 a.m., Capt. Flores cut the engines to check a ridge off Uncle Sam Bank. The colored fish finder in the wheelhouse was blank. Water temperature fluctuated between 61 and 62 degrees. We made several blind stops along the ridges and found a wide-open sand bass bite. I had never seen the sandies so thick! Every cast produced a bass over four pounds. All efforts for a 'tail proved negative.

We fished off and on through breakfast and lunch. Every stop we made brought more bass. Around 3 p.m., we made another northern move towards home, looking for warmer water. We were running approximately 18 miles off the Mexican coast and saw numerous California Gray Whales

It's a messy job, unloading the refrigerated holds of the American Angler, which explains the rubber suits worn.

Pink Lady Doornob lure and Penn International were twice responsible for stopping the boat on trolled jig strikes.

on their migration south. After dark, we spotted the lights of another boat, the first sign of other life since leaving eight days earlier. It turned out to be a large cruise ship on its way to Long Beach.

That night while anchored, "Mr. Hard Core," Mike Marino, tried his luck on black sea bass. For hours he hung out on the rails, soaking a mackerel or white fish on the bottom. He was using a Penn International with 100-pound-test line.

Around 4 a.m., he got bit. Whatever inhaled the bait peeled off close to 300 yards of line. With his harness and rod belt on, Mike did everything he could to apply the brakes. After the initial run, the line went limp and Mike retrieved an empty hook. The fish had spat it out somehow. What was it? Your guess is as good as mine!

DAY NINE

With no fish or warm water, we headed towards San Diego at full throttle. Shortly after another excellent break-

fast, some working birds caught deckhand Mike Brown's attention and he directed the captain in that direction. As we got closer, we could see the surface boiling with fish. About 20 jigs of various shapes and sizes hit the water simultaneously — and 20 instant hookups followed! It was a wide-open bonita bite. The fish were in the 10-pound class, so everyone got a good workout on these scrappers. It lasted about five minutes and we were on our way again.

Another patch of surface action caught the eye of the alert skipper as we continued north at full speed. This time it turned out to be a "log" barracuda bite. Many of the 'cudas hit the scale at close to eight pounds, with five to six pounds the average.

Hundreds and hundreds of California gray whales now were passing the boat towards their calving grounds. One of the largest killer whales ever seen passed us in mid-afternoon, its dorsal fin extending a good four to five feet. Chris Flores had seen several over the years but none

As the boat nears homeport in San Diego, refrigerated fish holds are unloaded to display the booty to dockside visitors who normally flock down to see what was caught. There is a ton of tuna here — several tons!

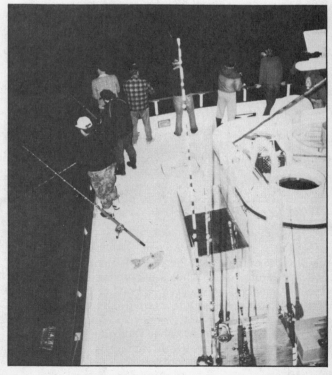

Nick Coleman fell just short of taking the jackpot fish with this 105-pound behemoth (left). Still, quite a trophy! (Above) When night fishing, you often don't know what's got your bait. Is it a tuna making that rod go bendo, or some bottom fish that you can add to the table fare?

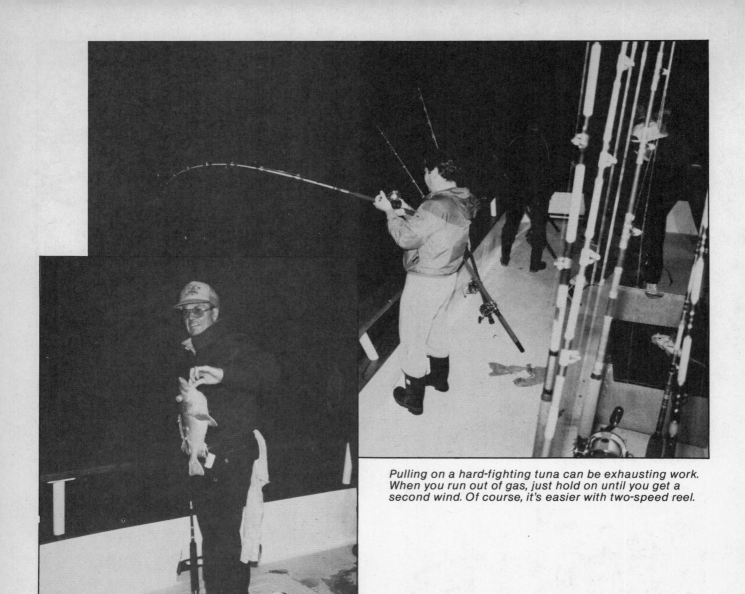

Pulling on a hard-fighting tuna can be exhausting work.
When you run out of gas, just hold on until you get a
second wind. Of course, it's easier with two-speed reel.

After a long boat ride, most anglers are itching to catch
something, even if it's bottom fish like this one (left).
If you want to fish 24 hours a day, you can go for it!

came close to the size of this one. Moments later we spotted two female killer whales paralleling the large male. Understandably so: he deserved two!

By late afternoon, the wind started to blow and the ocean got rough again. Koko and Donna had a hard time cooking our short ribs as the vessel bobbed and plunged through the waves. They managed a gold star feast with potatoes, green beans, homemade biscuits and peach cobbler for dessert.

The rest of the day and evening was spent cleaning my gear and packing it away. I then adjourned to my stateroom to reminisce about the good times and the couple that got away. No fishing trip is complete without a few getting away.

For most anglers, this was their first experience at long-range fishing. Some has been on overnighters and two had been on six-day trips before. Everyone, however, was past the novice stage by Day Four.

I remembered Jimmy McWilliams, by far the largest angler on board, struggling forever with a big tuna. Jimmy had never caught anything of this size. He eventually pulled the hook out of the fish's mouth.

Then there was Greg Bedoe, who had traveled to San Diego from Chicago. Amen to Greg's comments: "We don't have fishing like this in Chicago!" Jim Osgood, a Porsche mechanic from North California, was a part-time semi-pro freshwater bass fisherman. Jim was one of the two "experts" on board, since he had fished a six-day trip

The fish were fussy, at first eating nothing but mackerel. This meant you had to hook a mack, get it aboard before a tuna nailed it, transfer mackerel to your tuna rig, then cast out, then hook and fight tuna — maybe!

on the *Angler* the year before. Jim had an excellent trip and garnered his share of the fish. He was ready for another 10 days, right away!

DAY TEN

The excitement of arriving back home didn't make for a good night's sleep. Maybe it was just me, because the other folks looked a bit fresher. I got up early to take a shower and prepare to meet civilization again.

The deckhands also were up early and dressed in their rubber suits for the messy job of unloading the fish from the freezer holds. All the fish were frozen solid and in prime condition. For three hours they unloaded fish onto the deck. It was quite a sight!

We could see land to the east. It was Rosarita Beach, some 20 miles south of the California-Mexican border. The Coronado Islands were coming into view and only a handful of fishing boats were visible. It was a far cry from the thousands that are present during the hot yellowtail bite each summer.

By 11 a.m., the *Angler* was tethered to the dock. This was where it all began 10 days earlier. There was some hefty work ahead for everyone, getting the fish from the

boat up onto the landing. This is a "must" pitch-in feat for all.

The fish we sorted by numbers attached to their gill plates when caught. A corresponding number has been painted on the landing sidewalk and you sort the fish into piles next to the appropriate number. It took a good hour and a half to complete this task.

The line formed at the right for everyone to weigh his big fish. It also was time for some heavy bucks to be won in the form of the jackpot. Ray Bolduc of Placerville, California, took top honors with a 106-pound yellowfin tuna. Nick Coleman of Tujunga, California, was second at 105 pounds. My biggest was 81 pounds and I was happy as a clam!

I traded about two-thirds of my catch to the cannery at the docks for canned tuna. There was no way I was going to be able to polish off that much fresh meat. This is a convenience for most, especially if you don't live close by and have access to a truck to haul your catch away.

Final count for the 22 anglers was a whopping 434 yellowfin tuna, 5 yellowtail, 50 grouper, and 350 miscellaneous fish and sand bass.

This was a trip to remember. Lousy water temperature played havoc with us, but the excellent work of the *American Angler* crew put us onto some outstanding fish. This was a dreamed-about trip, 25 years in the making. No empty fish sack today!

Fisherman's Landing
2838 Garrison Street
San Diego, CA 92106
(619) 226-8030

Point Loma Sportfishing Landing
1403 Scott Street
San Diego, CA 92106
(619) 223-1627

American Angler Sportfishing
1357 Rosecrans Street, Suite D
San Diego, CA 92106
(619) 223-5414

H & M Landing
2803 Emerson Street
San Diego, CA 92106
(619) 222-1144

LA Harbor Sportfishing
Berth 79
San Pedro, CA 90731
(213) 547-9916

RODS & REELS

Custom Rod and Marine
1133 N. Federal Highway
Fort Lauderdale, FL 33304
(305) 561-5233

Penn Reel Company
3028 W. Hunting Park Avenue
Philadelphia, PA 19132
(215) 229-9415

Shimano Rods and Reels
One Shimano Drive
Irvine, CA 92718
(714) 951-5003

Sabre Fishing Rods
17100 Keegan Avenue
Carson, CA 90746
(213) 639-0200

ROD BELTS AND HARNESSES

Dick's Rod Belts
5638 Rockvale Avenue
Azusa, CA 91702
(818) 966-7707

Taniguchi Rod Belts
2272 Newton Avenue
San Diego, CA 92113
(619) 234-0431

Ripoff Rod Belt, Harnesses
P.O. Box 3270
San Dimas, CA 91773
(714) 592-4424

LURES AND JIGS

Bo-J Lures, Inc.
P.O. Box 1235
Ramona, CA 92065
(619) 789-2916

Doornob Lures
32232 Azores Drive
Laguna Niguel, CA 92677
(714) 496-7402

It's definitely an all-hands event, unloading frozen catch and moving it to numbered sidewalk spaces. Obviously, no one minded — no one was going home 'til job was done.

SUGGESTED TACKLE FOR 8-13 DAY LONG-RANGE TRIPS

REELS AND RODS

Rods should be of a good quality with an outstanding reputation, i.e., Sabre, Gator, Cal-Star, Fenwick.

3 - Light to medium bait rods with Penn 500, Shimano TLD 10 or 15 reels (or equivalent) with 20-, 30-, and 40-pound monofilament line.

1 - Medium bait rod with a Penn 113H, Shimano TLD 20 (or equivalent) with 40-pound monofilament line for mackerel bait or throwing heavy iron jigs.

1 - Short heavy rod for trolling or bottom fishing with Penn 114H, Shimano 4/0 (or equivalent) with 80-pound monofilament line.

1 - Heavy rod for live-bait fishing with Penn International 50 or 50W, Shimano Triton Beastmaster 30/50 or 50/80 (or equivalent) with 80- or 100-pound monofilament line.

OTHER TERMINAL TACKLE

2 dozen each 4/0, 2/0, 1, 2, 4, live bait hooks.
1 dozen each 6/0, 9/0 hooks.
1 dozen size 1/0 treble hooks.
2 dozen each ¼-, ½-, ¾-, 1-, 1½-ounce rubber-core sinkers.

1½ dozen 8-ounce sliding sinkers.
1½ dozen 8-ounce torpedo sinkers.
Several coils of assorted-weight wire leaders (30, 40, 80 & 100).
Lead sleeves for the assorted wire leaders and crimp pliers.
2-3 trolling feathers with double hooks.
3-4 wahoo lures (guppies, feathers, Doornobs, etc.).
8-10 heavy yo-yo type jigs (Salas, Sea Strike, etc.).
8-10 light casting jigs (Salas, Bo-J, Tady, Dick's, etc.).
8 regular and heavy-duty bait catchers (Lucky Joe, Handy Dandy).
2 dozen small black rings.

ADDITIONAL EQUIPMENT

Short rubber boots.
Hand towels.
Diagonal cutters and needlenose pliers.
1 set of repair drag washers for each reel taken.
Reel lube and/or oil.
Fishing belt (Taniguchi, Dick's, Ripoff, etc.) —
A MUST ITEM.
Extra monofilament line, especially in the lighter sizes.
Camera with lots of film.
Sunglasses, suntan lotion, hat.

Kidney harnesses are on author's "must bring" list, and made stand-up fishing for big tuna easier. Don't leave home without one, or risk harm.

CHAPTER 7

"CATFISH BY CANDLELIGHT"

Rod And Reel, Jugging, Limblining And Trotlining All Will Take This King Of The Watery Underworld

By Chris Altman

This 30-pound catfish was taken on trotline baited with cut shad and set in deep reservoir. For cats of this size, best bets are deep-water structures near the old river channel.

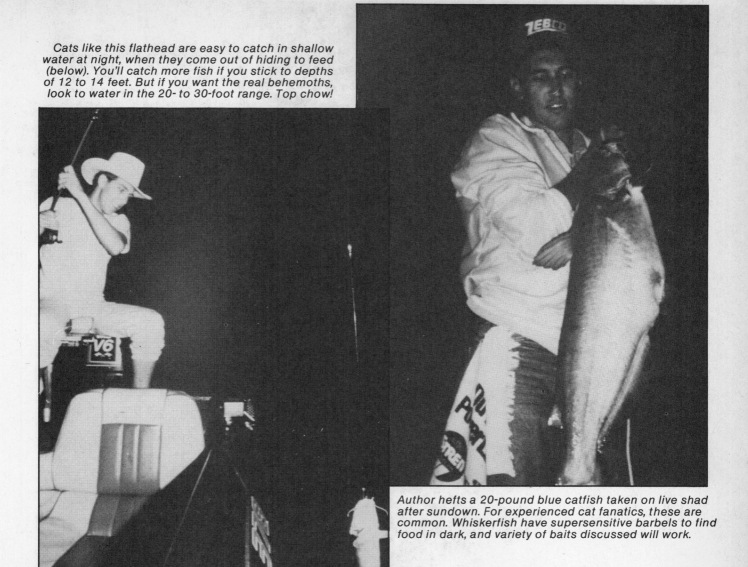

Cats like this flathead are easy to catch in shallow water at night, when they come out of hiding to feed (below). You'll catch more fish if you stick to depths of 12 to 14 feet. But if you want the real behemoths, look to water in the 20- to 30-foot range. Top chow!

Author hefts a 20-pound blue catfish taken on live shad after sundown. For experienced cat fanatics, these are common. Whiskerfish have supersensitive barbels to find food in dark, and variety of baits discussed will work.

CATFISH, it's been said, are America's bread and butter fish. Their often-enormous size, tasty flesh, voracious appetite, and bulldog-like fight make them an ever-popular gamefish. And even though most anglers pursue these whiskered denizens of the deep in a casual, Huck Finn, cane pole tradition, some chase their quarry with all of the enthusiasm of the most devoted bass fisherman. These anglers, America's catfish fanatics, know that there is no better time to hunt their bewhiskered quarry than after the sun has played its final hand of the day. For when the sun has set and shadows rule the land, the catfish is king of the watery underworld.

By nature, catfish are dwellers of relatively deep water. In most instances, however, the availability of forage in deep areas is sparse, whereas it is plentiful in the shallows.

Equipped with a set of barbels around the mouth which serve as super-sensitive olfactory (sense of smell) organs, these fish are readily able to feed at night. By following blood trails much like a shark, catfish can find a wounded, dead, or dying baitfish and make a quick and easy meal of it — all without the benefit of sight.

Thus, when the sun has set, most catfish will lumber from their deep-water, daylight holes to roam the shallows in search of prey. More so than any other gamefish, catfish are dependable. As sure as the world turns, a catfish can be depended upon to scurry from its deep-water, daytime holding pool to shallower water after the sun has set. And here, where they are feeding ravenously, the cats are most vulnerable to the sting of a steel hook.

The most common technique employed by casual cat-fishermen is certainly bank fishing. After selecting a fish-

Jug fishing is one of the easiest ways to catch a mess of catfish. It works particularly well on lakes that are stratified by temperature or oxygen levels. See text details.

When using jugs like quart-sized plastic oil containers, set hooks so they drift right on top of the thermocline. This jug is baited with a live bluegill — a hardy fish that will survive a day or so and is one of the top catfish baits where legal. Cats also eat other catfish.

ing site (usually for no good reason), anglers poke a few forked sticks into the shoreline and cast their baited hooks as far out into the lake or stream as possible. Their success, though relatively minimal when compared to that of a true catman, is usually sufficient to keep them coming back to their old tried-and-true technique.

But veteran catmen know there are more productive methods, ones which often produce scores of fish bettering the 10-pound mark each night.

Historically, trotlining has been widely regarded as the most productive catfishing technique in existence. Basically, a long, heavy line is stretched from bank to bank across a stream or buoyed in a reservoir. Shorter lines of about 18 inches are then attached to this main line at intervals of about 36 inches. Depending on the length of the main line,

trotlines are usually fitted with 25 to 100 hooks which are baited at sundown and then left for the night.

In the spring of the year, the most productive trotlines sets are normally in creeks, while main lake locations are better in the summer and fall. All things considered, the single most productive location for a trotline is on some type of structure adjacent to the inundated river or creek channel. You will catch more cats with a set in the shallows on the high side of the channel, but a trotline set at the base of a drop into the river channel will typically produce the largest fish.

While many commercial catfish anglers swear that trotlining is the world's most productive technique, one group of anglers takes quiet exception to that statement. Their favorite angling method also is an absentee technique

Nighttime Hot-Spots For Lake-Bound Catfish

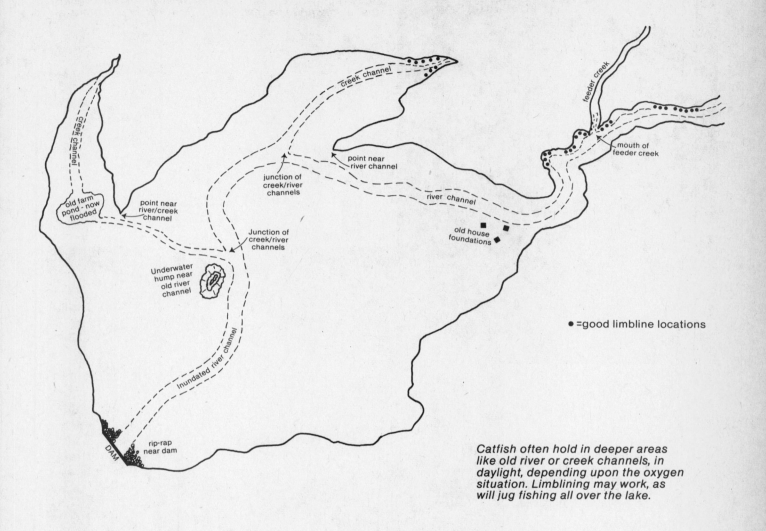

creek channel

feeder creek

creek channel

point near
river channel

mouth of
feeder creek

junction of
creek/river
channels

old farm
pond - now
flooded

point near
river/creek
channel

river channel

Junction of
creek/river
channels

old house
foundations

Underwater
hump near
old river
channel

● =good limbline locations

Inundated river channel

DAM

rip-rap
near dam

*Catfish often hold in deeper areas
like old river or creek channels, in
daylight, depending upon the oxygen
situation. Limblining may work, as
will jug fishing all over the lake.*

involving the use of scores of hooks. It is called limblining, and it is a deadly though seldom-practiced catfishing strategy.

For the most part, limblining is an extraordinarily simple technique. Basically, anglers suspend a hook from a small, green limb overhanging the river/lake edge so that it dangles just under the surface. The hook is then baited with a live baitfish of some sort. Three- to 4-inch creek chubs are most popular when seeking large numbers of catfish, but baitfish like 6- to 8-inch chubs, 10- to 12-inch suckers or carp, and 4- to 8-inch catfish and mud toms are used when hunting giant cats.

Once set, the baitfish swims on the surface, attracting the attention of the hungry predators ambling beneath. And when a catfish hits a limblined baitfish, chances are great that you will be able to put that fish into the boat no matter how large it may be. The live, green limb or twig to which the line is tied provides a tremendous amount of give. Thus, the fish has nothing to pull against, nor does it have enough space to wrap the line around some obstruction and pull free.

One of the keys to successful limblining is proper placement of the rig. Normally, the bait is presented on the surface in water 4- to 6-feet deep, and never more than 10-feet deep. In deeper water, catfish cruising the bottom will never notice the struggles of the baitfish above it. Increased limbline catches are had when the rig is placed just above or below a deeper pool, rather than along a half-mile stretch of shallow water. (The cats hold in the deeper pool by day and venture into the shallows at night to feed). Too, the best success is had when the bait is placed in the vicinity of

Taking the good-eating catfish may sound deceptively easy, but you must do your homework to ensure success. Anglers must know where deep areas are adjacent to shallow flats that concentrate baitfish sought by whiskery predators.

As size of catfish increases, color and distinguishing characteristics blur somewhat, making positive ID difficult. There's no mistaking the author's nice flathead in this case.

some underwater structure. Undercut banks, rocky overhangs, hollow logs, and brush piles are prime targets.

For anglers in the know, the sight of a small twig dancing over the surface of the water is a sure sign of catfishing success!

While some anglers prefer to hang their hooks from a taut line or a wispy tree limb, other catfish experts suspend theirs beneath a floating jug. Jug fishing not only is loads of fun, it is extraordinarily effective for anglers skilled in the technique. The reason for this uncanny productivity is that no other catfishing technique so easily covers so much water with so many hooks.

Jug fishing is a simple technique consisting of no more

than a few plastic jugs, each fitted with a length of twine and a hook. Though some anglers prefer jugs as large as gallon milk jugs or empty antifreeze containers, quart-sized motor oil jugs are nearly ideal. The length of line between jug and hook is the critical factor here, dependent upon the depth at which the fish are holding or feeding.

Throughout the year, catfish move from their daylight, deep-water holding areas to nearby shallow-water feeding grounds at night. Thus, for lake-bound cats, prime jug fishing areas include flats off of creek and river channels and points, while river-bound fish are more likely found in the shallows just above or below a deep pool. When jug fishing these spots, the baited hook should be positioned about a

Nighttime Hot-Spots For River Catfish

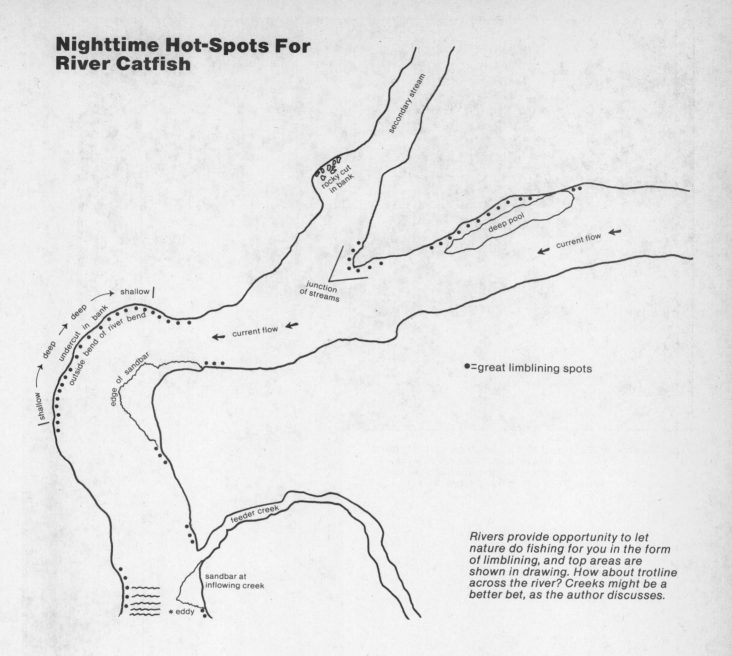

secondary stream

rocky cut in bank

deep pool

current flow

junction of streams

current flow

● = great limblining spots

shallow

deep

deep

undercut in bank

outside bend of river bend

shallow

edge of sandbar

feeder creek

sandbar at inflowing creek

* eddy

Rivers provide opportunity to let nature do fishing for you in the form of limblining, and top areas are shown in drawing. How about trotline across the river? Creeks might be a better bet, as the author discusses.

foot above the stream or lake bottom.

For the most part, jug fishing consists of baiting the hooks, dropping the jugs overboard, and then locating them again several hours later. Most often, lake anglers release the jugs in the back of a creek and collect them as they reach the lake. In steams, simply release the jugs above a set of riffles and then run downstream and wait for them to drift down to the boat. Of course, the missing jugs most often have fish on them — and the hunt begins! Catfish, when hooked on a jug line, tend to move into shallow water where they can rest without the floating jug tugging on them.

Jug fishing is perhaps the finest technique known to catch catfish in a thermally stratified summer lake. During the summer months, most lakes across the United States separate into three distinct layers of decreasing temperature. The epilimnion, or upper layer, is a freely circulating, well-oxygenated band of water which supports most of the life in the lake. The middle layer, or thermocline, is a narrow band of water characterized by a rapidly decreasing temperature. The lower layer, or hypolimnion, is a dead layer of water which is cold and virtually void of dissolved oxygen.

When the lake stratifies in the summer, the catfish often are forced to vacate their super-deep holding areas for the more favorable conditions above. And many times, the

Trotlines are perhaps the easiest way to catch a big bunch of catfish, and you must survey your state's fishing laws first. Up to 100 hooks may be baited and stretched across a tributary — one not frequented by boaters, that is!

Catfish of about three pounds make an ideal meal, once skinned and filleted. Prepare a bunch, as it goes quick!

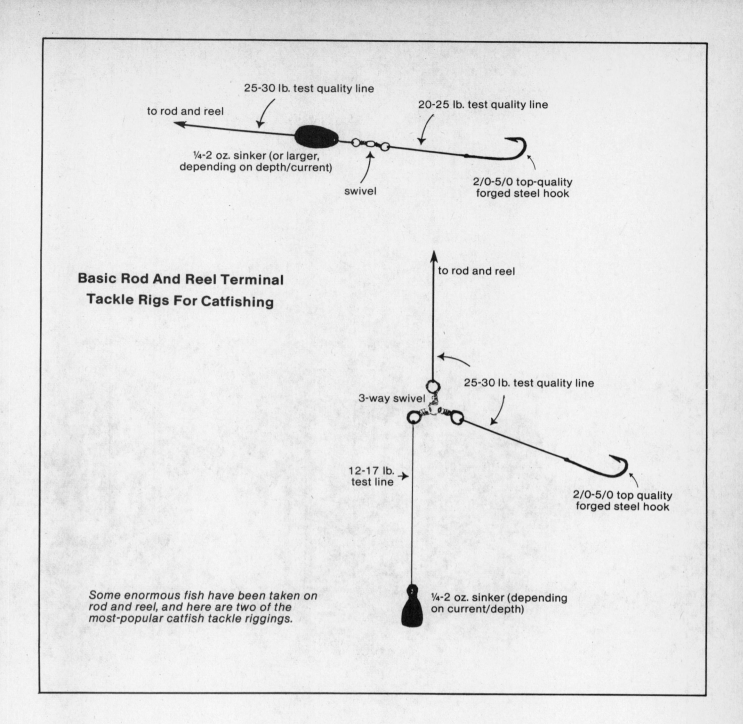

Basic Rod And Reel Terminal Tackle Rigs For Catfishing

25-30 lb. test quality line

to rod and reel

20-25 lb. test quality line

¼-2 oz. sinker (or larger, depending on depth/current)

swivel

2/0-5/0 top-quality forged steel hook

to rod and reel

25-30 lb. test quality line

3-way swivel

12-17 lb. test line

2/0-5/0 top quality forged steel hook

¼-2 oz. sinker (depending on current/depth)

Some enormous fish have been taken on rod and reel, and here are two of the most-popular catfish tackle riggings.

fish will suspend in the thermocline, holding to it just as they would to a physical structure. After locating the thermocline by cranking up the sensitivity on a depthfinder, jug lines should be set so that the baited hook rides just above it. In this situation, catfish may be found virtually anywhere in the lake, so you can actually let the jugs drift across the expanse of a giant lake and rake in the fish!

Anglers choosing to fish with rod and reel are not left out of this game. In fact, catfishing can provide some of angling's hottest rod and reel action. When a good school of cats is located, the fishing is fast and furious, and you truly never know when a 40-, 50-, or even a 100-pound cat will strike!

Rod and reel selection is crucial when hunting monster catfish. Most experts feel that medium-heavy, 6½- to 7½-foot, graphite/fiberglass composite rods are virtually ideal for catfishing. While 'most any baitcasting reel will suffice, Abu Garcia Ambassadeur 6500Cs and 7000s are the sport's favorites. Their wide spools will hold plenty of heavy monofilament, and the drags are sufficient for hefty cats. The 6500C is a bit smaller than the 7000, so it balances with most rods much better than the largest reel, plus it has a line-cut alarm (clicker) which is handy for catfishing.

The two most critical tackle components when catfishing are quality lines and hooks. A premium monofilament line, usually of 20- to 30-pound test, is crucial, and Berkley's Trilene Big Game is considered by many experts to be the

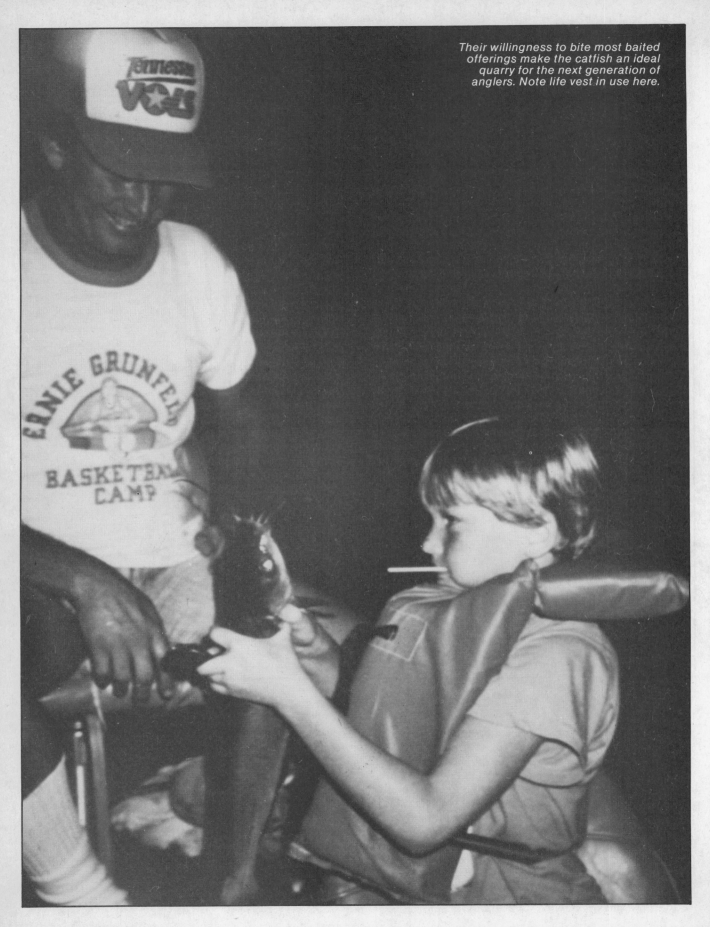

Their willingness to bite most baited offerings make the catfish an ideal quarry for the next generation of anglers. Note life vest in use here.

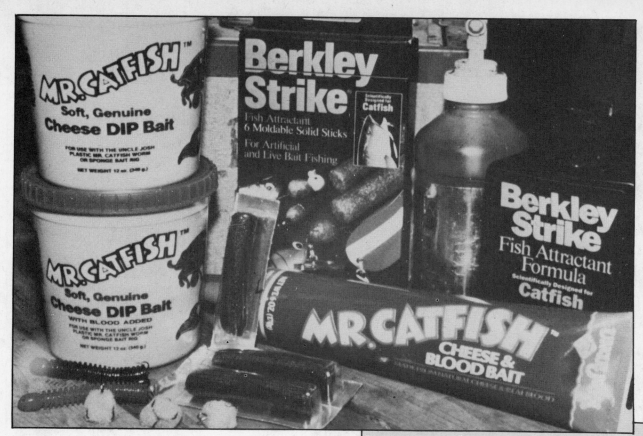

Although natural baits tend to be the most-productive of all, commercially prepared catfish baits are convenient and appeal to the whiskerfish's excellent sense of smell (above). While your rod and reel setups may vary with personal taste and your pocketbook, as standout is the venerable Abu Garcia Ambassadeur 6500C, as shown at right.

best catfishing line now on the market. A top-quality, forged steel hook of 2/0 or larger is mandatory, and you will hook more fish per strike if you use a hook with an off-set shank which rotates when the fish clamps down on it.

Simply concentrate your lake-bound efforts on structures near the old river channel, while looking to shallow areas above or below a deeper pool when fishing in a river or stream.

Catfish have long been associated with stinking dough baits, fish guts, bloody chicken livers, and road kills. If the truth be told, the three species of great cats in North America prefer a fresh, live bait. What is more, experienced catfishing veterans know that their greatest success will come when using the same bait which is most plentiful to the fish.

In many of the larger reservoirs across the country, shad are the finest bait a catman can slip on a hook. Gizzard and threadfin shad are commonly found in waters across the states, while the larger hickory shad or river herring (Atlantic and Pacific herring) are typically found in reservoirs and river systems with oceanic access.

Although difficult to keep alive, smaller shad like the typical threadfin are a superb live bait when rigged through the snout. Gizzard shad may be used whole, whether live or dead, or sliced into cut bait. Too, when wound on a small

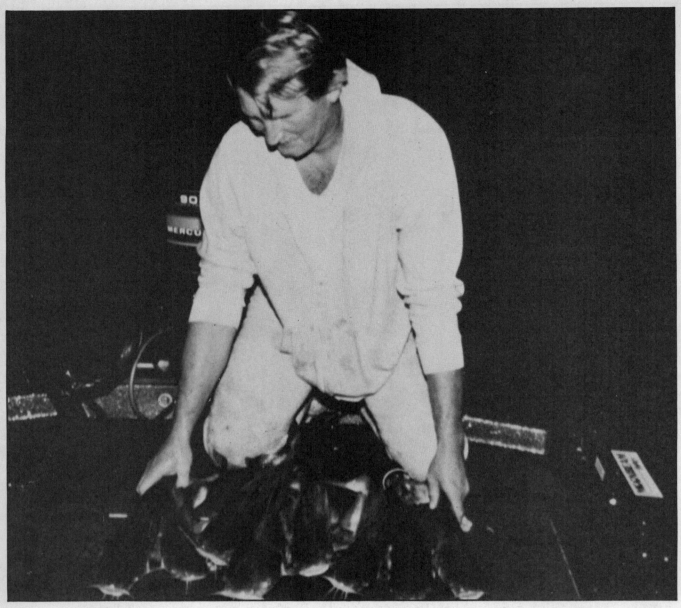

There's sure no problem with depleting the supply of catfish from lakes and rivers they populate. so feel free to fill your stringer or livewell with a mess of the leathery-skinned finsters.

treble hook, the entrails from gizzard or hickory shad are a messy but productive bait.

Where legal, live silver-dollar-sized bluegill are a terrific live bait for trotline or limbline use because they are extremely hardy and will live for a day or so on a hook. Other productive live baits include creek chubs, mud toms, and other small catfish (catfish are cannibalistic), small carp and suckers, nightcrawlers, catalpa worms. Whole crayfish are productive, but the white meat peeled from the tail is a virtual catfish magnet.

When collecting live bait is impractical or too time-consuming, commercial catfish baits are a viable alternative. Too, chicken livers, canned luncheon meats and even Ivory soap are productive at times...no doubt when the whiskerfish wants to clean up his act!

Nightfishing for catfish is a wonderful way to spend a lazy summer's night. And after seeing the monsters that these techniques so often produce, your bass buddies just might forgive you for it!

COMPARISON OF AMERICAN CATFISH

Species	Common Size World Record	Identifying Characteristics	Habitat	Bait Preferences
Blue *Icatalurus furcatus*	1-5 pounds average 10-20 pounders common World Record: 97 lbs. Missouri River, South Dakota 9-16-59 (rod and reel) –reports of 200-pound fish taken in the 1800s	Slate blue in color. Deeply forked tail. Long anal fin with 30 to 36 rays and a straight bottom edge.	Naturally occurring in the Mississippi drainage and rivers of the Gulf states. Prefers moving water, and is especially prevalent in most tailraces. Doesn't do well in most reservoirs.	Prefers fish, crayfish, and other natural baits. Will usually feed in swift-water "chutes."
Channel Cat *Ictalurus punctatus*	1-3 pounds average 10-12 pounders common World Record : 58 lbs. Santee Cooper Reservoir, South Carolina 7-7-64 (rod and reel)	Small fish usually olive with black spots. Larger fish assume a bluish coloration and are often mistaken for blue cats. Deeply forked tail. Rounded anal fin with 24 to 30 rays.	Prefers rivers and streams, but abundant in lakes and reservoirs. Very adaptable. Most common catfish in the United States.	Not nearly as finicky as blues or flatheads. Channel cats will eat virtually anything! Often caught by bass anglers using crankbaits.
Flathead Catfish (mud cat) *Plylodictus olivaris*	3-4 pounds average –fish over 100 lbs. taken by commercial anglers World Record: 98 lbs. Lewisville, Texas 6-2-86 (rod and reel)	Distinct flat head. Brown in color with darker brown mottling. Square tail. Short anal fin with 14 to 17 rays.	Prefers long, deep sluggish pools with a firm bottom. Though seldom fished for, American reservoirs support large populations of giant flatheads.	Flatheads are a solitary fish and a vicious predator. Flatheads demonstrate an overwhelming preference for large, live bait.

CHAPTER 8

LIVE BAIT TIPS AND TECHNIQUES

From Garden Worms To Hellgrammites, Naturals Take Tons Of Fish. Here's How To Do It!

By Chris Altman

Natural bait can produce fantastic results — in fact, perhaps too good. If you keep everything you catch, it's possible to deplete the fishery within the lake or river. Catch a meal, but be fair to the fish.

Not only productive, this technique is relaxing. This is usually more important to adults who dunk bait on a bobber rig — kids like more action.

Does live-bait fishing produce big results? Ask Tennessee's Gary Helms, who used a 14-inch shad to take the former world record striped bass. Monster weighed 60 pounds 8 ounces.

Photo courtesy Tennessee Wildlife Resources Agency

MENTION LIVE BAIT to many anglers and you're apt to get a look of disgust and curt remarks like "unsportsmanlike," "no skill required," and "boring."

It's unfortunate that so many fishermen harbor such terrible misconceptions about angling with live bait. It certainly is *not* unsportsmanlike — unless, of course, you keep every fish that you catch. It definitely requires skill, for you must present the bait where the fish are located to have any chance of success. And it definitely is *not* boring! In fact, fishing with live bait imparts a certain sense of expectation, as if a fish is going to grab your bait at any second.

Garden worms are particularly effective when fished on a slip sinker rig in a slow-moving stream or lake. When gamefish picks up the bait, there's no alarming resistance that causes fish to spit out hook.

The first step to live bait fishing success is understanding the various baits available, how to obtain them, then how to fish with them. This chapter on live baits and the accompanying illustrations of live bait fishing rigs will help make this first step easier for you.

WORMS

Of all of the live baits used in America, none is more popular than the worm. Common redworms and larger nightcrawlers will entice most every game- and rough fish in our waters, and as any youngster can tell you, most fish love them!

Although worms may be purchased at virtually any bait shop, they can be collected so easily that buying them should only be for the sake of convenience. Redworms may be collected by digging in any moist, fertile soil, such as that found in gardens or under rotting logs and leaves. As a boy, I used to spread layers of wet newspaper along the riverbank. In a few days, once the paper began rotting, the layers were full of plump redworms.

Nightcrawlers, too, may be collected quite easily, though the technique requires quick reflexes and some manual

Most youngsters begin their fishing involvement with live bait, and using an easy-to-see bobber helps kids see hits. A redworm under a bobber in bluegill country means action!

Crappie have a fondness for two- to three-inch minnows fished beneath a bobber with split-shot attached to get the bait down into the strike country. Lip-hooking keeps your minnow frisky longer. See text for more.

A with artificial baits, the size of your natural offering will dictate the size of gamefish caught. With some exceptions, big fish want big baits exclusively — it's not worth their effort to chase small stuff.

Giant Florida largemouths, like this 11-pound wallhanger, often succumb to a golden shiner up to a foot in length.

dexterity. What is more, catching nightcrawlers is often as much fun as fishing with them!

As their name implies, nightcrawlers creep by the light of the moon over most sodded areas. Your front yard probably harbors hundreds of them, and golf courses are wonderful worming spots. A thick evening dew will pull the crawlers from their burrows, but a quick sprinkling with the water hose will also accomplish the task and is much more dependable than the rain! Then, simply crawl along the ground while shining a bright flashlight a foot or so in front of you. When you first see the gleam reflecting from the worm, grab quickly or they'll disappear in the blink of an eye.

Worms may be kept nearly indefinitely when stored correctly. Put them in a covered container with holes in the top and filled with rich, loose soil or worm bedding that's kept moist but not wet. Sprinkle a tiny bit of corn meal on the surface each week for the worms to eat, keep the container cool, and the crawlers should thrive until you're ready to use them.

For the most part, redworms are used when fishing for species with small mouths — like bluegill, bream, trout,

Natural bait, as with artificials, is most productive in early morning and late evening, when fish are most active.

Chubs are particularly attractive to catfish, but this "freshwater chicken" also will take worms, shad, crawdads.

Catfish are abundant in North American waters, and show preference for live or cut bait. But they will surprise the bass angler occasionally by hitting a big crankbait.

and perch. For members of the panfish family, redworms usually are slipped on a very small hook and suspended under a small bobber or float. When fishing for trout in a stream, pile a few worms onto a hook (and nothing else, except for a tiny split-shot when needed for casting distance) and drift it through a swift water chute.

Whole nightcrawlers are a better offering for big-mouthed fish with big appetites — like bass, catfish, and walleye. When fishing live crawlers for bass and walleye, most anglers use a "walking sinker" or bottom-bouncing rig and hook the worm once through the head so that the body trails out behind to flap and wiggle enticingly. Catfish are lured to giant gobs of nightcrawlers usually rigged on a 1/0 hook fitted to a slip-sinker rig.

No matter the live bait you use for whiskerfish, you must present it at the optimum depth. Otherwise, you trust in your luck that a passing fish will scent bait and hook up.

A big 'un coming aboard, Gramps! Hooked through the head, a deeply fished nightcrawler wriggled irresistably — bang!

MINNOWS

Most fish to which American anglers give chase consume minnows and small baitfish as their primary food source. As a result, minnows are one of the finest live baits an angler can slip on a hook. Too, minnows are one of the only natural prey species which are prevalent during the cold weather months, so these are your best choice for winter angling.

Small tuffy (or fathead) minnows in the two- to three-inch size range are tops for taking crappie, walleye, sauger, and white bass, as well as smaller specimens of most other gamefish. Common shiners and creek chubs of three to six inches are favorite baits for chasing largemouths and smallmouths in areas north of Florida, while golden shiners, sometimes up to a foot in length, are the favorite bait of Florida's largemouth lunker hunters.

Minnows may be netted, trapped, or purchased at most bait shops. The easiest method to obtain a few dozen minnows is to use a wire minnow trap: a cylinder constructed of wire mesh with funnels leading into either end. Baited with stale cornbread or rolls, the trap is dropped into a calm hole of deeper water in virtually any creek and left overnight. You will catch more minnows if you position the trap so that the openings on either end face upstream/downstream rather than across the current.

Rainbow trout like this nice four-pounder prefer the taste of a juicy 'crawler, this one slow-drifted through riffles.

The torpedo-shaped walleye frequent deep structure during daylight hours, so your natural bait must get down to 'em.

Seining minnows also is quite simple in most shallow creeks, though it requires a little more work than a wire trap. Using a minnow seine — a piece of small-mesh net tied between two sticks — simply walk upstream while poking the sticks between crevices and overturning rocks. Occasionally, stop to remove the minnows and crayfish from the net and drop them into your minnow bucket.

The key to keeping your minnows active is to maintain sufficient levels of dissolved oxygen in your bait bucket. The easiest method to accomplish this is to change the water in the bucket frequently. When fishing, keep a hole-laden bait bucket (the inner portion of a two-piece metal bait bucket) hanging in the water. If you're using a styrofoam or other solid bucket, change the water often, keep it cool by adding a few pieces of ice, or use a small battery-powered bait aerator.

A bottom bouncing rig tipped with a feisty nightcrawler did the job on this hefty spotted bass. Rig stays weedless.

A six-pound walleye will make your fishing trip memorable, and they're fond of leeches, minnows or big nightcrawlers.

Crayfish this size are super for just about all types of gamefish, and are easily caught by turning over rocks in streams with net below. They're unsociable, though, as big ones crunch small ones. See text for help.

Creek minnows in the four- to six-inch category are trophy producers for smallmouths when fished over deep structure.

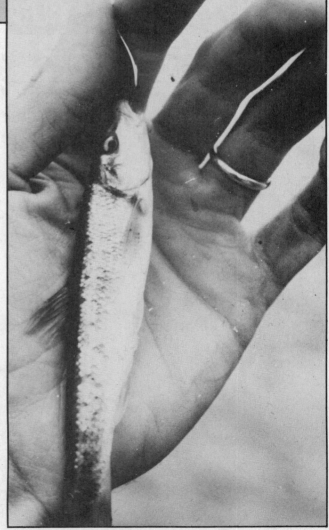

Basically, there are two ways to hook a minnow. One is through the lips, a rig used most often when the bait is presented in a moving fashion so that the angler can cover more water. This through-the-lips hooking method prevents the bait from being dragged backwards through the water and drowning.

When fishing a stationary rig, minnows most often are hooked through the back just behind the dorsal fin so that the bait can swim naturally. When using small minnows, be sure to use a light wire hook so that you do not critically injure the bait.

Grasshoppers make excellent bait for panfish, bass, other species. You can catch them easily by hand or with a net. Fish 'hoppers on light wire hook with bobber-rig.

All gamefish are predators, feeding on smaller fish of virtually all species. Hence, minnow or even fish going up to 12 inches or more are prey for fish of large size.

Crappie fishermen typically suspend their live minnows beneath small bobbers. When fishing for deeper fish, a slip-bobber rig is preferred, as it allows for easier casting. When probing true deep-water structures, a two-hook crappie rig (see illustration) often is used. The heavy sinker on this rig, when fished directly under the boat, allows the angler to accurately present his bait to deepwater structures such as stumps, sunken brush piles or fish attractors, and channel breaks or ledges.

Anglers fishing for walleye, bass, and catfish most often resort to using a bottom-bouncing rig of some sort. Work this down points, over flats and reefs, or along channel breaks and ledges.

Guides in the smallmouth-rich state of Tennessee use a simple but effective rig to fish live, four- to six-inch, creek and sucker minnows at depths where the bronzebacks lurk. Two small split-shot sinkers are crimped on the line 18 to 24 inches above the hook, but the sinkers are separated by about six inches of line. Then, using a long line (which must be adjusted to fit the changing conditions), anglers drag these minnows over the bottom along points and rocky ledges by slow-trolling with an electric motor.

This 55-pound, former Tennessee state record striped bass was taken on a giant live shad below the heated discharge of a steam plant. As text notes, match bait size to fish.

ounce is attached to the line a few feet above the hook. This rig is then dropped to the desired depth, or a few feet off of the bottom, and the rod then held in hand or placed in a rod holder.

CRAYFISH

Whether you call them crawdads, crayfish, or mudbugs, one thing is certain: They're one of the finest live baits you can slip on a hook! Although most commonly used as bass baits, everything from walleye to catfish to drum to carp will readily feed on these delicacies of the deep.

While some say that only soft-shelled crayfish are worthy of use as bait, I feel just as confident with a hard-shelled one. Crayfish are not as common in lake bottoms as you might think, and I honestly believe the crustaceans are a food which will not be passed over once spotted by a fish.

It is obviously easier to cast artificial to surface-feeding stripers — not using bait to catch 'em deep. But there are times when fish are down deep. Then what?

Though not true minnows, shad are one of the most abundant baitfish in America. Although the most difficult live bait to support, shad are the top choice of hybrid and striped bass — two open-water species which feed predominantly on these baitfish. Preferred sizes are three- to five-inch threadfin shad and four- to eight-inch gizzard shad. Too, in tailrace areas below dams where they tend to congregate heavily, shad is the favorite bait of catfish anglers.

In most instances, there is only one way to capture shad: with a throw- or cast net. These circular nets are thrown so that they spread open to a diameter of 10 to 20 feet and sink rapidly, thus capturing bait in the net. Throwing cast nets is rather difficult, but a wise investment of your time if you're a serious live bait fisherman. Once captured, shad are placed in a large, circular bait tank of about 30-gallon capacity fitted with an efficient aeration system.

Typically, anglers after striped bass and hybrids use two basic rigs when fishing live shad. In the spring, when fish are cruising shallow flats, a free-line presentation is desired. This consists of nothing more than a nose-hooked shad and 100 feet or more of line trailing behind the boat, which is eased over the top of likely areas. For deeper, suspended fish or those holding near the bottom, a heavy sinker of about an

Author Chris Altman used a live shad to lure this 25-pound striped bass, and the bait is still on the line. You can get a sense of proportion in size of bait vs. gamefish.

Fishermen associate big stripers with cold weather and water, but there can be exceptions. Fish in the 20-pound range need plenty of feed and live bait will take 'em.

I've watched smallmouths actually move rocks after seeing a crayfish scurry underneath.

Easily collected by overturning rocks in 'most any creek in America, crayfish can be kept in a bait bucket half-full of cool water. Leave the pinchers intact, and put a few leafy twigs in the bucket to provide hideouts. These critters are not too friendly, and the larger crawdads will often pinch the smaller ones in half!

When used, crayfish most often are hooked through the tail from bottom to top and rigged on a walking sinker rig. Cast the bait/sinker combination onto a point and let it sit for a few minutes. Then reel the bait forward a few feet, pause a few minutes, and repeat the series until the bait is under the boat or to the bank — or until something big and ugly tries to tear the rod from your hands!

Success with any species depends on knowing its habitat and behavior, then presenting a natural offering or imitation in likely areas. Stripers this size primarily eat fish.

Bobber Rig
— used to suspend a live bait in relatively shallow water.

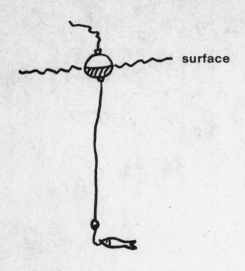

surface

Slip-Bobber Rig
— used to present suspended live bait in deeper water.
— slip rig puts weight of bobber at the end of the line to allow for easier casting.

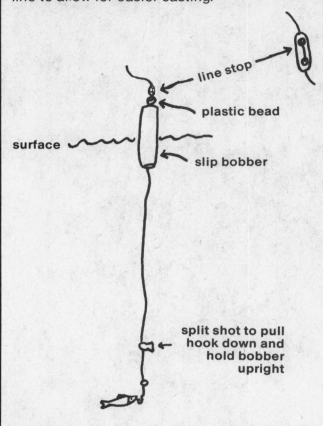

line stop

plastic bead

surface

slip bobber

split shot to pull hook down and hold bobber upright

2-Hook Crappie Rig
— used to probe deepwater structures (stump beds, channel breaks, etc.) when fishing for deepwater crappie in summer and winter.

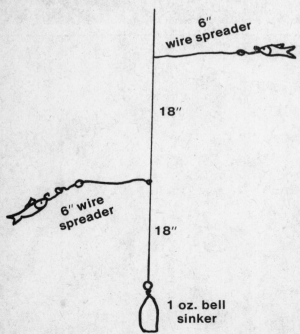

6" wire spreader

18"

6" wire spreader

18"

1 oz. bell sinker

Live Minnow Smallmouth Rig
— developed by smallmouth anglers to present live minnows to smallmouths holding on deep structures.
— this long line/little weight method gets the bait down to the fish without using large sinkers which might spook the smallmouths when they run with the bait.
— this rig is normally slow trolled over points and channel breaks or ledges in 20-40 feet of water.

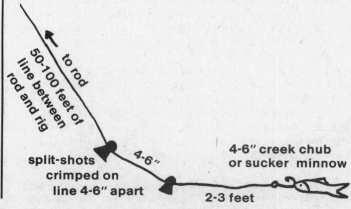

to rod

50-100 feet of line between rod and rig

split-shots crimped on line 4-6" apart

4-6"

4-6" creek chub or sucker minnow

2-3 feet

Shad is far and away the favorite bait of hybrid and pure striped bass, and nose-hooking keeps the bait lively longer. You can use a cast or seine net to catch baitfish. See text.

Part of the fun of fishing with live bait is that you're never certain exactly what's likely to hit. Could be a bucketmouth bass like this lucky lady angler nailed.

Before you can get 'em in the net, you've got to get 'em on the hook. Natural bait works better than anything else, but you must match your bait to size of fish you're seeking.

Though difficult to throw, cast nets are tops for catching live minnows, which tend to school. They're used most often by striper/hybrid anglers chasing after shad species.

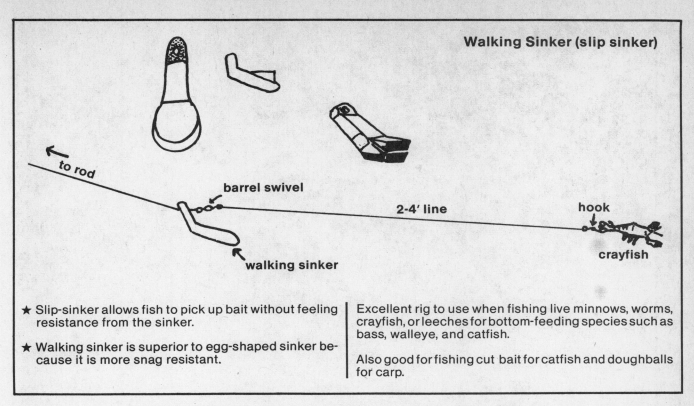

Walking Sinker (slip sinker)

to rod

barrel swivel

2-4' line

hook

crayfish

walking sinker

★ Slip-sinker allows fish to pick up bait without feeling resistance from the sinker.

★ Walking sinker is superior to egg-shaped sinker because it is more snag resistant.

Excellent rig to use when fishing live minnows, worms, crayfish, or leeches for bottom-feeding species such as bass, walleye, and catfish.

Also good for fishing cut bait for catfish and doughballs for carp.

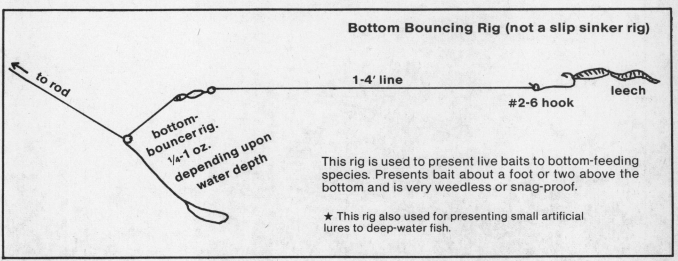

Bottom Bouncing Rig (not a slip sinker rig)

to rod

1-4' line

leech

#2-6 hook

bottom-bouncer rig. ¼-1 oz. depending upon water depth

This rig is used to present live baits to bottom-feeding species. Presents bait about a foot or two above the bottom and is very weedless or snag-proof.

★ This rig also used for presenting small artificial lures to deep-water fish.

LEECHES

Used primarily by Northern anglers in search of walleye and bass, leeches are exceptionally effective in streams and rivers in which they occur naturally. For the most part, only ribbon leeches are used by fishermen. When hooked through the head, ribbon leeches squirm and undulate for hours on end, while most other leeches are virtually lifeless.

Leeches are easily captured by placing a few pieces of raw meat or dead baitfish in a coffee can, pinching the mouth almost shut, and then sinking the can overnight. Next morning, pick the can rapidly up out of the water (with the mouth upwards!). Leeches, like crayfish, may be kept in a bucket half-filled with cool water.

When drifted through riffles and swift water chutes in a stream, leeches usually are rigged with nothing more than a single split-shot. Anglers fishing leeches in a lake or reservoir most often suspend the leech beneath a bobber or rig it on one of the bottom-bouncing rigs.

CRICKETS and GRASSHOPPERS

Crickets are superb live baits for panfish as well as trout. In many areas, enough crickets can be caught by turning over rocks and logs (watch out for spiders!), but usually it's most convenient to buy them by the hundred from a local bait shop. Grasshoppers are great baits for bass and catfish. During the summer months, catch them by hand or net in hay or tall grass fields.

You need to get up into the shallows in most cases to find schools of bait, which seek protection from larger predators. It takes practice to throw net correctly, and weights take it down quickly.

Grasshoppers are best kept in a regular metal or plastic minnow bucket (not a styrofoam one) with a small, hand-sized opening. Crickets are best stored in a cricket cage available from most tackle stores. Both species of insects may be kept for several days in a cool, shady place. Add a little cornmeal for food and a tiny bit of water. Crickets tend to feast on each other if you don't supply food.

Most often, crickets and grasshoppers are slipped onto a fine wire hook (into the tail, through the body, and out just behind the head), then fished below a bobber rig. In streams, these insects are productive when drifted through riffles and the eddies below them.

SALAMANDERS/WATER DOGS/ SPRING LIZARDS

Where available, these creatures are tremendously effective baits for almost every species of gamefish. You can virtually always catch fish with them...and they often produce big fish, especially lunker largemouths and "mule" smallmouths!

Spring lizards can be found beneath damp rocks near wooded creeks. The tan, brown, green, and black ones are much more effective than brightly colored ones. Bright coloration on a prey species is a warning to predators that they are either poisonous or bad-tasting.

When retrieved, you hopefully will find a bunch of nice baitfish trapped in the net. Now you must keep them alive in a livewell or aerated bait tank, or a bucket in which water is changed frequently. See text details.

Do you think catching a big bass like this little guy did will make him a fisherman for life? You bet! And live bait could be just the way to get him started in fishing.

Most often, these creatures are hooked through the front of the head with a #2 to #4 light wire hook and fished on one of the bottom-bouncing rigs.

By no means are these the only living things you can use to entice your favorite gamefish to hit, but they are the most popular. Other live baits include waxworms, mealworms, and grubs (used primarily for bluegill and bream); frogs and large tadpoles (bass, walleye, and pike); catalpa worms (available for only a few weeks in the summer but excellent bass and catfish baits); hellgrammites (great baits for most stream and river gamefish); and for hunting truly large bass, muskie, pike, and catfish, many anglers use carp,

Once caught, shad are placed into large, circular, well-aerated bait tank, which helps reduce incidence of "red nosing." Shad are difficult to keep alive and kicking.

Walleye and its cousin, the sauger, are...well...suckers for a leech, nightcrawler or minnow presented on a bottom-bouncing rig down deep.

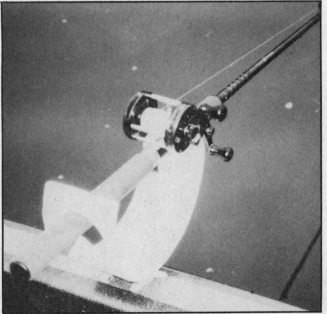

Rod holders, like this one made from PVC pipe, are handy tools for the live-bait angler using more than one rod.

suckers, and shad in the two- to three-pound range and bluegill or goldfish about the size of a silver dollar.

Whether you are teaching your little boy or girl how to fish or enjoying an evening on the water, live bait fishing is a fun and extremely rewarding angling technique. Use it to complement your artificial lure techniques and you will be well on your way to gaining a better understanding of your favorite gamefish.

One final point: Fishing with live bait demands a certain responsibility on the part of the angler. By removing too many fish, it is possible to harm the population of gamefish in any lake or stream. And because live bait anglers are presenting natural forage creatures to the fish, you can literally decimate a population of fish should you decide to keep everything you catch. Please, keep only those fish you need and release the others...immediately and unharmed!

You'll need to do plenty of pre-fishing work before you ever drop a cannonball over the side, but the results — big fish in daytime hot weather angling sessions — justify the labor involved. Long rods help keep line away from the boat and facilitate tighter turns. Keep your baits off the bottom to avoid hangups.

CHAPTER 9

TROLLING TIPS FOR DEEP RESERVOIR LUNKERS

When The Mercury Rises, Fish Drop To Their Comfort Zones. Learn Here How To Catch 'Em!

By Don Wirth

THE DOWNRIGGER CABLE sang a monotonous song as I trolled the deep Kentucky reservoir. It was the first of August and so hot you could cut the air with a butter knife. When the 98-degree air temperature became too much, I'd dunk my hat in the lake and flop it back on my head for some relief. The lake was dead-calm and the humidity intense.

Most of my buddies had started night fishing a month ago, but I believed deep summertime trolling was a method that should be tried. After all, they do it in the Great Lakes. Why not in this 140-foot, slick-bottomed lake?

The graph showed a thick band of life between 35 and 45 feet. I was using two downriggers placed at 30 and 38 feet, plus a big trolling plug on wire line that was hitting about 38 feet. With a surface temperature of 93 degrees, I knew the reservoir water would be warm at moderate depths. I'd have to get down there to find cool water.

I made a wide turn and the port downrigger line snapped free as the rod buckled over in its holder. Fish on! I immediately grabbed the rod and felt something solid thrashing down deep. It ran away from the boat and peeled monofilament off the wide-spool reel. Part of the fun of summer reservoir trolling is never knowing exactly what you're hooked into, but I knew one thing. This fish was big. Very big!

Hot, muggy and still — a perfect day for trolling?!?!? As a matter of fact, yes! Suspended fish are your targets.

I reeled and drew the fish upward. Finally I could see it, thrashing like a big snake, throwing its head back and forth like Godzilla in those monster movies. It was a muskie and a good one. Its eyes seemed to cut through the water and pierce me with their cold, malevolent stare.

The fish circled the boat and I drew it close enough to net it. Going into a panic, the fish shot downward. The rod bent nearly double and the big trolling plug caved in, hooks straightening. It popped to the surface like a toy boat and the fish was gone, back to its deep-water lair.

With shaking hands, I rerigged the rod and started trolling again. The only way to get over losing a fish that good would be to catch one bigger, I figured. I'd long wondered what would happen if you tried downriggers during hot weather, and I was determined to experiment with it. So far, I had not been disappointed.

Downriggers were born on the Great Lakes, where fishermen use them for trout and salmon. The once-barren mega-lakes became salmonoid paradises back in the Sixties when coho, chinook and other species were introduced into the Great Lakes in a bold experiment destined to succeed. Fishermen discovered that new equipment and techniques were necessary to reach the deep fish, especially during hot weather.

I'd often wondered why downriggers had never gained widespread popularity here in the Southeast, where deep, clear reservoirs usually devoid of cover are the rule. Lakes like Center Hill and Dale Hollow in Tennessee, Cumberland in Kentucky and countless others are typified by large size, little brush or wood cover, superclear water permitting excellent upward visibility for the fish, and tough fishing conditions during hot weather. Almost all species of fish tend to move offshore and suspend out over river channel dropoffs, points and submerged islands, making casting for them unproductive. Most of the reservoirs mentioned have literally no daytime fishing activity on them during the summer. It's virtually all done at night, mostly bass or walleye fishing; then, the fish move up out of deep water and scatter along the rocky banks to feed.

But the nature of suspending fish intrigued me. I had often seen big schools of walleye, trout, even muskies stacked up "like cordwood" on my graph during a hot summer day. If they would move shallower and scatter at night, exactly the opposite was true during the day. I guessed this might make them easier to target. The right presentation might get them to bite.

I was aided in my quest by Fred McClintock, a Pennsylvania native who moved to Tennessee to be a guide on famed Dale Hollow Reservoir. Dale Hollow provided the ideal locale for downrigger research. The classic highland reservoir, this beautiful lake contained many species of fish and had oodles of offshore structure that held them.

Reflected clouds are hardly disturbed by the slow troll of this boat. A trolling plate is a wise investment, as it keeps the engine from loading up at slow speeds.

This trolling angler keeps a close eye on his graph, as following the old riverbed is key to finding suspended trophies, baitfish. Water is more highly oxygenated, a critical factor in summer.

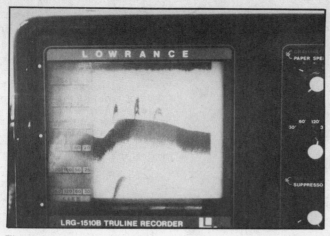

These big hooks are muskies, hanging out on the edge of channel dropoff. It's a perfect spot for trolling plugs.

Fred had the ideal reservoir trolling boat, a 17-foot Aluma-craft Backtroller with a 40-hp Evinrude. The V-bottom aluminum boat was big and roomy, with tiller steering and all downriggers and electronics at Fred's fingertips. We usually ran two downriggers, sometimes with stackers (high lines clipped to the main line), a rod and reel with wire line, and sometimes a flatline or two (no cannonball or wire). This permitted us to troll anywhere from 10 to 140 feet deep, if we wanted to.

One of the first questions the downrigger angler wants to know is, "How deep should I run my cannonball?" I could tell you the depths we typically fished during the summer here in Tennessee, but that might not be much help to the reader in other parts of the country. Once you're on the water, your first task should be developing a temperature profile of the broad area you plan to troll.

Based on general knowledge of the species you're after, you can usually tell in which area of the lake (lower, middle, upper) you will probably find them. For example, once the surface temperature reaches the mid-80s at Dale Hollow, you can bank that the rainbow and lake trout will be at the lower end of the lake. Likewise, I'd troll for the lake's big muskies in the middle of the reservoir, because this is where deep weedbeds occur. You can't make broad generalizations about where all species will be during hot weather, but by studying their habits and asking questions of knowledgeable anglers in your area, you can target in on their most likely locales.

Let's say you're going after a muskie — not a bad way to spend a day! First, you find out what broad area of the

Dale Hollow guide Fred McClintock lowers thermometer to learn temperature profile of lake. He's had great success on this big reservoir, which hosts variety of gamefish.

Big walleye are best caught on overcast days, early or late, but you can even troll for them after dark descends.

To the surprise of many, you CAN find trout suspended below the thermocline in a highland reservoir — if, of course, there's oxygen. See chart on following pages for preferred temperatures.

reservoir would have the best shot at holding these toothy fighters. Next, get a drop-probe thermometer, the old-fashioned kind with a long string attached, and move about in this area, dropping the probe to various depths and recording the temperatures you find there in a notebook. You'll want to know temperatures at depths from, say, 20 to 40 feet for warm-water species, and down to 120 feet or so for trout and salmon, if they're available in your region. This is a time-consuming process, but be patient: The information you log will be invaluable in eliminating unproductive water and helping you zero in on the fish you're after.

A good topographic map of the reservoir is a must. Often you'll have to spend a day, two days, a week slow-trolling areas shown on the map. The information you derive from this process will help you in the months and years to come, for you'll find by comparing the map with your graph

(another indispensible trolling tool) that many maps are liars. Conditions change over time, and a great many topo maps show features that may no longer exist. Make note of any changes you find with a marker pen for future reference.

Avoid big-lipped crankbaits when downrigger fishing, as they make depth control imprecise. And you MUST know depth at which your bait is swimming or depend on luck.

A flasher or dodger is used ahead of the lure to attract trout when downrigger trolling. Present lure above fish.

Flutter spoons are lightweight, colorful and ideally suited to downrigger fishing; color suggestions in text.

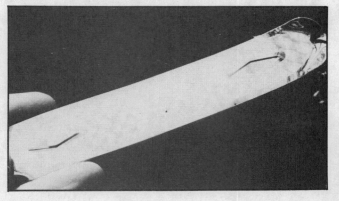

Smallmouth bass will strike lightweight flutter spoons without hesitation — IF you get them down to the right depth. Fred McClintock got an eight-pounder while he trolled, and says truly big fish are waiting — ones that've never seen a lure!

So when do we start fishing? Calm down. Reservoir trolling is a new ballgame. If you want to succeed at it, you've got to do your homework and sometimes write your own set of rules. And don't look for help from your buddies. They'll think you're crazy!

You don't need a giant selection of artificial lures to properly troll for trout, walleye, smallmouth bass, muskies and other deep summer species. Flutter spoons, those lightweight flashes of brilliant color from the Great Lakes

These flutter spoons have hammered surfaces, resembling the scale pattern of baitfish, plus reflecting light.

Minnow imitations have thin profile to match baitfish, and light weight/shallow lip make them ideal for trolling.

Big plugs like the Bomber 600 (top) and Hellbender are ideal for deep trolling. Latter has flashing blade, too.

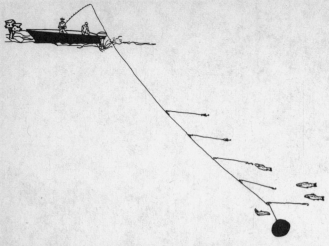

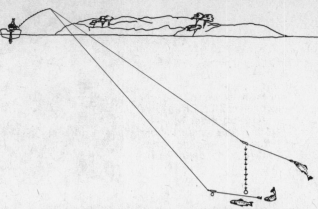

If fishing strange lake without time to take temperature readings and study topo maps, the multiple depth trolling system improves chances of finding fish at some depth. You'll need depthfinder to keep your rig off lake bottom.

Sinker release system of downrigger fishing sacrifices the weight when fish hooks up, as it is freed from the line to sink. This frees line to make for more enjoyable fight with big fish from deep water. See text for alternatives.

region, are, overall, your best bet for downrigger trolling. Their advantage is they offer precise depth control since they have little weight of their own which would sink them below the level of the cannonball. At a slow speed, their action — darting, flashing, fluttering like a dying baitfish — is perfect. We've caught everything from lake trout to muskies on them.

For bass, walleye and muskies, hard plugs can often turn the long day of trolling into a memorable one. Toothy fish like muskies crave those big wooden Pikie's and similar wobbling plugs. Walleye have a fondness for long, slim minnow plugs like the A.C. Shiner and Rapala.

On downriggers, avoid crankbaits with long lips. These divers run below the level of the cannonball and can get you in trouble, hanging up on deep weeds and running below the depth of the fish. That's an important point: Try to fish at or slightly above the depth of the fish you're after. Many of them refuse to move downward to strike your lure. Upward visibility, remember, is excellent at the depths all but the deepest fish will be using.

To get you started, I'll tell you some of the lures we've had the best success with: flutter spoons in white, black/orange, chartreuse; small Pikie Minnows in black and white; Rapalas in silver; the dodger/squid combo in just about any hot color. All of these are available through the larger mail-order houses like Cabela's if you can't find them in your area.

Most non-Great Lakes boats are ill-equipped for trolling. The typical bass boat, with its low sides and big outboard, is a prime example. There's no place to mount the downrigger and those big V-6 engines troll too fast, and load up frequently. Use a smaller engine and invest in a trolling plate. This gadget bolts to the lower unit and contains a swinging metal plate which slows down your trolling speed considerably. When running to another spot under full power, the plate swings up, providing little top-end loss.

A trolling speed indicator, also available by mail, is a tremendous help. The tendency is to troll too fast. Study the chart provided and learn to deliver the proper presentation for the species you're after.

Now that you're equipped with the right lures, have

Muskies, also known as "water wolves" by veteran anglers, are just one of the species you can catch by using a downrigger. Find their preferred water temperature and go get 'em!

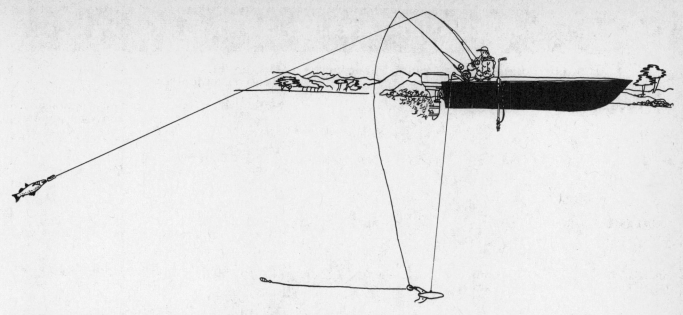

Typical downrigger or cannonball is secured to downrigger spool with wire cable, and fishing line is secured with tension-release clip. When fish hits line attached to cannonball, line pops free so angler fights fish and retrieves cannonball later by cranking downrigger handle. Second line is trailer, trying different depth.

taken a temperature profile of the lake and have a big box of graph paper on standby (yes, I still prefer the paper graph over the liquid crystal units for deep trolling), know this: Each species has its own preferred temperature range.

Going back to our hunt for a big muskie, the chart tells us that 65 to 75 degrees is ideal for this species. Check your notebook to find the depth range encompassing this temperature range, lower your cannonballs accordingly, troll at the proper speed and you're in business. In Tennessee during August, for example, we might find muskies hanging from 30 to 40 feet. If you have only one downrigger, run the cannonball at 35 feet. If you have two, run them at 38 and 31, or something close. And remember, these figures pertain to my own home lakes, not necessarily yours. Only by checking out the temperature profile of the reservoir will you zero in on the correct depth.

The thermocline is an important, if invisible, structure. But sometimes its importance can be overestimated. Many reservoirs lack oxygen below the thermocline in hot weather. But others have oxygen at extreme depths. The latter are typically where rainbow, lake and brown trout may

thrive. These species occur deeper than most other gamefish in these lakes. I've heard fishermen swear that fish will not bite if they go beneath the thermocline. In many highland reservoirs, this simply isn't the case.

Typically, most lakes that have oxygen problems are extremely fertile due to the massive quantities of plankton growing in them. In hot weather, when this plankton dies off and decomposes, oxygen can be seriously depleted. However, most highland reservoirs are infertile — this is what makes them so clear. Thus, it's possible for gamefish to be above or below the thermocline, making downrigging even more attractive.

Haphazard trolling will seldom get you a trophy fish. If you simply don't know where to start in hot weather, I'd move offshore and locate the old river channel on the main part of the lake. This usually has some current flow, making it more highly oxygenated than other areas. Baitfish and predators alike will suspend at or close to the channel dropoff, usually at a depth corresponding to their comfort zone.

Long points which run a good ways out into the reservoir

Brown trout tend to hang out a little higher than rainbows, and may be taken with minnow imitations shown on other pages. Many state records were taken thanks to trolling devices.

SUMMER TROLLING CHART

Species	Temperature Range	Trolling Speed	Line Length Behind Cannonball	Best Lures
WALLEYE	55 - 70	2 - 4 mph	50 - 150 ft.	flutter spoons, minnow imitators
MUSKIE	65 -75	3 - 7 mph	50 - 150 ft. (clear) 6-15 ft. (murky)	flutter spoons, Pikies, other plugs
SMALLMOUTH BASS	60 -70	3 - 5 mph	50- 150 ft.	flutter spoons, small crankbaits
RAINBOW TROUT	50 - 60	2 - 4 mph	25 - 50 ft.	flutter spoons, minnow imitators
BROWN TROUT	55 - 70	2 - 4 mph	50 ft.	minnow imitators
LAKE TROUT	45 - 55	1 - 3 mph	4 - 10 ft.	flutter spoons, dodger & squid

Source: Fred McClintock, Celina, Tennessee

Big walleye like this 11-pounder will move shallower on overcast days and at night, chasing baitfish. If you know this, then you're set when it comes to trolling for them. When they suspend deep, find their layer.

Deep-water reservoir trolling is a whole new ballgame, but one that offers tremendous potential.

Author Don Wirth took this beautiful muskie from 36 feet of water during August. Fish was suspended near hump.

also offer superb trolling potential. Take care to swing your boat far enough out so that your cannonball doesn't hang up on the shallow areas of the point.

Submerged islands, rockpiles or high spots (humps), especially those far from shore, can hold good fish if their depth is right. Predators often use them as halfway stations between the channel and the shoreline. Also look for deep weedbeds (especially for big muskies), flooded timber (keep the cannonball above the timberline) and submerged roadbeds.

One fact of life about summer fish in reservoirs — they'll usually be suspended. Some of the best trollers I've encountered believe there's a reason for this. Predatory gamefish often suspend because they're conserving their metabolic energy. Rather than go on the prowl for food, they suspend in a particular area where forage is likely to pass by. This is why you so often see big hooks on your graph over the channel dropoff, off points, over humps, and the like — such areas are ideal holding places and migration routes for baitfish. The predators instinctively "know" that they're in a good spot for a meal, and they'll sit it out until baitfish happen by.

I believe that once fishermen put more time into reservoir downrigger trolling, the records will begin to fall. Fred McClintock caught a smallmouth nearly eight pounds while trolling the Dale Hollow river channel — on an eight-inch muskie lure! And he believes far bigger fish are suspending out there — fish that have never seen a lure. Until anglers are willing to forego their normal bank-chunking behavior and attempt something different, we may really never know what's out there — hanging, waiting in deep water.

CHAPTER 10

SUCCESS SECRETS FOR SAUGER

This Bottom-Hugging Cousin Of The
Walleye Is Called Many Names,
Including Good Eating!

Tailrace areas found below navigation and large reservoir dams are ideal places to find sauger — when mercury dips. Usually the first to arrive in fall are the smaller males, followed by egg-laden females that spawn in the spring.

Great stringers of sauger like one at left are fairly common along major rivers in the Midwest during the late season. Go dressed for the cold or your outing will be miserable. (Above) Tested sauger lures include deep-running crankbaits, leadheads and grubs, weight-forward spinners, and metal sonar baits. Get down deep!

By Soc Clay

"**Y**OU'LL ONLY SEE a few of us old-timers down here this time of the year," Bernie Christian remarked, wiping the tip of a cherry-red nose that appeared to be nigh onto freezing.

For hours, he and a half-dozen other anglers scattered along the rocky shoreline had been dropping artificial offerings into the turbulent waters below a navigation dam on the Ohio River. The reason they were enduring the icicle winds and general discomfort of the chilly January day splashed in the shallows at water's edge a few feet distant.

There, on metal stringers tied with long cords attached to allow for the constant wave action along the boulder-strewn shore, swam a number of uniquely colored fish ranging in size from about 15 inches all the way up to one going nearly four pounds.

"Ain't many folks that know about wintertime fishing on these big rivers," the grizzled old salt continued as he turned the handle of the spinning reel, slowly. "And there ain't a handful of fishermen in the country that know about jack salmon," he added.

A handful, indeed, I thought, stooping to pick up Bernie's stringer to admire the bronze-and-copper-colored fish that many old-timers who live along the nation's large river systems call sand pike, jack, spotfin pike and gray pike, as well as the jack salmon title.

The scene on the cold winter riverbank occurred nearly 20 years ago. Christian and the few other anglers spread out along the shore of the tailrace were among the first

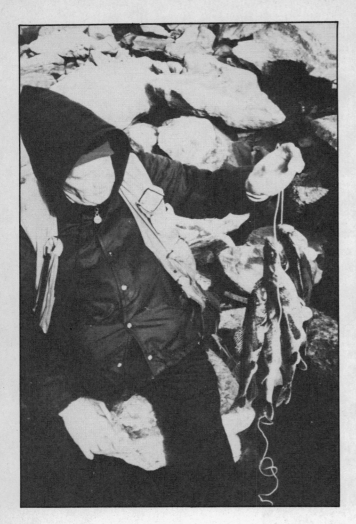

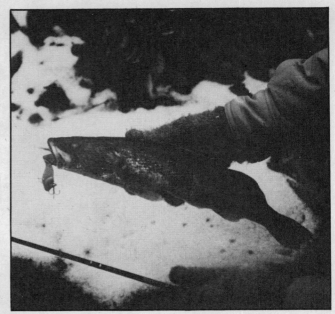

For those dissatisfied with winter football watching, the sauger is made-to-order. This husky fellow, being gripped by gloved hand with snow in background, went after deeply presented crankbait. Remember to slow down your retrieve.

Rocky shorelines (left) are great places to find sauger in rivers and big reservoirs during frigid times of the year.

wave of America's modern-day sauger fishermen. Today, the winter view along some of the country's large rivers has changed dramatically.

In what appears to be an insatiable quest to find good fishing on a year 'round basis nearer to home, more and more anglers are discovering the bleak, gray-colored days of winter along some of the large rivers in the U.S.

Sauger *(Stizostedion canadense)* are a close cousin to walleye and are located in rivers and some large lakes found west of the Appalachian Mountains from northern Mississippi to the southern edge of Canada's Hudson Bay. The Ohio and Mississippi River drainage, including the Missouri River, are principal strongholds for the species in this country, but a number of large riverine lakes dotting the upper South and northern Midwest also contain fishable populations of sauger.

Until recently, sauger were considered America's most mysterious gamefish. Long-time river anglers who can remember catching jack salmon as far back as the 1930s recall they weren't exactly certain what kind of fish they were bringing to the net. What they *did* know, however, was this fish was about as good eating a finnester as swims in fresh water. They also were aware that only when the water turns to the chilly side does this fish get active.

Joel Vance, a widely read magazine and book author who also is the Information and Education Chief of the Missouri Department of Conservation, says that most anglers who catch sauger from the lower reaches of the Missouri River and along his state's border with the Mississippi often confuse the identity of this species with walleye. This confusion, he notes, probably is the reason the state record for the species — 4 pounds 6 ounces — is on the small side.

William M. Clay also notes this confusion between the two species in his *Field Manual of Kentucky Fishes* (1962, Dunn Press, Louisville). He writes that while the coloration of the mature sauger is clearly different than that of its near relative, the walleye, smaller, immature fish of both species look a great deal alike without close study. In addition, sauger taken from certain water conditions often are pale, rather than distinct in coloration. This adds to the confusion of identification. As Vance notes, no doubt many larger sauger have been caught in Missouri and other waters that were mistaken for nothing more than a braggin'-size walleye. Few probably realized they had just landed and eventually ate a sauger that might have been a state record!

Besides being one of the best tasting of all freshwater

gamefish, sauger are becoming increasingly important as a niche-filling species for open-water fishing during the so-called off-seasons of late autumn, winter and early spring. Additionally, the species has caused a refreshingly new focus by both anglers and fishery agencies along some of America's great waterways.

Currently, the 1989 edition of record fish compiled by the National Freshwater Fishing Hall of Fame lists a total of 25 states that count sauger in their record fish listings. Of these states, record-class sauger producers are pretty much evenly divided between rivers and reservoirs, with the nod going to rivers (14 for rivers, 11 for reservoirs).

Noted angling author A.J. McClane, writing in *McClane's New Standard Fishing Encyclopedia* (1974, Holt, Rinehart and Winston, Inc.), reveals that sauger taken from the upper reaches of the Mississippi and Missouri rivers are, on average, much larger than sauger caught from the Ohio, Arkansas and Tennessee river systems. McClane suggests the possibility of a sub-species as an explanation for the size difference.

A sub-species? Perhaps. The all-tackle world record for the species is 8 pounds 12 ounces, caught from the Lake Sakajawea in North Dakota in the autumn of 1971. South Dakota and Nebraska also show state record weights for the species in the seven- and eight-pound class. However, in recent times as more and more anglers begin to fish for and learn about sauger habits and movement patterns, even larger fish are beginning to show up on record books in the southern reaches of the species' range.

Get Petit, a fishery biologist and writer who works for the Tennessee Wildlife Resources Agency, says he is suspect of the parentage of any sauger exceeding six pounds. He suggests the possibility of natural crosses occurring between male sauger and female walleye in the wild. This cross creates a hybrid called "saugeye," which can achieve weights upward to 10 pounds. Faint markings of both parents are evident on saugeye, which could add to proper identification in the field.

Presently, the 1000-mile-long Ohio River receives wide acclaim as one of the best places in North America to catch great numbers of sauger during cold weather months. The middle section of the Mississippi and the lower one-third of the Missouri River also are prime locations for producing great numbers of sauger once water temperatures drop below 55 degrees in autumn.

Millions of sauger, and the saugeye crosses which occur when a sauger male mixes it up with a walleye female, now inhabit large rivers and reservoirs found in the many states listed at the end of this chapter. Write for info.

A lone sauger fisherman tries his luck on the Ohio River during late season. These bottom-hugging fish orient on some type of structure, so you need to find humps, rocky points and the like to have the best chance of success.

Anglers have learned the key to finding catchable numbers of sauger is to select large, murky rivers that are being used for commercial navigation. They concentrate on the tailrace areas below the river barriers, beginning in October. When water cools to about 60 degrees, smaller sauger are the first to be caught, leaving anglers to believe the male of the species is the first to arrive at the winter feeding areas. By late October or early November, the larger, egg-carrying females begin to pile into the tailrace areas in great numbers. These fish stay in the tailrace throughout the winter or until water temperatures begin to warm up in March, when some of them leave to locate spawning areas.

Fishermen line the banks of the tailrace during this period, casting ⅛- and ¼-ounce leadhead jigs dressed with two- and three-inch Mr. Twister-type plastic grubs into the swift currents. The key to locating and catching sauger is to probe the river floor with bottom-hopping lures, searching for humps, a drop or ledge area. The plain leadhead jig is popular with most sauger anglers because it works best on the bottom and can be retrieved very slowly, and is inexpensive. The latter is important, because in a typical day's fishing, dozens of rigs are surrendered to rocky bottoms.

At Kentucky and Pickwick lakes, sauger fishermen commonly use one-ounce jigs to carry a grub or live minnow dressing quickly down to deep water in the reservoir, or through the currents in the tailrace. Sometimes fishermen in this area tie a small length of monofilament to the jig eyelet and attach a tiny treble hook to the other end, which is imbedded in the tail of the grub or near the tail fin of the minnow.

In the Ohio River, sauger fishermen sometimes opt for tying a ⅛-ounce jig with a two-inch plastic grub to the end of their line, then attach a ¼-ounce jig with a three-inch grub some 12 to 16 inches farther up the line. Not only does this two-lure combination provide extra attraction,

On an overcast, chilly morning, the author holds aloft fruits of cold-weather fishing. Number of state or world record sauger that have been eaten as braggin'-size walleyes is unknown, but it's doubtless happened.

Note the unique spotted coloring of the sauger on this stringer, taken from below a navigation dam on the Ohio River. Males are smaller fish.

A jig and grub fooled this sauger into biting, and tight-line technique is required to feel the subtle hit when lure is sinking. Inexpensive rig is welcome, since you will lose many to rocks.

the added weight is enough to keep the offering on the bottom during the retrieve, even in swift currents.

Boating fishermen often use a vertical jigging motion to take limits of sauger from spots away from the shoreline, even in tailrace areas. One-fourth to ⅛-ounce metal jigging spoons and a ½-ounce Silver Buddy — a sonar-type lure — are the two most used artificials on some middle-American river systems.

The trick is to locate some type of bottom structure such as a ledge, a hump or something solid like a wall, pier and so on. A depth finder is handy for such, but an LCR or graph is much better. Once one or more spots are found, some fishermen drop marking buoys; craftier ones use shore markers for location coordinates so they can remember the exact location without sharing the prize.

The boat then is positioned directly above the structure and lures are lowered to the bottom on a tight line. Begin a vertical jigging motion that lifts the lure about a foot before it is dropped back. Users of the Silver Buddy fine-tune the lift by pulling the lure up with the rod tip until the first vibration is felt — usually about six inches — then lower the lure back with the line tight. When vertical jigging for sauger

Rock-strewn shores bordering tailraces are good spots for seeking sauger when mercury recedes. Just a few years ago, a turnout like this would have been phenomenal; now, it is common sight during winter.

during the cold water season, 90 percent of all strikes occur while the lure is falling. Tight-line techniques that permit the angler to feel the light bite of the sauger during the drop are critical to success.

Beside tailrace areas, the mouths of major tributaries also are good places to locate sauger during the off-season. Here, again, the bottom is the target and most fish will be caught where there is an underwater ledge or hump area with current flowing across the top.

For years, sauger fishermen believed sauger were found only in water below 15 feet deep. But a recent study con-

ducted by a hydro-electric generating station at Greenup Dam on the Ohio River discovered that sauger often surge to the bank during the night, cruising in water less than two feet deep. To date, however, few fishermen have learned how to capitalize on this nocturnal feeding behavior.

Most sauger are caught in reservoirs with trolling techniques or by anglers fishing for other species. At sprawling Kentucky Lake, fishermen have developed specific methods for catching this bottom dweller during summer months. The key is pinpointing their locations along bends and steep drops in the old river channel. Frequently these spots

Boaters are pretty much forced to find schools of fish during warmer months, when fish are 'way down. But in winter they come shallower, orienting on structure. Obviously, fish finders are big help to boaters.

will be found near wide flats where sauger may be coming to feed during the night.

Downriggers are used to carry an assortment of slow-wobbling crankbaits, jig-and-grub combinations, and sonar-type metal lures to the level where the fish are holding.

Fishing pressure on most reservoirs is light for this species, because few anglers can find the large concentrations of fish that are available on many rivers once water temperatures cool off during the late season.

Anglers who prefer to use live bait will find some action throughout the autumn and winter periods but best results come when water temperatures drop into the mid- to high-

30s. Fished on a #4 light wire hook with enough weight to sink the offering through the current and hold it on the bottom is the standard technique. Some fishermen also use spreaders so that two minnows at a time may be fished.

Just how many sauger are swimming in America's rivers and reservoirs? Few studies have been conducted as yet to answer this question. But in Tennessee, wildlife agency personnel sampled the waters below Pickwick Lake Dam several years ago. They determined that more than a million sauger were living in the first half-mile below the river barrier. Oddly, bank fishermen were complaining that the fish had moved out because they weren't catching many!

STATES WITH FISHABLE SAUGER POPULATIONS

ALABAMA
Alabama Dept. of Conservation & Natural Resources
64 N. Union St.
Montgomery, AL 36130
(205) 261-3471

ARKANSAS
Arkansas Game & Fish Comm.
2 Natural Resources Dr.
Little Rock, AR 72205
(501) 223-6300

COLORADO
Dept. of Natural Resources
Div. of Wildlife
6060 Broadway
Denver, CO 80216
(303) 297-1192

GEORGIA
Dept. of Natural Resources
Game & Fish
Floyd Tower East, Suite 1358
205 Butler St.
Atlanta, GA 30334
(404) 656-3524

ILLINOIS
Dept. of Conservation
Lincoln Tower Plaza
524 S. Second St.
Springfield, IL 62706

INDIANA
Div. of Fish & Wildlife
607 State Office Bldg.
Indianapolis, IN 46204
(317) 232-4080

IOWA
Iowa Dept. of Natural Resources
Wallace State Office Bldg.
Des Moines, IA 50319
(515) 281-6155

KENTUCKY
Dept. of Fish & Wildlife Resources
One Game Farm Rd.
Frankfort, KY 40601
(502) 564-4336

MICHIGAN
Fisheries
Dept. of Natural Resources
P.O. Box 30028
Lansing, MI 48909
(517) 373-1280

MINNESOTA
Dept. of Natural Resources
Fisheries
P.O. Box 12
St. Paul, MN 55416
(800) 328-1461

MISSISSIPPI
Dept. of Wildlife Conservation
P.O. Box 451
Jackson, MS 39205
(601) 961-5432

MISSOURI
Dept. of Conservation
P.O. Box 180
Jefferson City, MO 65102
(314) 751-4115

NEBRASKA
Game & Parks Comm.
I&E
P.O. Box 30370
Lincoln, NE 68503
(402) 464-0641

NORTH CAROLINA
N.C. Wildlife Resources Comm.
Div. of Boating & Inland Fisheries
Archdale Bldg.
512 N. Salisbury St.
Raleigh, NC 27611
(919) 733-3633

NORTH DAKOTA
N.D. Game & Fish Dept.
100 N. Bismark Expressway
Bismark, ND 58505
(701) 221-6300

OHIO
Ohio Dept. of Natural Resources
Div. of Wildlife
Fountain Square
Columbus, OH 43224
(614) 265-6305

OKLAHOMA
Dept. of Wildlife Conservation
Fisheries
P.O. Box 53465
Oklahoma City, OK 73152
(405) 521-3721

PENNSYLVANIA
PA Fish Comm.
P.O. Box 1728
Harrisburg, PA 17105
(717) 657-4519

SOUTH CAROLINA
SC Wildlife & Marine Resources Dept.
P.O. Box 167
Columbia, SC 29202
(803) 734-3886

TENNESSEE
TWRA
I&E
P.O. Box 40747
Nashville, TN 37204
(615) 360-0500

WEST VIRGINA
Dept. of Natural Resources
Fisheries
1800 Washington St.
East Charleston, WV 25305
(304) 348-2771

WISCONSIN
Division of Tourism
Dept. of Development
123 West Washington Ave.
Madison, WI 53703
(608) 266-2161

CHAPTER
11

HANG HAWG STRIPERS IN HOT WEATHER

Find The Cool River Waters And Forget About Depth —
You'll Find Huge Stripers There!

River bluffs, often hold stripers, which sulk in the deep holes adjacent to them during high light periods of the day. At such times, you'll have trouble luring a strike. Early in day and late evening are best times.

Tailwaters with a cold-water discharge offer great summer potential for giant striper. Author likens them to "cold-seeking missiles" that will go where they must to find the oxygenated, coldest flow in the river. See text for more.

By Don Wirth

T HE FIRST ONE was all silvery-slick, like a street hoodlum with a pair of stolen Adidas. The second darted and pulsed, charged with the electricity of the hunt. And the third — the third was impossibly big, riduculously large for its surroundings, like a '62 Oldsmobile in a parking lot full of Hyundais. They glided past my boat in water so shallow, the biggest one's back ripped the surface.

They were striped bass. It was summer. I was fishing a cold, shallow tailwater, a river only frequented by corn and Velveeta chunkers after stocker-size rainbows.

The fog was so thick it nearly choked you, and every-

thing was dripping wet. Up ahead, a great blue heron, perched like a lawn statue on a rotting tree, suddenly took flight, its wings laboring against the damp air. What a setting for a horror movie, I thought. *Attack of the Giant Stripers!*

I cut the engine on my aluminum boat and dropped the trolling motor. The current was dark and heavy and quickly pulled me downriver. A big gravel bar lay just ahead. I pulled line from my battle-scarred Ambassadeur to double-check the drag: 30-pound Silver Thread slid reluctantly from the spool. I quickly checked the hooks of the nine-inch prop bait for sharpness. As the boat drifted closer to the bar, I made a two-handed cast with the eight-foot rod. The plug landed without style or grace, but with a big, wet *splat!* One, two, three times I ripped it, and the big prop blades churned and sputtered loudly. As I drifted a few more yards, I heard a splashing, and quickly reeled in for my shot at a big striper. A lone flyfisherman materialized through the fog, looked at the musky-sized topwater hanging off my rod tip, and shot me a suspicious glance. What did I think I was going to catch on a plug that big, in this dinky little stream?!?

Around another bend, to a rocky bluff where the current slowed. I turned and shot a cast close to a knobby tree that had fallen off the bank and was dangling haphazardly from the rocks. I ripped the lure across the current and a branch

See that timber that didn't quite make it downriver? In low-light periods when current is swift, you should cast to the submerged limb tips as stripers will wait to ambush unwary baitfish. Keep boat clear.

Using casting net is author's preferred practice to collect live bait like skipjack herring that stripers particularly like. Shad are more difficult to keep fresh. Use a livewell additive to prevent red nose.

reached out and grabbed it. Damn, a great cast ruined, I thought. I jerked the lure clear and it spun out into the eddy. Reeling quickly to take up slack, I noticed something out of the corner of my eye. A flash, something not quite right, a sign that big things were about to happen.

The surface erupted in a savage blast, not the compact smack of a bass strike, but a strike that looked like somebody had dropped a Volkswagon off a bridge. I instinctively buckled the rod, and the fish reacted with violent thrashing, throwing water nearly back to the boat. Again and again I set the hooks, and the striper began moving upriver, slowly at first, like a steam locomotive leaving the station, then faster, faster, water droplets streaming from the reel, rod arching and pumping. This was a good one, a genuine bad boy, and I thought of that Oldsmobile fish I'd spotted earlier. I kept pressure on the fish but resisted the temptation to thumb the spool.

The striper began surging toward the opposite bank. Lucky for me, I thought, because the bluff side of the river was full of line-busting trees. She powered for a shallow shoal and a silvery shower of shad peppered the air. Now she was on top, thrashing and trying to get sideways so the current could help her in losing the lure. My trolling motor scraped bottom. I put more pressure on the fish and miraculously turned her back to deeper water. She powered downward and I let her run, then worked her back around

Heavyweight stripers like this 30-plus-pounder gravitate to rivers in hot weather, where they can be taken on huge topwater baits like nine-inch Cordell RedFin at right.

sent the big lure sailing out of her jaws. It shot into the side of the boat so hard, it split from head to tail. I sank to my knees as the fish sulked in the current, then confidently swam upriver.

Most striper fishermen put their tackle away when summer arrives. A few hit the water at daybreak and sunset, drifting live bait or hoping for an occasional surfacing fish. But once the sun has established itself in the sky, they leave the water to the party-bargers and water skiers. Stripers, they say, don't like the summer heat.

I'm here to tell you that the hottest part of the summer can be the most explosive time to hang a big striper. It's not merely a sometimes thing — you can practically go to the bank on it!

MOVING WATER

The key to big stripers in summer is moving water; not the slow-paced current found in reservoirs, but serious current, river current. There are important reasons for this. Stripers love cold water — experts agree that somewhere between 50 and 60 degrees makes for active striped bass. To go to water anywhere near that temperature range in many reservoirs, especially in the Southwest and Southeast, the striper will find itself in a world of trouble. If it goes deep enough to find cool water, it will probably go beneath the oxygenated zone of the reservoir. And a striper can't make it without oxygen. This dilemma is known as "the squeeze" among striper fanatics. In fact, it's such a problem in some states that fisheries personnel have stopped

Red and white lures are attractive to big stripers in clear water. This one hit a Zara Spook with modified — as in beefed up — hooks, hardware epoxied to body.

in a slow circle. That's when I got a good look at her. This fish was no Oldsmobile — she looked more like a stretch Mercedes! I'd landed stripers close to 40 pounds in this river, but this striper was totally out of the league. Fifty? Maybe bigger!

Suddenly I felt weak-kneed. The fish made another long run, and I used this opportunity to clear the floor of the boat of tackle boxes and loose lures. I unhooked the gaff from its holder and waited, waited while the line pulled from the reel and the rod buckled under the weight of the fish. Finally, I pulled her around one more time, and she was within three gaff-lengths of the boat. Her back was as thick as two railroad ties, and I admit to being nervous as hell.

I leaned over, gaff in hand, as she began to roll over onto her side. That's when she whipped her head around and

Doug Hannon may be known as "Bass Professor" for his work with largemouths, but he'll cast a fly to a summer striper. Fished down deep, these imitations score well.

Another good thing about catching a big striper from a cold river is you usually can release him alive and in good shape to fight again another day. Hannon does that in this case.

If you figure to keep your hawg fish, your equipment should include a gaff. Hopefully, you'll be more successful with its use than was author Wirth.

stocking striped bass in favor of the more heat-tolerant hybrid.

But oxygen is no problem in a river. The very nature of current, with its tumbling action, guarantees oxygen from top to bottom in many areas of the river. And river water is generally significantly cooler during the summertime than in a reservoir. In mid-Tennessee where I do much of my striper fishing, a reservoir near my home might easily attain a surface temperature of 90 degrees; even more in the dog days of summer. On the other hand, a river not far from this reservoir might never get hotter than 80 degrees on the surface.

Of course, even 80 degrees can be too hot for active stripers, so the trick becomes looking for the coolest water you can find in the river. Often this occurs in a secondary river or tailwater.

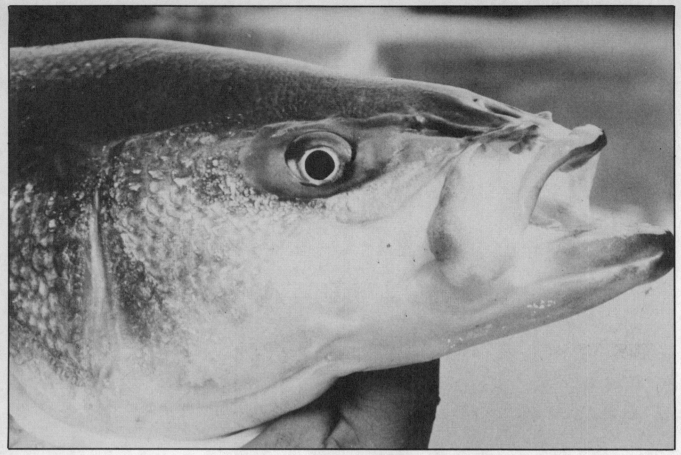

Huge stripers will work in packs, herding baitfish like cowboys did cattle on the ranges of the West. Once they're corralled, the baitfish would be consumed in feeding frenzy that'd blow fish six feet in air.

COLD AND CLEAR

I've talked with striper fishermen from California to the East Coast, and many report seeing big stripers in cold, clear tailwaters during the summertime. This is no fluke. Many of these tailwaters dump into a larger, warmer river, or reservoir. You've heard of a heat-seeking missile? Think of the striper as a cold-seeking missile in summer. It will travel long distances and move into unlikely places in its quest for cold, highly oxygenated water. If this means moving into a shallow tailrace, a trout-fishing spot, so be it.

If you have stripers in your area, check to see whether or not they've been stocked in a major river. If they have, once summer arrives, look for connecting secondary rivers that feed into the major river. The coldest of these will contain striped bass — big ones, too.

The hardest part of fishing these shallow tributaries during hot weather is believing the stripers will be in there. You'll probably motor past hordes of waders and bank fishermen dunking a smorgasboard of assorted treats for trout. Like the flyfisherman I drifted past that fateful foggy morning, they may look askance at your heavy-duty tackle and major league lures. Let 'em dunk Niblets for six-inch rainbows — you're after something serious!

If the fish are there, and the water isn't muddy from a recent rain, you'll know it. You'll see them. It's hard for a 20-, 30-, or 40-pound striper to hide in a place this small.

GENERATING EXCITEMENT

One of the facts of life about tailwater fishing, whether you're after trout or stripers, is that conditions will seldom be the same two days in a row. That's because the river will rise or fall, depending upon the generation schedule at the dam. Ideal conditions for big stripers, to me, are fast current, clear water and moderate depth. Water up in the trees — high water — is bad news: I've seldom connected with stripers in this situation. But water high enough on the shoals to permit me to motor upriver without busting my lower unit is not only convenient, it is ideal for stripers.

Those shoals are super-important when the current is moving fast. Current draws everything in the river up shallower. It brings baitfish, trout, rough fish like carp and suckers, and stripers up onto shallower structure. Long, shallow shoals are my Number One place to fish for big stripers in the summer when dams are generating electricity. This is part of the disbelief system of summer striper fishing. They're supposed to be in big, deep reservoirs, not on a three-foot river shoal. But you'll see big wolfpacks working up and down the shoals, corraling baitfish like cowboys in a movie.

The trouble with super-shallow shoal stripers is they are hard to catch once the light hits the water. For this reason, I fish the shoals while the river fog is still dense in the morning, and again when it begins to gather in the evening.

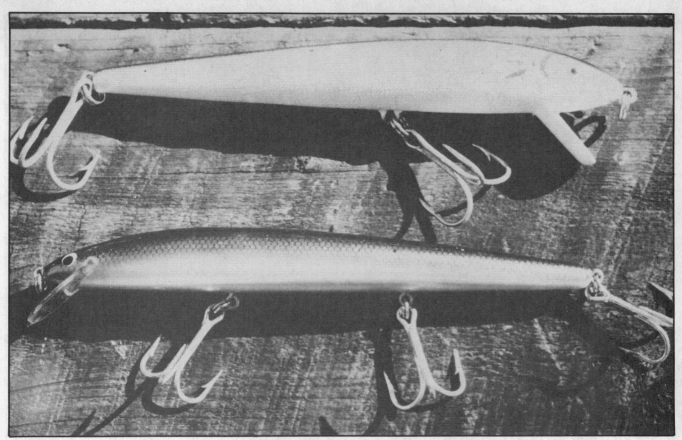

Topwater minnows in the jumbo category may get you savage strikes — like a Volkswagen falling off bridge! Prop bait (far left), popper (far right), chugger (third from left) and wounded minnow imitations are producers.

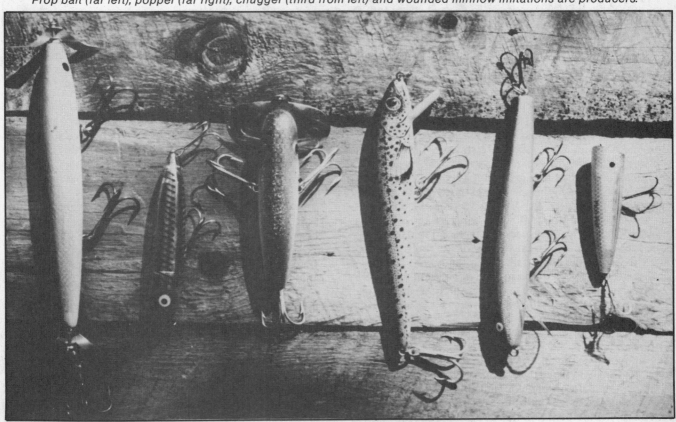

As the fog clears and the sun begins to penetrate the clear river water, switch to quieter lures for big stripers.

During times when the sun hits the water, I'll switch to what I call mid-depth runs. These usually occur below or above a shoal, and are typified by a straight chute of water averaging from six to eight feet in depth. In the rivers I fish, anything deeper than that is a hole. The runs represent a compromise between the shoals and the holes, to my way of thinking. I think the fish use them when the current is strong and the light high. They'll hang around shoreline trees and big rocks, and, especially, in midstream trees that have tried and failed to wash downriver. If you're floating downstream through one of these runs and spot the telltale dark shadow of a fallen tree in midstream, don't float too close to it. Move the boat off to one side and cast toward the tips of the branches. Often you'll see a big striper, or several, move out to examine the lure.

Some of the biggest stripers stay in the deepest holes in the river, but seldom far from a shallow shoal. I've watched them blow shad six feet into the air right at the edge of a shoal, and am convinced they sit and wait for the baitfish to enter the hole. Often when you first enter an area like this, you'll notice the savage splashing of a feeding striper. This isn't merely coincidence: When you passed over the shoal

with your boat, you spooked baitfish, which ran into the hole, which quickly realized they should have stayed put. In fact, you can deliberately generate striper activity by repeatedly running back and forth over a shoal with your boat, then settling down to casting the closest adjacent hole.

Don't think of stripers as big, silvery largemouth bass. They don't stick close to structure like largemouths will. They will occasionally use structure, especially fallen trees, as feeding stations, because in a river such areas attract a ton of bait, but more often than not, you can catch a striper in open water. They follow the baitfish.

TOPWATERS ARE TERRIFIC!

There are all kinds of lures fishermen use to catch stripers, but to me, topwaters are the top choice in summer, especially in these cold rivers. Big prop baits, stick baits like the Zara Spook, poppers and chuggers — you name it, they'll eat it. The striper is not a picky eater. I do like a light-colored lure, however, such as white or silver. And I've found stripers have a strong attraction to red, especially as a secondary color. One of the most popular striper topwaters

Live bait is great for cold-river stripers. This bruiser ate a foot-long skipjack herring drifted over shallow bar.

is the big Cordell RedFin. Cast it out and reel it in slowly, with the rod held high, so that the bait wobbles back and forth across the surface, sending out a telltale wake.

The problem with many topwater lures is that they aren't stout enough to hold a giant striper. On bass-sized topwaters such as the Spook, I'll remove the standard hooks, replace with bigger ones, then epoxy the hardware and screws back into the body of the lure. I caught my biggest tailwater striper, a fish of 39 pounds, on a modified Spook. A buddy I fish with frequently went to the same spot the next morning and caught a 42½-pounder on the same lure!

As a rule of thumb, fish your bigger, noisier topwaters in the low-light periods, and your smaller, less-obtrusive ones when the sun comes out. Action typically falls off dramatically after mid-morning and usually won't pick up again until evening — the striper simply doesn't like strong sunlight.

For heart-stopping action, fish these places after dark. Use a noisy topwater and you may be rewarded with the biggest striper of your career — if you can stand having a trophy blow a hole in the water next to your boat in the dark!

BAIT IS GREAT

Live bait, while not as exciting as topwaters, can turn the head of a sulking striper in a cold, clear river. I like to use a cast net to get big shad and skipjack herring, a tarponlike fish over a foot long that stripers can't resist. Hook these and let them swim on a flatline behind your boat as you drift with the current. The bigger baits may require a heavy sinker to keep them down. Set the hook immediately when the striper hits and enjoy the ride!

River forage species such as shad require extreme measures if you hope to keep them alive and kickin'. Many striper fanatics use a large, circular, aerated bait well to prevent the circle-swimming shad from "red-nosing" and losing their appeal to the stripers. Treat the water with a livewell potion such as Jungle Labs' Shiner Life.

BELIEVE IT OR NOT

Summer can be absolutely the best time to catch a huge striper, if you fish cold rivers and believe in the magic of topwater lures and live bait. Remember, the striped bass goes where it must to attain what it needs: Cool, highly-oxygenated water. You should go there, too. Believe it or not, you'll find the action you've been looking for!

Redfish this size give a fine account of themselves on light spinning tackle, making them favorites with flats fishermen. The redfish will take a variety of lures that are presented in front of feeding fish cruising shallows.

CHAPTER 12

RETURN OF THE REDFISH

A Three-Year Hiatus And Gamefish Status Have Thankfully Restored This Hard Fighter!

By Chris Christian

THE FALLING TIDE pushed strongly against Jim Ising's 18-foot center-console Sea Squirt, but it was no match for the big electric trolling motor on the bow. Easing us a little closer to the oyster-laden point, Jim sent his plastic-tailed jig to its outside edge. Mine wasn't far behind.

I don't think either of us pumped the jig more than a half-dozen feet before we were locked up with another hard-fighting redfish.

It was getting repetitious and, as my throbbing right wrist would attest, a bit painful. We'd been working back and forth across this small point for the better part of two hours and seldom did one of us go more than a few casts without hooking up with a redfish. They just kept on coming, drawn to the deeper water of the point as the falling tide stripped water from the shallow mud and oyster-laden flats around it.

My present fish, a good bit bigger than the others we had taken, wasn't giving my wrist much of a break. Turning down current, it launched into a blistering series of short bulldog runs that strained my light spinning rig to its limits. It was a good five minutes before I was able to reach down with a pair of needlenose pliers and free the jig from the 15-pound-plus red.

"That's enough for me, Jim," I remember saying as I exchanged my spinning rod for a cold can of the beverage

Polarized sunglasses will assist flats fishermen who are using sight-fishing method described in text. You must approach quietly, author says, as flats fish are spooky.

that made Milwaukee famous, then began massaging my aching wrist.

"This is going to be my last one, too," Ising replied, as he tussled with yet another red. "I never thought I'd get tired of catching redfish, but I certainly have today."

Long ago memories of past and better times? Hardly. In fact, the incident happened less than 12 months ago, and the same scene has been repeated on a number of trips since then.

Capt. Tony Lay puts the strain to his rod-holding wrist as hefty redfish tests tackle. "Poor man's bonefish" is found over wider area than bones and rate highly on fighting ability.

This redfish is about finished — as was the entire fishery just a few short years ago. New laws and the vigorous enforcement of them restored fishery. Season is closed for three months to protect spawning cycle.

It's safe to say that Florida is currently undergoing a redfish revival of no small proportions. In fact, veteran Sunshine State anglers might readily admit that the current population of redfish is the best it's been in decades!

At about age 2 for males, and 4 for females, they mature into spawning-capable adults and migrate to the deeper waters of the Atlantic and the Gulf of Mexico. From there, they return annually to spawn in and around barrier islands and passes. The resulting fry move to the shallow estuaries to complete the reproductive cycle.

The vast majority of sportfishing for reds centers around the juvenile fish in the shallow bays and estuaries. With a rapidly expanding number of sport anglers, combined with virtually no size and bag limits, it became evident that stocks of these redfish were being caught faster than they could be replaced by spawning adults. This is termed "recruitment-overfished," and can lead to the collapse of a species.

This alone was cause for grave concern among fisheries managers. But in 1985, the commercial catch suddenly skyrocketed to over five million pounds, due entirely to the demand for blackened redfish. These fish, however, were not the shallow-water juveniles; instead, they were the mature, open-water adult spawners — fish far too large and coarse-fleshed to be kept for food by the sport fisherman, which thus far had been relatively safe from overharvest.

The combined pressure from sport and commercial fishermen proved too much for the reds, and the species was in imminent danger of a complete collapse!

Today, after a three-year closure, redfish stocks have rebounded vigorously. And, to keep them there, Florida has granted them gamefish status, free from the nets and black skillets that could plunge them to the verge of collapse once again.

Under present laws, anglers are allowed to keep one redfish per day between the lengths of 18 and 27 inches, with a

While prowling the flats and blind casting in deep water, light spinning tackle in the 8- to 12-pound class is ideal for top action on flat redfish.

full closure on the species during March, April and May. The new law forbids all sale of redfish.

For anglers whose idea of a successful trip is a cooler full of fillets, redfish may not rank up there with a number of other desirable species. But, for those looking to experience some of the most exciting light-tackle angling around, here's a look at the two most popular techniques for taking them: sight fishing and blind casting.

SIGHT FISHING

Spotting a redfish cruising slowly along a shallow flat in search of a meal, and then making a precise cast with an artificial bait, has often been called "poor man's bonefishing." There are a lot of similarities.

Like bonefish, reds will spend the low-tide periods in deeper holes and cuts. Once rising water begins to cover the shallow flats, both species will move up onto them to forage for crabs, crustaceans, and other delectables. Both can be spotted by sharp-eyed anglers armed with polarized glasses, and will reveal themselves by their wakes, small puffs of mud (called muds) made as they root in the bottom, or they may even display their tails above the surface as they root out a critter from his hiding place.

Once an angler spots his fish, he maneuvers into casting position with the aid of a push pole and flips his lure beyond the fish, in order to retrieve the bait across its line of sight.

While bonefish are definitely the more glamorous species, known for their lightning runs when hooked, redfish don't take too much of a back seat. One factor certainly in the redfish's favor is his availability. While bonefish are restricted to the southern portions of Florida, reds are available virtually anywhere along the Gulf and Atlantic coasts.

Top sight-fishing areas for reds occur along most of the

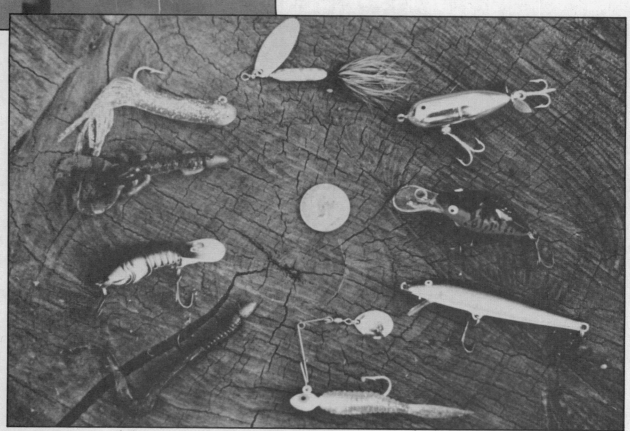

Plain bucktail jig is top choice when sight fishing for reds that've moved up onto flats to feast on crustaceans. You need to cast jig beyond feeding fish, then retrieve.

These are just a few of the many artificial baits redfish will take when they move onto shallow flats to feed. If these look suspiciously like lures used for freshwater gamefish, you're right on!

west coast of Florida from Flamingo to Pensacola. Along the east coast, peak areas range from West Palm Beach to Daytona Beach, although some excellent fishing can be had in the backwaters of the Intercoastal Waterway near St. Augustine. In all areas, the procedures and equipment are much the same.

The first requirement is a shallow-draft boat that can be poled in waters as shallow as 12 inches. Aluminum boats are not the best choice, since they tend to be a bit too noisy and can spook shallow-water fish.

A good spinning rod in the 6- to 6½-foot range, spooled with 8- to 12-pound line, is more than adequate. More reds on the flats will be under 10 pounds. Line capacity for red-

fish need not be much more than 125 yards. Many experts attach a 12-inch length of 20-pound monofilament as a shock leader, but doubling the last foot of line with a spider hitcher seems to work about as well.

An effective list of lures for the flats need not be a lengthy one: Redfish on a flat are there to eat and will take virtually any small lure that can be hopped past their nose. One of the best is a plain ¼-ounce bucktail jig with a slightly flattened head. Commonly called "skimmer heads," they're available in many area tackle shops. Color combinations of white/brown, white/green, and white/pink work well.

Some anglers prefer to tip the jig with a small piece of

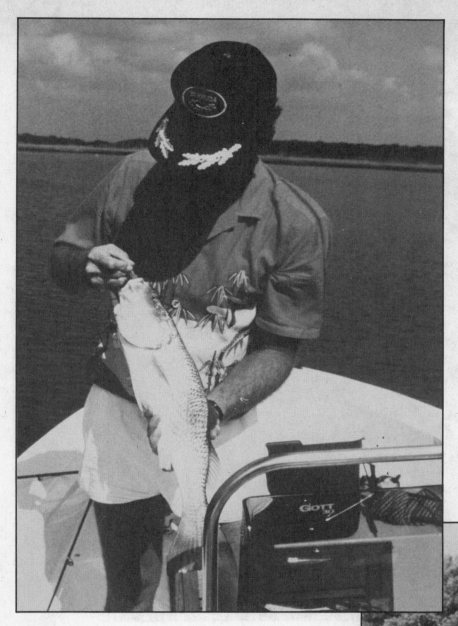

This school-sized redfish fell to a tube lure that imitates juvenile squid. Redfish that fall within the legal 18- to 27-inch length are called "slots." Anything bigger or smaller must be released unharmed. Establishment of "slot" limit, and ban on commercial fishing, have saved the species from extinction.

Poling shallow flats in search of feeding redfish has been termed "poorman's bonefishing," but there's nothing poor about the sport. Pole allows for silent approach, to keep from spooking the fish back into deep water. While you're poling, keep an eye out for approaches to flats; fish the deeper areas with crankbaits during low tide for more fun.

Author removes crankbait from an undersized redfish that fell during outing in Florida's middle west coast. This is a prime area for redfish, due to maze of oyster bars. Crankbaits are ideal here, as they float free of snags when you bump them off the bottom. Jigs tend to hang up. See text for hot color info.

shrimp, since it is felt that the redfish has relatively poor eyesight and might need a bit of scent to zero in on the lure. I've found this unnecessary, except when the water is particularly turbid. Redfish have better eyes than they're given credit for.

Plastic-tailed jig and grub combinations are equally effective, especially in pearl white, pink, clear with silver glitter, motor oil-red flake, and flourescent lime green. In waters with a lot of weed growth, a four-inch plastic worm or curly tailed grub can be deadly when rigged Texas-style, just like freshwater anglers rig plastic worms for

largemouth bass. Another top bait for grass-covered flats is the ¼-ounce gold Johnson Silver Spoon.

Live-bait anglers will find a small shrimp placed a foot or so under a popping cork works quite well, but remember that treble hooks are not allowed when using live bait for redfish. Instead, use a short-shanked 1/0 single hook.

Not all flats will hold redfish. The best will generally be those that lie near deeper water, giving the reds easy access and a refuge during low tide. Although reds will begin moving onto the flats as soon as the flood tide provides enough water, peak periods will be the last three hours of the tide,

Deeper channels along shallow flats are prime places to find redfish as tide falls. Redfish will move into deeper water, but still will feed.

This angler has opted for a flyrod to present large bucktail over a relatively shallow oyster bed. The hungry reds will routinely rise to a tempting morsel and smash it hard!

and the first hour of the ebb tide. Once the tide has begun to fall, the fish can get very spooky and tend to shy away from even expertly placed casts.

While sight fishing for reds on a rising tide can be an exciting method of taking these battlers, the most effective tactic for straining the wrist is often blind fishing on the dropping tide. Flats fish tend to scatter as flood waters cover the flat, but once the water starts to fall, they may concentrate in the deeper cuts off the flat, giving the angler the opportunity for several hours of fast action in a relatively small area.

BLIND CASTING

The same basic tackle as used in flats fishing works quite well, but many anglers find lighter graphite rods in the six-foot range a bit easier to handle. You'll be doing far more casting here than on the flats and a lighter rod is an asset.

One can also use the same basic array of lures, and indeed, bucktail jigs and plastic-bodied grubs are top choices. However, in areas where a sharp dropoff exists, a better bet is a small crankbait.

One of the best-kept secrets among Florida's redfish experts is that reds are suckers for many of the same

Author says that the best-kept secret among Florida's redfish experts is the deadly effectiveness of crankbaits. Those that imitate shrimp or crustaceans are best bets.

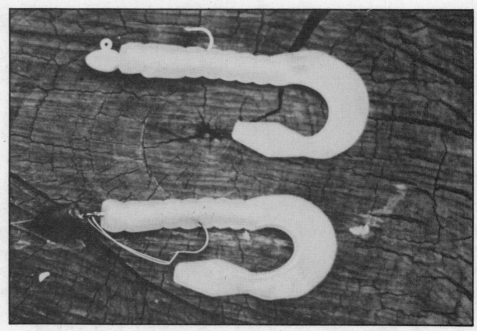

Curly-tailed plastic grubs are deadly medicine for reds. They can be rigged with an exposed jig head, as shown at top, or shifted to a weedless rig when working grass flats.

crankbaits used for largemouth, smallmouth, and spotted bass!

Some of the most effective models are the Bass Magnet, Mann's Deep 10 and Deep Stretch 10, and Mann's Crawfish, although any floater/diver that can reach depths of six to eight feet should work quite well. Best color combos are pink, reds, and browns, possibly because they imitate crustaceans.

One thing that should be done to any crankbait intended for redfish is to replace the standard wire hooks with similar-sized models in a plated, extra-strong size. Eagle Claw XX and 4X models are preferred by many. A 10-pound red can destroy a light wire hook.

Crankbaits are particularly effective when working over oyster bars and rock and gravel spoil banks — two premier redfish hotspots wherever they are found near a shallow flat — because when the retrieve is stopped they will float free of snags, while jigs tend to hang up.

Blind casting is most effective after the first two hours of the falling tide, all the way to the end of the tide. This is when the reds leave the shallows and seek deeper water to await the flood tide that will allow them to return to the shallow flats.

In actual practice, blind casting for reds is much like working a shoreline for bass. And as such, a strong trolling motor is a definite asset in assuring proper boat position.

Casting a shoreline for reds is much like fishing for largemouth bass, the author says. A strong electric trolling motor is a major asset when it comes to fighting the tide and keeping boat in casting range. See text.

Locating low-tide reds is easy — at least as long as you've found some of the flats they feed on during the flood tide. Look for channels, cuts, holes, sharply dropping shoreline, and any other deeper water in the immediate area of the flats. The best spots will invariably have oyster bars, or some other form of hard-bottom structure on them. Reds dislike soft marl bottoms in deeper water.

My basic procedure is to cast the crankbait to the shallow section of the drop and work it slowly toward deeper water. Most reds will be holding right on the actual dropoff to deeper water.

Anglers who stay on the move won't have any trouble locating reds in this manner. Particular spots for attention are the mouths of shallow tide creeks, deep-water points extending off flats, and the edge of channels cutting across flats.

Once redfish are contacted, it's a good idea to work the area thoroughly, since there are likely to be more down there. In fact, there may be enough to literally wear an angler out!

While the future of redfish looked bleak in the Sunshine State just a few years back, there's no doubt that strong conservation measures, and gamefish status, have definitely resulted in the return of the reds. Thankfully!

CHAPTER
13

SUMMERTIME'S SIZZLING SAND BASSIN'

It May Be The Only Game In Town When Temperatures Climb. Beat The Heat And Fill The Freezer!

It's not unusual on a sand bass trip to take some nice halibut, especially if you're fishing anchovies.

Sometimes the summer sandies get a bad case of lockjaw, generally a sign that school is new in the area. If you don't get bit, pull anchor and move to more agreeable school, which likes the plastics tipped with squid.

These are just a few of the rubber baits author has used to good effect on sand bass. He's high on twintail baits from Worm King, shown at top and second from bottom. See text.

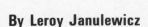

By Leroy Janulewicz

SUMMERTIME IN Southern California means sizzling temperatures and smoggy streets. Tempers get short and relief from the heat is hard to find.

The saltwater angler gets lucky when the temperature starts climbing, however. That's when one of the most-sought-after species of good-eating gamefish comes in close. To beat the summertime sizzle and provide some great barbecue fare, grab your gear and jump aboard a half-day or twilight boat going after barred sand bass. The species moves in about June and stays around 'til the end of August, providing good sport for the short-run skippers fishing from the numerous inexpensive landings all along the Southern California coast.

The barred sand bass is a mysterious fish. Not much scientific research has been done on their migration habits. We do know they migrate to Southern California to spawn, then leave without notice. Some angling experts speculate that the sand bass come all the way from Baja, changing their skin coloration during this long trip. I've caught several different species of bass in Baja, but none of them resemble the sand bass in coloration or tooth structure, so I tend to discount this. Many novice anglers confuse the sand bass with its cousin, the calico or kelp bass. Sand bass can vary from a beige to a light gray, with several bars running the length of the body in light green or brown.

Sand bass have a couple of nicknames: "grumpy" or "twister." Why? When one hits the deck, "grumpy" will

What a good way to beat the sizzling summertime temperatures — a twilight run close by for good-eating sandies. When they school up, they're pretty uniform in size. Larger bass like plastics.

puff its gills out to make it appear larger. When being reeled in, the sand bass will twist in small circles, like a rock cod on a gangion.

They are not the most intelligent species of bass, but can be very stubborn when they don't want to bite. Conversely, when the water conditions are right (the optimum water temperature is between 69 and 72F degrees), it's not uncommon to catch a sandie on every cast, depending on the volume of bass under the boat. That's when it really gets fun!

It can be very frustrating to see thousands of twisters on the fish meter, and no takers! If this should happen, chances are the school is a new batch of bass that just moved into the area, and is getting acclimated to the spawning grounds. If you run across such a school of tight-jawed bass, pull anchor and look for a school that's more willing. Sportfishing skippers do this all the time. They may move the boat

only a couple hundred yards and locate another school that produces a wide-open bite.

Sand bass usually are found in depths from 40 to 100 feet, and prefer a flat sandy bottom to fit their spawning needs. California's minimum size limit is 12 inches, with a bag limit of 10. Sand bass can run up to 8 or 9 pounds, with some even larger. Like other saltwater and freshwater bass, the females are larger than the males. I've fished sandies for many years, and no matter what size they are, it's always a blast on light tackle!

I've found that fishing for sandies at night usually is more productive. Powerful lights hung over the side of the boat will attract sand bass like a magnet, and a good supply of live anchovies for chum will keep them around for hours.

Sand bass fishing is a light-tackle affair. Leave all that 30- and 50-pound gear at home. Many fishermen even use

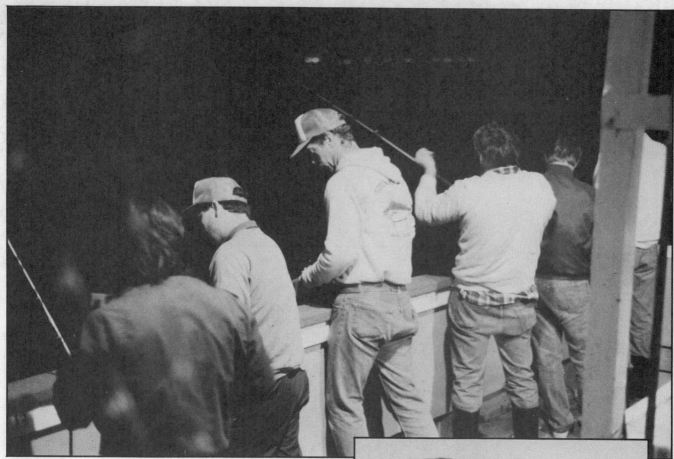

Author's longtime fishing buddy, Danny Jones (ball cap, right) watches line sink during nighttime trip. You'll generally get bit on sink, so if your line stops, reel down and slam it! (Right) Current and depth of fish will determine size of leadhead to use, and sometimes tipping Worm King with a frisky anchovy will produce remarkable results. See text.

their freshwater outfits for sandies, but I prefer a light saltwater outfit. On several twilight trips, I've caught large barracuda, halibut and white seabass. I like to be prepared for the unexpected, as well as for a big grumpy!

I've found that rods in the 6- to 6½-foot length, rated for 15- to 25-pound line, work well. CalStar's Model 195 (6 feet, 8- to 20-pound) or Model 196 (6½ feet, 10- to 25-pound) are perfect. Sabre and Fenwick also have a variety of good sand bass sticks. It's a matter of personal taste. Matched with a small reel like Shimano's TLD-5 with 15- to 20-pound line, you have a dynamite twilight sand bass outfit!

There are several proven methods for catching grumpy bass, but I really have to laugh when I see all the unorthodox methods being tried on a typical twilight run. After I bag a limit, these novices always ask for the secret of my success.

Grumpy bass get excited about the plastics made by Mr. Worm King, Marvin Bendalin shown holding a performer.

If the sandies are being extra tough, give 'em a try with a live or fresh dead squid. Jighead is hooked as shown.

Variety of colors will work in both iron jigs and plastic baits. Ask at landings what the top producer is, then stock up. Bring bait hooks, sinkers, too. You never know!

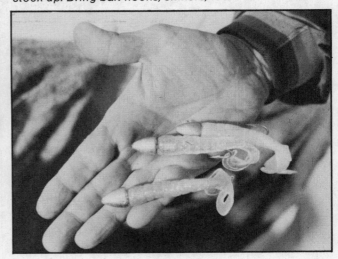

After a few minutes of instruction and tackle modification, they're sacking 'em up, too!

When you get into a school of willing spawners, there's nothing more fun than catching grumpies on artificial lures. Artificial baits usually will catch the larger sandies, and maybe win a jackpot or two. Soft rubber lures work best. Worm King Products makes a top producer in a twintail model. Chartreuse, root beer, pink and brown bait are the hot colors. I always take along several different colors, as you never know which will work right off the bat. Ask your skipper which color has been most productive lately, then go from there. If that starter doesn't work, keep changing until you find the right one.

Baits like Worm King's lure require a leadhead; the current will determine the size to use. Usually a ½- to ¾-ounce leadhead will work in the quiet summer currents. At times a small piece of strip squid pinned on the Worm King setup will help entice the sandies to bite.

When fishing the artificial rubber lure, I first find out how deep the bass are. The fish can range from 20 feet down to the bottom. Most of the school will be gathered under the lights and spread out 30 to 40 feet around the boat. To give the lure a more-natural look, I cast out about 50 feet, put the reel in gear and let it sink to the depth of the school. Most times you'll get hit on the sink. If your line goes slack, more than likely you picked up a sandie. Reel in the slack and let him have it! Sand bass have pretty hard mouths, so don't be afraid to set the hook hard. If you didn't get picked up on the sink and you're headed for the bottom, start to retrieve the twintail at a very slow crank. When you drag the rubber lure through the school, you'll know when you get hit. Sandies are very active feeders when hungry for artificials!

When fishing iron jigs for sand bass, I always use the light models. I usually wait until the bass school builds up really thickly under the boat before throwing iron, or if the

These are definitely a pair of grumpies, and good-sized ones, at that! When water conditions are just right, you can catch grumpies all day long.

The IGFA All Tackle World Record for sand bass is this 13-pound 3-ounce freight train caught by Robert Halal at Huntington Flats off Southern California using a Worm King plastic. Do they work?

plastics aren't getting bit. I've had good success with the EX6 and CB1 models of Killer Jigs in scrambled egg and blue-and-white colors. Fish the iron just as you do the soft rubber lures. The light iron will flutter down on the sink, and with a very slow retrieve, it drives the larger bass crazy! Salas and Sea Strike lures also have many lightweight models to entice a big grumpy.

When you find a school of sand bass that won't give the artificial a second look, it's time to switch to live bait. My choice is a live anchovy with egg sinker setup. The size of the anchovies will determine hook size. Take along sizes #4, #2, 1/0, 2/0, 3/0 and 4/0 for any unexpected change of anchovy sizes. Better safe than sorry!

Usually a ½- or ¾-ounce egg sliding sinker will work with a slight current. Pinch on a small splitshot about 18 inches up from the hook to keep the egg sinker from sliding down on the hook. You want to keep the anchovy as natural as possible. For best results, gill hook the anchovy.

Use the same fishing method as the artificial, but let your line sink to the bottom and rest there awhile. A sandie may come along and pick it up, or a nice big halibut may suck it up — extra steaks to bring home!

If you're fortunate enough to have some brown bait (herring) in the bait tank, and the bass are running on the supergrumpy size, use a 3/0 or 4/0 hook with the same sliding egg sinker setup. The bigger bass just love those brown baits. Hook the brown bait just above the anal fin for best results, and let the bass run for 15 to 20 feet before setting the hook.

Although the International Game Fish Association (IGFA) only recognizes this hearty migrator in the All Tackle World Records, grumpies are fun to catch, at times challenging and excellent eating. When the sand bass come in, they're likely to be the only game in town. Don't drag your heels on those hot summer nights — cool 'em on a twilight run for summertime sandies!

CHAPTER

14

TROPHY TIME FOR MUSKIES

When It's Icy, Blustery And Miserable For Fishermen, You Might Take Your Biggest Muskie!

By Don Wirth

Fall is prime time for muskies, according to guide Fred McClintock, who caught this nice one from a Kentucky lake using the huge jerk bait hanging from the fish's jaw. Jerk baits kill you!

The muskelluge is known as the "fish of 10,000 casts," and one Fred McClintock had mounted was worth the effort.

Muskies are mean, moody fish equipped with lots of sharp teeth that make use of wire leaders mandatory. See text.

THERE ARE FISHERMEN...and then there are *muskie* fishermen.

Fishermen lie awake at night before a big fishing expedition. Muskie fishermen may never go to bed at all when their quarry is biting. Fishermen cast until their arms are sore. Muskie fishermen cast until their shoulders, backs, even legs are begging for mercy. Fishermen don't mind spending $5 for the latest plastic crankbait. Muskie fishermen spend hours carving their own fish-catching creations out of wood, knowing that the fish they're after must be enticed by something extra special.

If, in the eyes of some, fishermen are crazy, then muskie fishermen are raving lunatics!

But there's a reason for their madness. The muskellunge is America's premier freshwater gamefish. Its savage disposition and moody behavior makes fishing for muskie both exciting and incredibly frustrating. Often called the "fish of 10,000 casts," the muskie will sulk for days, then suddenly go on a feeding rampage that will decimate schools of baitfish and leave fishermen with busted lines and broken hearts. Then, just as suddenly, it will return to its holding area and watch with disinterest as forage and lure alike pass by.

Muskie fishermen agree that the best time to go muskie fishing is any time they can, but for many, the choicest period of all is during the fall. When the leaves begin to turn and there's a chill in the air, many turn their thoughts to football and tailgate parties. Not muskie hunters. They'll begin a long, often lonely vigil to their favored muskie haunts, casting endless hours, grateful for a followup, ecstatic when there's a strike.

"I've often broken the ice off a lake in the late fall when I'd go muskie fishing," says Celina, Tennessee, fishing guide Fred McClintock. McClintock, a Pennsylvania native, is experienced in the ways of both Northern and Southern muskies, having caught more than 250 legal-sized fish in

Late fall, when the lake is lonely, can produce top muskie action, author says. It's often best when you must break the ice of the lake surface to launch your boat; look to weeds, shallow bars, shoals.

five states and Canada. His largest is a 36-pounder caught while trolling on Dale Hollow Reservoir, where he guides.

"Down South, many lakes and rivers in Tennessee, Kentucky, Virginia and West Virginia have fair to good muskie fishing, although our fish don't usually have the size potential that they do up North," McClintock says. "And here, the term 'fall' is relative. Because many prime Southern muskie waters are deep, clear highland reservoirs — lakes which often lack extensive cover — lake temperatures remain warm for long periods of time. Muskies may remain very deep until November or December. Up North, you can catch them shallow in the fall."

McClintock is serious about his icebreaking exploits on Northern lakes in the fall. "I've hit the water at daybreak on many, many mornings to find the ice has covered the lake. I'm always glad to see this, because it signals the possibility of a big muskie. People may think you're nuts, but if you use your boat to bust up that ice and start casting, you might catch the biggest muskie of your career."

Fred loves to fish for muskies when the surface temperature falls below 40 degrees in the fall. "If you can catch the temperatures somewhere from 35 to 39 degrees, or even if the surface has frozen with a thin sheet of ice, you can score big on muskies up North. Down South, surface temperatures may not get down this low, even in the dead of winter. Dale Hollow, where I fish for smallmouths, walleye, trout and muskie, seldom has surface temps much lower than 39 degrees. In an extremely harsh winter, it might freeze over in the backends of the tributaries, but that would be in February."

The thought of arriving at an upstate New York muskie lake at dawn to find a cold north wind blowing and ice on the water is enough to make most anglers turn their car heaters up a notch and head back to the house. Not McClintock. "You've got to suffer if you want to catch muskies," he swears. "But when you finally connect, man, is it ever worth it!"

McClintock gets muskie fever in the fall when surface

In Southern reservoirs, the water is still warm as leaves begin to change, and trolling often is necessary to reach deep, suspended muskies. Guide McClintock here tries big plugs deep on Tennessee's Dale Hollow Reservoir.

Does reservoir trolling produce? How about this 26-pounder, soon to be released by McClintock. Artificials are better than live bait for muskie, as latter leads to gut-hooking and makes it impossible to release fish.

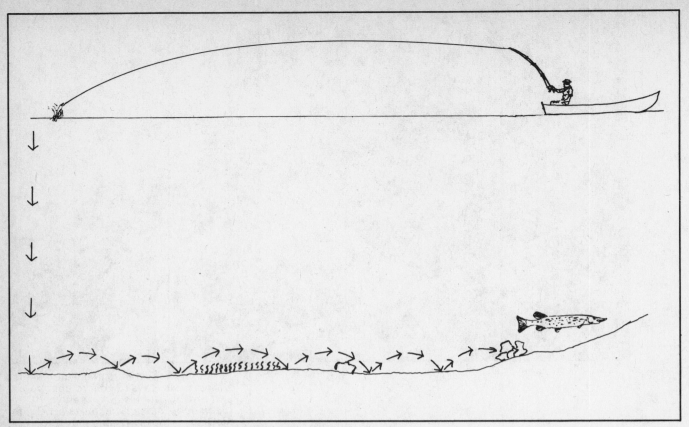

Before water temperature drops, enabling top-line predator to come shallow, you may have to search subtle structure to find suspended fish, those places overlooked by most anglers: deep weeds, subtle dropoffs, small rocks and the like. In Northern Lakes, counting-down a big-lipped, deep-diving crankbait that's bounced on bottom often works.

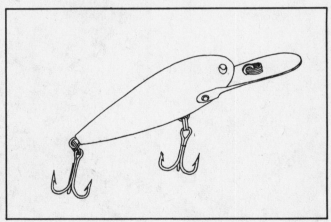

Big baits for big fish — that's what muskie hunters believe. But the size of some baits, particularly homemade jerk baits, seems to indicate suicidal tendency on part of angler who has to cast and retrieve the "logs!"

temps start dropping into the 50s. "Up North, look for weed beds. Stay with these places as the water drops another 20 degrees through the fall months, and pay special attention to the last green weeds — these are the ones that will often hold fish the longest." Reservoirs such as Chataqua in New York contain massive weed beds and millions of muskies. But many other muskie haunts may not hold large quanties of vegetation. "You've got to fish what you've got, and if you don't have weeds, then big rocks are a good bet," believes Fred. Rocky areas in a river or reservoir to check out include submerged shoals and islands, plus rockpiles and boulders adjacent to deep water.

"The more I fish for both muskies and smallmouth bass,

the more I realize how much alike they are in their habits," McClintock observes. Being a guide on Dale Hollow provides him plenty of opportunity to observe both the world record smallmouth (11 pounds 15 ounces) came from this superclear reservoir, and it holds muskies approaching 50 pounds. Both species, McClintock feels, require a deep-water access. "This is especially important to remember in the fall, because whether you're fishing for smallmouths or muskies, you may catch 'em in shallow water one day, only to find that they've disappeared the next. More likely than not, what's really happened is that the fish have dropped to the nearest available deep water."

Both fish are highly oriented to breaklines, places with a rather abrupt depth change. "They'll move out and sus-

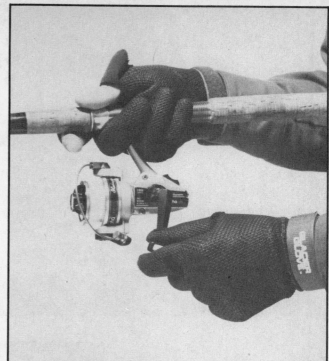

Technology has made freezing days in late winter more bearable. Gore-Tex oversocks (above) are waterproof, they breathe and are worn over wicking, insulating socks and under boots or shoes...aaahhh! Glacier Gloves for anglers are either slit or full-finger textured neoprene (above right), same as worn by scuba divers. Polypropylene liner is available for full-finger models, which sell under $50. Du Pont's Magnum 14/40 is designed for heavy cover and easy casting. Braided nylon is favored for jerk baits, as it has no stretch to kill action imparted by fisherman.

pend off a channel drop, weedline, ledge, submerged roadbed or any other area close to shallow water that has a distinct depth change. Of course, when they're deep, they're catchable, but not nearly as catchable as when they're up shallow.'' McClintock must resort to trolling in deepwater reservoirs such as Dale Hollow, but finds that in Northern lakes, casting is the rule. Both methods require skill and concentration. Both can produce.

When Northern muskie lakes get cold and fishermen break out their longhandles in the fall, McClintock suggests fishing the shoreline to 10 feet deep. "They'll be shallow, and those last few days before iceup can really turn them into a feeding frenzy. Late October/early November is traditionally when many huge muskies are caught in

the Northern states. To do it right, you've got to fish from dawn 'til dark, no matter how cold, sleety or snowy it is. That's one reason why so few big muskies are caught: There aren't too many fishermen willing to fish for them when they're at their peak.''

Want to start an argument among muskie fishermen? McClintock says the easiest way is to tell them what lures are the best for big fish. "Every muskie maniac I've ever met has his own pet lures," he laughs, "and I guess I'm no different."

Fred's "pet lure" is an ominous-looking stick of cedar that he hand-builds, using a lathe and hand tools. "I'm a real fan of jerk baits, and this lure is a 'jerk' that weighs about four ounces," he says. "It has 5/0 Mustad hooks

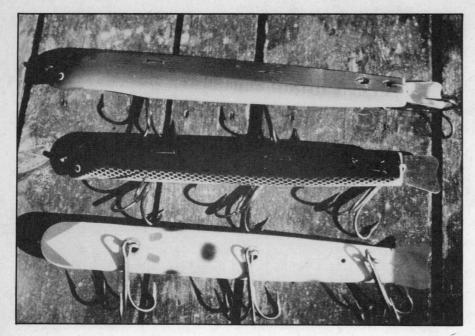

Big jerk baits such as these sticks handmade by guide Fred McClintock take more big muskies in fall than any other bait. McClintock says all of his 30-plus-pounders hit these.

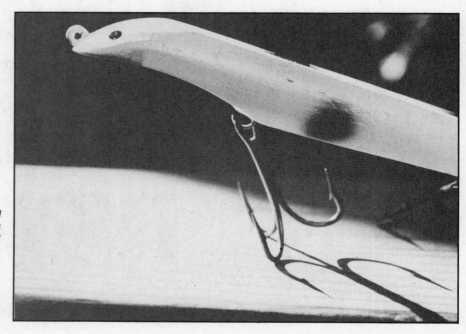

This closeup of a McClintock-carved bait reveals strong hardware and a graceful curve that imparts a gliding action to imitate a wounded baitfish.

held in place with heavy-duty cotter pins. The lure is about nine inches long and always painted one color — black."

Jerk baits are popular lures among many muskie hunters. "They get their name because of what you have to do to make them work," Fred explains. "You cast 'em out and then take up the slack and jerk, jerk, jerk. When you pull, they dart like a wounded sucker. Jerk baits are one reason why there aren't more muskie fishermen — they'll kill you, working them day in and day out!"

McClintock uses a short, powerful rod to work his jerks. "You can't hope to fish these heavy baits on regular tackle," he says. "Get a jerk-bait rod such as the one made by Skyline, an Ambassadeur 5500C or Daiwa Millionaire

high-speed baitcasting reel, and a spool of braided line such as 36-pound Cortland Musky Master, and you'll be in business."

Braided line is something many anglers believe has gone the way of the buggy, but it's ideal for jerk baits. "Braided line has almost no stretch. When you jerk, you want the lure to dart. These baits are so heavy that any stretch in the line kills their action. Monofilament line would leave a jerk bait just sitting there grinning at you."

Repeated "jerking" can nearly kill even the most avid fisherman, Fred attests. "I've come off of the lake in the fall, when the fishing is hot, and be so sore I was almost crying. But jerk baits will catch more big muskies than all other

Scenery is spectacular during fall muskie fishing forays, which are made even better if you catch one of the bad-tempered "water wolves." Problem is, you can't count on 'em to hit!

lures combined. I'm convinced of it. I've caught nearly every one of my 30-plus-pounders on them."

Topwaters are another excellent choice for fall muskies. "Most fishermen think that you can only fish a topwater when the water's warm, but muskies will prove you wrong," he swears. "They'll hit a big prop bait, even a buzz bait, when the water's icy. There are few sights more humbling to the fisherman than that of a 30-pound muskie blowing up on a topwater. First the water humps up, then they just annihilate it! They'll jump right out of the water trying to blast it."

Many muskie fishermen swear that live bait is the best bet for fall, but McClintock prefers throwing artificials.

"They'll hit a big sucker or chub minnow, but the problem is, you can't swing at them right away or you'll miss them. What happens then is a long waiting period for the fish to swallow the bait. Most muskies, regardless of their size, are consequently gut-hooked when using live bait. This means that the fish can't be released, and for muskies especially, that's bad news. The muskie is always the top-line predator in the water, no mattter where it occurs, and in nature, top-line predators are never abundant. If you use artificials, you can usually release the fish to fight again."

Rivers offer excellent muskie fishing in the fall, and are often overlooked by all but the most persistent anglers.

All of these artificials have taken muskies, including the bucktail spinners near top and spinnerbaits/buzzbaits at bottom. But for humbling topwater action, go with jerks.

Guess which color Fred McClintock prefers for his jerk baits? He must have taken a page from Henry Ford's book on the Model T — "You can have any color you want, so long as it's black." Silhouette is what muskie will see.

"Rivers hold tons of structure, which makes them both easy and hard to fish," Fred observes. "For one thing, you pretty much know exactly where a muskie is going to be in a river. He doesn't like curent, so he'll hold in the slack pools and eddies. He's fond of fallen trees, rocks and weeds, and these are liable to be abundant in a river — so abundant that you have too many casting targets to cover a lot of water." McClintock believes that muskies are far more structure-oriented in rivers than in lakes or reservoirs. "I can't emphasize enough how important it is to fish the slack areas and places with heavy cover in a river," Fred says. "Cover breaks up current and attracts bait, both of which are vital for muskies."

Other places where muskies can occur are around boat docks, bridge pilings and sunken timber in both lakes and rivers. But in areas where this fish is popular, such spots can be hit very hard. "Spend a little time casting to these more-obvious places, but spend more time seeking out 'subtle structure' such as a change from living to dead vegetation, a shallow dip off a big gravel flat, or an area with several types of cover close together. Most fishermen won't notice these kinds of places, and the bigger muskies may be on them."

Pressure, Fred believes, can be what makes muskie fishing so tough in most lakes. "I can always tell a lake that hasn't been fished with jerk baits, 'cause I'll usually bring up a lot of muskies the first time I fish it," he says. "But these fish learn over time. They learn to avoid fishermen and their lures. This is why it takes so much time to connect. Muskie fishing has declined tremendously in the past few years, simply because there are so many more people fishing for them."

McClintock points out that Muskies, Incorporated, a national muskie fishing organization emphasizing catch and release, has largely been responsible for the release boom among muskie anglers nationwide. "Today, many muskie addicts are releasing legal-sized fish. Some are releasing trophy-sized muskies, as well. We're realizing that the muskellunge is a very precious resource, one that can be easily depleted."

Are *you* up to the challenge? Are *you* willing to break through the ice and cast giant lures until your body cries for mercy? Are *you* willing to subsist on coffee and Twinkies for days or months at a time while you look for the fish of your dreams? If you are, welcome aboard! I'm heading for muskie country come daybreak!

When muskies move shallower in winter, they're susceptible to topwater offerings that are jerk, jerk, jerked!

The shed outside McClintock's home groans under weight of a true wallhanger, proof positive that jerk baits work!

CHAPTER 15

KING-SIZED CRAPPIE CHALLENGE

Slabs Are Fine Eating And Easy To Catch With Traditional Or New-Fangled Methods

By Soc Clay

Early day crappie fishermen show off their catch from a typical winter's day of jigging for the excellent table fare. While fish haven't changed, there's been huge increase in number of anglers who hunt them.

NEWLIGHT, SPEC, PAPERMOUTH, Calico bass — whatever name you care to call it — *Pomoxis* (more commonly known as white or black crappie) is getting to be one heckuva popular gamefish species across much of America.

This fine-eating fish is so easily caught during the spawning season of mid-spring that it's caught the eye of the fishing promoters, boat and motor manufactures, tackle companies and tourist groups.

Crappiethon USA, a highly successful promotion in much of the eastern half of the U.S., has been credited with creating a new wave of interest in this sportster that, at its best, shows little sport in the fighting department. Yet the thought of dropping a baited hook into the water with the possibility of dredging up an eight- to 10-inch fish that might be worth $50,000 gets folks to thinking crappie fishing in a hurry!

Even without the incentive of financial gain, crappie have long held the title as America's family fish. In fact, kinfolks have grown up fishing together for this species, mainly because everyone from kids to grandpa can, at one time or another during the course of the season, easily catch a full stringer.

In the past, about the only time you found the average fisherman trying for crappie was during the month of May, when huge schools of the species invaded the shoreline of lowland lakes searching for a place to spawn.

Nowadays, it seems you've got to have sophisticated boats and fishing gear to score on crappie. But when they come into the shallows to spawn, anyone can find huge schools.

Once water temperatures hit 65 degrees, it's time for whole families to hunt for woody areas favored by spawning crappie. Males will lure a female or two onto their beds, and all you need do is find the right depth.

Hair jigs are deadly for late-winter crappie, but don't impart too much action. Charley Guffy finds prime spot, then presents fine hair jigs slowly at one-foot intervals.

Women and kids make up a big portion of today's crappie fishermen. The sport has grown tremendously, despite the lackluster reputation crappie has as a fighting fish.

This slab is a real horse! A frisky minnow on light wire hook usually works when right depth has been found. See text for tips on the white coffee mug system.

Flooded buckbrush, stumps, lay-down trees and the like were the targeted area once water temperatures warmed to about 65 degrees. Back then, anyone armed with a johnboat, long cane pole, a short piece of line, cork bobber, a long-shank, light-wire hook and a lively minnow the size of a man's little finger was all set up for crappie fishing. And, nine times out of 10, he came off the lake at day's end with a heavy stringer.

Such simplicity is mostly ancient history today. The new crappie promotion that has swept the countryside has elevated crappie in the ranks of desirable gamefish species. No longer are fishermen confining their efforts just to the spawning season. Like other forms of angling in America, the sport has evolved into a year 'round activity.

Because of the increased interest in crappie and because fishermen now expect to catch crappie at any time of the year, a brand new industry has emerged around this tasty panfish. New, wide-deck boats allow mom, pop and all the kiddies to assault a sunken brush pile, stake bed or dropoff in style and comfort. Whisper-quiet outboards and trolling motors permit anglers to slip up on shallow-holding crappie. Ultra-sophisticated electronics pinpoint the location of fish, almost from top to bottom, and some units show them in color, at that! There's been new line development and special rods and reels, and tackle boxes made especially for crappie fishing. And fishin' poles — my gosh, you can't believe how dainty yet strong and sensitive they are, until you pick up one of these super-lightweight creations.

These men used pencil and red/white bobbers over spawning beds in early Seventies, a technique that works to this day. Get yourself good eating!

With the aid of electronics, crappie movement can be traced through the seasons like a footprint in new-fallen snow. Nowadays, it's not unusual to talk with anglers who schedule a week's vacation time in order to hit the first wave of crappie action that usually occurs in late February and early March on lakes that remain free of ice for much of the winter.

Essentially, crappie movement in reservoirs and rivers is caused by two factors: food supplies and comfort levels. This usually means that during the dead of winter, crappie take up a holding position in fairly deep water where temperatures and dissolved oxygen content are desirable, yet somewhat close to a food supply. In simplistic terms, crappie go deep during mid-winter and mid-summer. The times in-between are spent moving to the shallows in spring to spawn or pursuing baitfish into coves, creek arms or backwater areas in autumn.

On large riverine reservoirs like Kentucky Lake, the crappie's instincts cause it to move out of wintertime holding areas in the main lake and begin to move into the mouth of major creek arms. Their eventual target is the headwaters, where warmer water and good spawning sites await. But since the water still is cold at this time of the year, the crappie's movement is slow.

Chasing crappie is a year-round affair these days, and use of fishfinders has helped boat-owning set to locate big school that herd and feed on baitfish. See text for info.

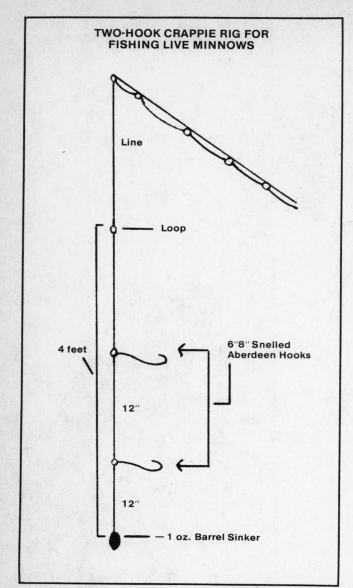

TWO-HOOK CRAPPIE RIG FOR
FISHING LIVE MINNOWS

Line

Loop

4 feet

6"8" Snelled
Aberdeen Hooks

12"

12"

— 1 oz. Barrel Sinker

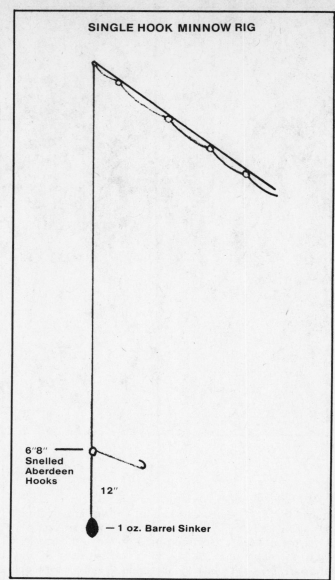

SINGLE HOOK MINNOW RIG

6"8"
Snelled
Aberdeen
Hooks

12"

— 1 oz. Barrel Sinker

Some anglers prefer to make up several rigs with short line of about four feet length. These are ready for use at differing depths, until you find crappie school. Above right is a single-hook minnow setup.

Because they're a schooling fish, sometimes large numbers of the fish will emerge on a single creek arm, holding to deep-water ledges or steep bends in the creek channel. During this period, both the smaller male and the larger female bunch together.

By using depth finders, graphs and LCRs, early season crappie chasers check out known holding areas and explore new places regularly, trying to locate one or more concentrations of fish.

Once found, both live minnows and jig-and-plastic-grub combinations are dropped among the slow-motion fish, keeping the bait presentation positioned right at or slightly above the school of fish. As a general rule, crappie will often swim up several feet to feed, but rarely go down even a foot.

Until only a few years ago, most early season crappie fishermen going after king-sized crappie (also known as slabs) relied almost exclusively on live minnows fished on a two-hook rig. The rig consisted of a one-half to one-

ounce-barrel sinker tied to the end of the line with two, six- to eight-inch snelled. Aberdeen-style, light-wire hooks attached at intervals of one and three feet above the sinker. This rig is ideal for fishing deep structure and the two-hook placement allows some latitude in finding the best fishing depth.

The downside of fishing live bait and two hooks in crappie cover — and they *love* anything wooden — is that they get hung up a lot. That's the reason most experienced live-bait fishermen use 20- to 30-pound-test lines, which allows them to straighten the light wire hooks and pull them free without losing the whole rigging.

On the other hand, John Stephenson, a long-time crappie guide from Jackson, Tennessee, believes a rig that features a one-ounce barrel sinker at the end of the line and a single snelled hook tied on about a foot above is ideal for fishing sunken brush with live minnows. He notes that when the hook becomes snagged, he simply drops the heavy sinker with his rod tip which usually pulls the hook free from below.

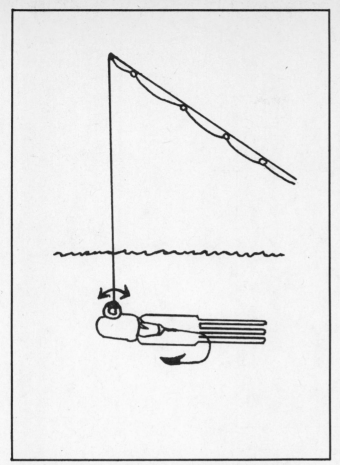

For success with tube jigs, it's essential that jig lie level in water. Adjust angle of line by moving improved clinch knot forward or backward until jig lies as shown.

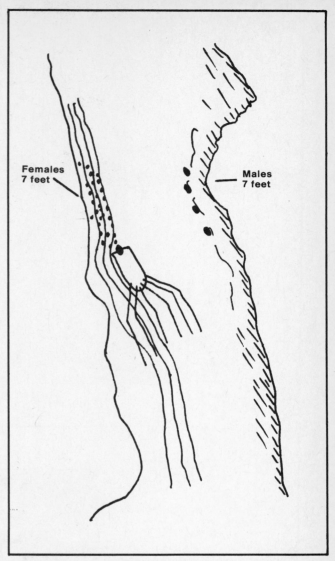

When male crappie take up station in spawning area, anglers spider-troll for larger females at same depth, but along ledges, drops or across flats where they school up and await favorable temps before going to spawning site.

Over the past few years, more and more crappie fishermen are discovering that tube jigs are murder on king-sized crappie during the early season, when the angler can fish straight down into cover.

What makes these rather simple-looking lures so effective is that they don't have to be jigged, danced, hopped or swum to catch fish. In fact, the less movement the better.

The absolute key to fishing tube jigs for crappie, however, is that they must hang straight across — perfectly horizontal — in the water, rather than slanted up or down. This is accomplished by using an improved clinch knot and slipping the knot backward or forward until the right angle is achieved. See the illustration for a visual explanation.

One of the reasons crappie poles are so long is to allow the angler to stay back away from the cover, thus cutting down on the possibility of spooking fish. This is not so important when crappie are holding to cover or structure in deep water. But when fishing clear water or when crappie are near the surface, it's a good idea to back off and make longer casts to the target.

For live bait presentation, this means using a bobber. Traditionally, natural-colored cork has been a favorite among most experienced crappie anglers. Brightly colored floats are easier to see, but some fishermen are concerned that flashy colors can spook fish when they are shallow or the water is clear.

Anglers who prefer artificials for this kind of fishing usually opt for casting Mr. Twister-type grubs or flat-tail plastics, allowing the offering to sink to the desired level before beginning a slow stop-and-go retrieve.

As the water warms in April, a new method for determining the level at which crappie are suspended entails the use of a plain white coffee mug. Once water temperatures reach 55 degrees, the male crappie begin to take up positions along brushy, weedy or stump-dotted banks or flats where they will eventually entice one or more females to spawn. Anglers have learned that this position will almost always be two feet below the point that light penetrates in the water. On murky reservoirs, this can be as shallow as three to five feet. On clear-water lakes, crappie can spawn upward from 20 feet.

To determine where the light penetration ends, anglers tie a length of line to the handle of a white cup and lower it into the water. The line is marked the instant it disappears

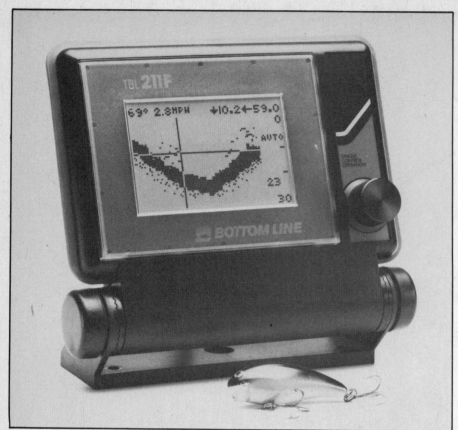

Bottom Line's 211F flasher/graph LCD has simplified control and displays water temp, boat speed, water depth. Such is required for winterime crappie angling, when fish are deep.

Ultralight line makes best sport you can get out of crappie, and Fenwick's Liteline is targeted to this market. Many anglers who seek crappie in the thick brush or flooded timber will seek heavier line. With it, they can pull light wire hooks free without losing the entire rig. Much depends on what the fish are preferring.

Back when hair was short and socks were patterned, crappie filled the waiting stringers of late spring anglers. While socks and hairstyles may've changed over time, desire for this tasty fish hasn't.

from sight. The bait or lure then is fished two feet below this level throughout the pre-spawn period that usually lasts for about a month.

Interestingly, while the smaller male of the species will hang out at this depth around the actual spawning area, the big, slab-sized females will school up at the same depth and either cruise throughout the lake arm or take up a holding position along breaks. But it will be at the same depth the male is holding to.

To cash in on the bunched-up, king-sized females, some anglers are using a spider-type rod holder that can accommodate up to six cane poles or rods. Lures or live minnows are attached to lines which are trolled very slowly across flats, along shallow breaks, through the middle of creek arms or just about any place in the lake. The idea is that once a school of fish is located, the numerous baited rods will catch a number of the fish in a very short time. One angler describes this technique as "vacuuming fish!"

Fishermen searching for jumbo crappie in highland reservoirs learn early on that instead of moving great distan-

ces in and out of creek arms to reach shallow water in late winter and early spring, crappie are more apt to move vertically.

A big slide that has carried trees and brush off the adjoining hillside, depositing cover and structure deep into the reservoir, can be a real honey hole year 'round. That's because while there is spawning potential in the shallow, upper layers of the slide, the deep, bottom half offers the security of deep water.

Crappie fishing guides like Charley Guffy, who fishes highland reservoirs such as Kentucky's Lake Cumberland on a regular basis, enjoy the challenge of the early season and Charley often registers his best catches during the in-between season that separates true winter from true spring.

For cold-water fishing, Guffy goes all out for tiny hair jigs. But first, he locates a brush-covered slide, sunken brush pile or stump bed found on the edge of a ledge or drop in water ranging between 10 and 30 feet. Vertical jigging is the key to success for catching the fish in deep water, he notes. Guffy likes to pull his boat directly over the target

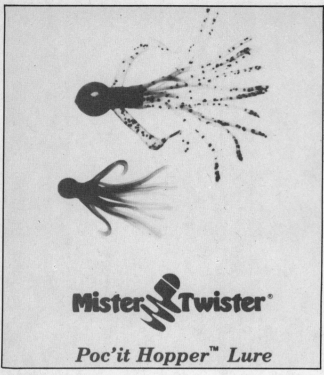

Combination squid/tube/salamander lure from Mr. Twister is aimed at crappie fishermen. Jighead fits snugly into cavity in head of Poc'it Hopper, which comes in two sizes.

What a way to get a crappie fisherman started — a 91-piece outfit from South Bend that has everything you need: two-piece, five-foot glass rod, spincast reel, line and more. In fact, fishing combo even has practice plug.

There are now four colors of Crappie Candy, a synthetic bait from Johnson Fishing's Bass Buster line. It's edible fish food with water-soluble flavoring to attract crappie.

Bait Box Grubs from Bass Buster are synthetic, but made to look like the real thing. They come in three colors and appeal to panfish via scent and sight. Bait stays on hook.

area and tie off or drop an anchor. He then drops a 1/32nd or 1/24th-ounce leadhead tied with short strands of brightly colored hair hackle to the bottom, raises it a foot, waits a while and, if nothing happens, he raises it another foot.

This procedure is continued upward until a fish bites, the cover runs out, or the lure can be seen. Two or three times is all that is needed to determine if crappie are holding in the cover or if they will bite.

When water temperatures are below 45 degrees, the Kentucky native advises anglers to fish super slow and lift the rod tip the instant the least little difference is sensed in the line. "Cold-water crappie often suck the lure into their mouths, making it very difficult to detect a bite." Guffy notes. For this reason he recommends light lines and a very sensitive rod.

Fishing for slab-sized crappie ain't for everyone, of course, but then maybe it is. A quick check among the top pro bass anglers in the U.S. turns up nearly 100 percent of these anglers who actually take time off from their busy schedule to put a few of these fine-eating fish in the cooler during early spring.

Give it a try!

1989 CRAPPIETHON SET RECORDS, EXPANDS IN 1990

The 1989 Johnson Reels' Crappiethon USA reached an all-time participation high with over a quarter-million anglers involved and over $1.5 million distributed in cash and prizes.

The annual Crappiethon tournaments are traditionally held on America's best crappie fishing lakes in the North, South, Midwest and Southwest regions from January through June. Each lake holds both a one-day tournament and a 60-day tournament in which people try to hook tagged fish for prizes. In 1989, thousands competed in one-day tournaments, while close to 300,000 participated in the 60-day tournaments across 36 locations. "Never in the history of fishing have so many anglers paid an entry fee to fish in one type of promotion," said Ken Clary, president of America Outdoors, Inc., the parent company of Crappiethon.

Beginning in 1990, the tournament trail increased from 36 lakes to 42 lakes, four of which are in new Crappiethon states, Minnesota and Wisconsin. "We've expanded from our first year in 1984 when we had three events," Clary said. "We've made steady progress and have become a leader in the fishing tournament business for panfishermen."

Funds collected from the Johnson Reels' Crappiethon USA tournaments under the name of the Mariners Conservation Program were donated to the Fish America Foundation for specific conservation projects around the country. "We are proud of our conservation efforts," said Clary, "and hope to increase them each year to promote the future of fishing."

The 1990 Crappiethon Classic is slated for Smithland Pool, Kentucky, on June 2. The top three teams from each of the one-day tournaments qualify for the Classic and will compete for first place and $40,000 in cash and prizes. The top five teams that weigh in the 20 largest crappie will receive $40,000, $6,000, $2,000, $1,500 and $500, respectively.

Smithland Pool, just south of Paducah, will be off-limits to qualifiers from April 1st until the day before the tournament, the only official practice day.

"This is the world series of crappie fishing," says Clary. "These fishermen represent the cream of the crop of more than 20,000 crappie anglers who tried to qualify for the Classic in 42 one-day events."

The events begin Friday night, June 1st, with a seminar in the lake area. At this gathering late registrants will be signed up, tournament rules discussed and the crowd entertained by fishing and equipment experts. The Classic will officially kick off next morning and last through the weekend.

Johnson Reels' Crappiethon USA one-day tournaments are open to any team, so long as one member is of legal age in each particular state. Johnson Reels, sponsor of Crappiethon, is a division of Johnson Fishing, Inc. Both are located in Mankato, Minnesota. For more information, contact: Ron Sundborg, Johnson Fishing, Inc., 1531 Madison Avenue, Mankato, MN 56001.

CHAPTER 16

THE BARRACUDA ARE BACK

Called A Variety Of Names, This Sporty Gamester Has Returned To Southern California's Fishing Grounds — And It's About Time!

By Leroy Janulewicz

Author holds a brace of keeper 'cuda, indicative of the comeback species is making all along Southern California. 'Cuda kill baitfish even when full.

Keeping barracuda flat makes filleting much easier, preserves maximum amount of tasty flesh. 'Cuda are great on the barbecue, or smoked after marinating.

Anchovies certainly will catch slime sticks, but handling catch isn't so easy as with iron jigs. You have to remove hook and, on undersized 'cuda, handling them removes protective slime barrier that could cause them to die later. Too, it takes more time going to bait tank.

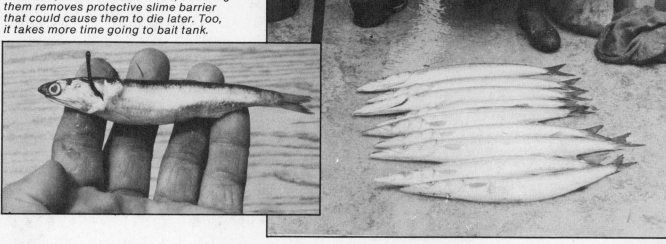

BARRACUDA HAVE finally made a comeback, and that's the best news California saltwater fishermen have heard in years! It comes after many years of famine. For example, when I started the exciting sport of saltwater angling as a 9-year-old some 34 years ago, my father and I used to catch barracuda as long as I was tall! Those were the good old days, with limits of 10- to 15-pound barracuda the norm, rather than the exception. But for some reason, the numbers and the size of barracuda then fell off. Now, the years of work by the California Department of Fish and Game are finally paying off. Whether it was the larger legal size imposed, or the close scrutiny for illegal net boats, it's improved the fishery all along the Southern California coast.

Barracuda migrate from Baja each year around June, then spawn along Southern California's coast and outer islands. They stay around for the whole summer before heading back south of the border.

The species has acquired many nicknames from old-timers: "slime sticks," "logs," "cuda," "pencils," and "poor man's wahoo." Whatever the name, they are a kick in the pants to catch!

California has a legal size limit of 28 inches, and I wish I had a dollar for every pencil (short 'cuda) I've released in the past. I wouldn't have to worry about winning the lottery! Fishermen who do keep short fish are cheating themselves and will hurt future barracuda fishing for everyone.

Like their big brother, the great barracuda, these logs are voracious feeders. They are opportunistic, too, eating whenever they can, day or night. The 'cuda's menu consists of anchovies, sardines, squid and any other species of baitfish.

On one long-range trip, I witnessed a mile square full of logs — 'cuda in the 8- to 10-pound class — having a field day feeding on red tuna crabs. What a sight! I've come to the conclusion that even if a 'cuda's stomach is stuffed, it will still attack and kill a baitfish without eating it. That's where fishing with artificial lures comes into play.

Barracuda are predominantly surface feeders, but can be caught near or on the bottom when the surface temperature cools or the current slows. When a school of bar-

That's some impressive dentition, and a 'cuda is only too happy to bite the hand that feeds it! Use caution when you remove lightweight jigs, hooks from these toothy critters.

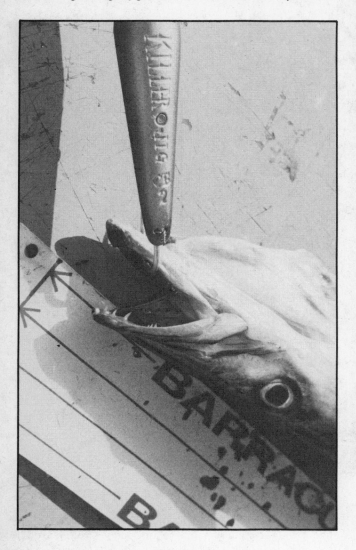

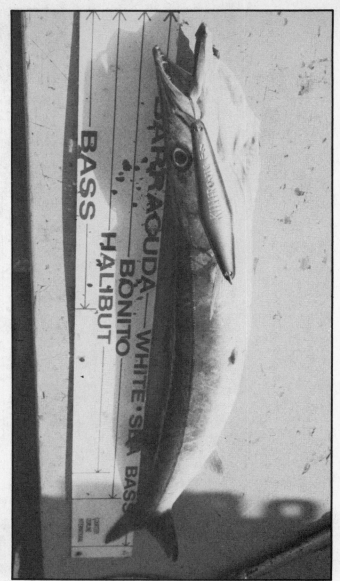

Virtually all sportfishing boats have measuring sticks on board, noting the legal minimums. Don't cheat and keep an undersized 'cuda, author says, as it hurts the species.

racuda are in a wide-open feeding frenzy, the ideal way to fish them is with the iron jig. Barries bite best when there's a slight chop on the water, with water temperature between 68 and 71 degrees.

There are several advantages to fishing iron. The jig, especially the single-hook style, can be quickly and easily removed from a 'cuda's mouth. If the fish is too short, you can release it unharmed. Just hold onto the jig and shake the pencil off back into the water. By releasing the fish in this manner, you don't have to put your hands on him — or you'll understand where the 'cuda gets the nickname of slime stick. The barracuda has a very thick, slimy, protective film on its skin. If this film is removed by handling, the fish could die when thrown back.

Using the iron jig will also give a fisherman more fishing time. You don't have to bait up with an anchovy on every cast, or replace a hook. Barracuda have a nasty set of teeth and are notorious for cutting the best brands of monofilament line, as well as fingers! So be extra careful when removing the jig.

If you need to handle the 'cuda, whether it's short or of legal size, hold the fish with an old towel or a burlap fish sack. This will minimize removal of the 'cuda's slime, and keep it off your hands. Regardless, wash your hands before your next cast. I've seen many fishing outfits slip through the best fishermen's hands.

Barracuda, especially the big logs, seem to be partial to blue and white, black and white, purple and silver, chrome,

Dick Aker, ramrod of Dick's Killer Jigs, must spend lots of time on water "field testing" his new jig designs. The fact that he loves fishing has nothing to do with it, of course. Like the author, he favors rods up to eight feet long for log barries.

No, this isn't a messy sight — these 'cuda were just tipped from horizontal fish sack in readiness for filleting. Bleeding will keep flesh firm, author advises.

and solid white jigs. There are several jigs to choose from in these colors. I've had my best success with Dick's Killer Jigs CBI, Salas Jigs 2x 200, Tady AA, and Sea Strike 33. Whichever you choose, the lightweight models are barracuda favorites. The heavier models don't seem to work as well in my past barracuda outings.

When fishing iron, I've found that a slow retrieve works best for the big logs. The light jig swims better; perhaps that's its appeal. Lighter jigs drive the fish crazy, just wait and see for yourself!

When your jig gets bit, don't set the hook like you were bait fishing. Keep winding on the reel, and don't pump the rod. Make sure your reel drag is fairly tight before making

There's a nice limit of log barries, nailed by author on a Sabre rod and Penn 500 reel spooled with pink Ande.' After handling a 'cuda, be sure to wash your hands or the rod might take a header over the rail. That's a big $$ loss!

Another problem with using bait is that you'll frequently gut-hook barries, which makes survival after release iffy. It's tough to hook them in their tough jaws. See text.

the cast. Using this method will bring the 'cuda to the boat like a torpedo when you turn his head.

I only use conventional reels when fishing the iron, because of the drag system and the grinding power when retrieving a hooked 'cuda. The Shimano TLD 10, TLD 15 and Penn 500 are among my favorite reels when fishing for big 'cudas. These reels are strong and dependable. I use 25- or 30-pound test line. Ande line has been a longtime favorite for its dependability and strength. Ande line in clear and pink colors works well when fishing iron for barries.

The most successful barracuda fishermen use rods in the 6½- to 8-foot lengths. I've found through the years that the longer rod will enhance your casting distance, especially when throwing a light jig and using heavier line. Always watch your backcast with a long rod. The most popular barracuda jig rods have been from Cal Star and Sabre. While both rod companies have several jig rods in their lines, the Cal Star Model 6480 in the 8-foot length and

Sabre Model 580 8-footer are my favorites for log barracuda.

If possible, when you have landed a bunch of nice 'cuda, try to keep the fish flat. Lay your fish sack on the boat deck. When barracuda are crammed into the sack, they also curl; makes it harder to fillet them than if they're straight.

As to caring for your catch: in the straightening process, the flesh inside will tear and the fillet won't hold together as well. I've seen lots of nice logs turn to mush after being filleted. I also like to bleed my barracuda prior to sacking them. These two steps will keep your catch fresh and firm.

Don't let anyone tell you that barracuda are poor eating! They are excellent barbecued, as well as smoked. If you don't believe me, just check the prices of barracuda next time you're in the local fishmarket!

When you don't get away for the long-range trip to Baja, give the poor man's wahoo a try for some local summertime fun! It's top sport with a good tasting result!

Off the Southern California coast during summer, barracuda provide top sport for several months. They migrate into the spawning grounds in huge numbers, a comeback that's a credit to fish and game officials.

When a 'cuda hits your iron jig, don't slam the hook home. Rather, with drag screwed tight, you commence to crank on the reel handle. Thus, when you turn fish's head, he comes to the boat like a torpedo.

CHAPTER 17

GET THE DROP ON FALL & WINTER BASS

BASS Pros Larry Nixon & Tommy Martin Tell How To Improve Your Take On Cold-Water Bigmouths

By Terry Freeland

Larry Nixon, all-time leading money winner on Bass Anglers Sportsman Society tournament trail, shares some of his fall bass-catching techniques.

Tommy Martin, perennial qualifier for BASS Masters Classic who, like Nixon, hails from Hemphill, Texas, prefers a pork trailer when bass are sluggish.

Author (left) unhooks quality bass that hit vertically jigged spoon during fall while suspended over hump author has fished previously. (Above) Chunky bass like this await patient anglers who find stacked-up schools, then put spoons right on their heads. Fish won't move much.

VERTICAL JIGGING isn't fancy. It has none of the glamour of topwater fishing. Nor is the adventure of throwing crankbaits there, either. But for fall and winter fishing, jigging is one of the most effective techniques you can use to put fish in the boat — sometimes lots of them!

To be able to catch bass, you first must find bass. At few times of the year will electronic locators play a more important role in catching bass. A fisherman without a flasher, straight-line graph recorder or Liquid Crystal Recorder will have to rely on knowledge of the lake he plans to fish — not to mention just plain luck. "Vertical jigging is a locator game," says Larry Nixon, BASS Tournament Trail all-time money winner. "You want to pinpoint your structure, and you need some kind of information about what depth the fish are holding."

Finding this depth is easily accomplished by turning on the locator and motoring across the lake, watching the locator for signs of the bait and fish. It's now a simple matter of moving to structure which has similar depth and begin looking for active fish.

One mistake common to anglers new to using elec-

tronics is not turning the sensitivity control up high enough to give a good detailed reading. For example, a flasher unit should display a distinct "second echo" to show the power is properly adjusted. The deeper the water, the more important this becomes or your readings may be incorrect. Consult the directions which came with the unit for detailed information about this adjustment.

Electronics give the angler the advantage of being able to bypass all water which is essentially fishless. "Use of electronics is the most important aspect of bass fishing after a guy learns the fundamentals," adds Nixon.

During fall and winter, bass form tight schools and it is important to know the seasonal locations they prefer. "I always find the fish on some kind of definite *something,* like an underwater bridge, or a channel bend in a creek, or a long point that has an underwater channel swinging in close to it," confides Nixon. "I like to stay deep because that's where the concentrations of fish are."

Former Bass Masters Classic champion Tommy Martin concurs on fish holding structure. "In the fall and winter months, I feel that bass start relating more on real *vertical* type dropoffs which drop 20, 30, even 40 feet deep. Spoon

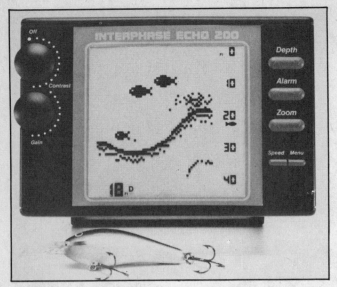

Interphase's Echo 200 is low-priced LCD fishfinder with variety of features and four-button operation, including ability to zoom-in on any quarter of screen down to 320 feet. Fish alarm and symbols distinguish big, small fish.

Bottom Line's flasher unit mounts in dash and is furnished with 18-degree transducer for bilge mounting that gives through-the-hull readings. You'll be able to read break-line and bottom, essential for success on winter bass.

In winter, you'll find bass orienting or "stacking up" on vertical type of structure (left), as opposed to summer bass that favor a more-gradual slope. Pinpoint accuracy with jig, spoon is required to succeed.

fishing can be real exciting," he says. "Many times I've pulled up to a vertical drop, or an outside bend in a creek channel, and caught 20 or 30 bass."

Not surprisingly, both Nixon and Martin have favorite spoons. Martin prefers a Hopkins spoon in ½- or ¾-ounce sizes. "When the fish are active and I want more action in the lure, I go to a shoehorn-style spoon," he adds. Nixon says he favors "the CC Spoon and the Shoehorn Spoon."

The Hopkins spoons, long a jigging standby, have traditionally been the hammered-finish variety, but a recent addition to the line promises to become another standard for the vertical-jigging enthusiast. The Hopkins Smoothie series features a polished surface and the addition of prismatic tape, with a different tape color on each side of the spoon. Obviously, this gives the fish a new look and the double color combination makes the lure work under a variety of different water clarities. Some other effective jigging spoons include the Dixie Jet, Krocodile, CC Spoons,

Kastmaster, Bomber Slab Spoon and Mann-O-Lure.

Different spoons have different actions. It pays big dividends to experiment and learn the performance of each spoon in your tackle box. "You've got to play with the action while spoon fishing," Nixon advises. This means you need to vary the lift and drop of the spoon enough to find the one bass prefer on that given day. One day the fish may want a sharp snap of the lure to trigger a strike, while on another they may hit a nearly motionless spoon. Concentrate on the amount of movement you impart to a spoon. By changing deliberately through a series of different motions and retrieves, the fisherman will often discover the one the bass prefer. Experimentation is a key ingredient to successful bass fishing.

Detecting strikes while spoon jigging is a learned experience. Strikes can vary from nearly nonexistent ticks to knuckle-busting jolts. Strikes from active fish are easy to detect and will almost always occur on the drop. Tommy

There is a wide variety of spoons on the market today, and virtually all will hang bass under the right conditions — which you, the angler, must determine. In right photo, spoons are (from top): Flutter-craft, Krocodile, Hopkins Shorty, and a second Krocodile, this one with prismatic tape. Same lineup appears below, with a silver standard Hopkins at far left, and a Dixie Jet (third from right). In below right photo you'll find Kastmasters, Little George, and others. Shoehorn-style are easy to identify by distinctive shape.

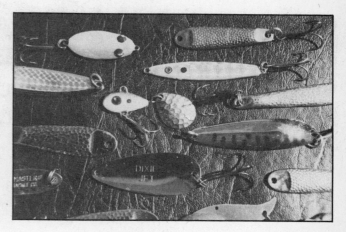

Martin declares the fish will often whack a spoon hard. "Sometimes you can see the line jump a foot," the Texan says enthusiastically. "The complete opposite is true of bass in very cold water. Some special attention is needed to catch those inactive fish."

Martin tells of a special trick for that situation. "Something that's worked for me, that a lot of fishermen aren't familiar with, works when the fish are three or four feet up off the bottom. I let the spoon fall vertically to the bottom until my line goes slack, then reel up about three to four feet while holding my rod tip completely still. This lets the line unwind. When the spoon starts unwinding in clear water, or semi-clear water even, it gives off a lot of light, and it produces movement. Bass often hit the lure while it's unwinding."

A key factor to producing strikes in cold water is the amount of movement imparted to the spoon. Cold water slows a bass's metabolism and this should be considered when vertical jigging. "In the wintertime, something you have to watch out for is imparting *too much* action," says BASS pro Larry Nixon. "Be careful when you are spoon fishing if the water is real cold, say down around 43-44 degrees. A lot of times I'll just get it right on the bottom and raise it about six inches, then let it fall back. I then just pick it up off the bottom maybe a couple of inches and hold it still. You'll be sitting there and it'll just go 'thunk.' Set the hook!"

Tommy Martin offers the same advice. "When the water is in the low 50s or even high 40s, I've had better results pulling the spoon up six to nine inches and just letting it fall back down. Don't jerk or rip the spoon up off the bottom. I think a lot of fishermen tend to put too much action, too much movement, into the lure."

To be a successful spoon fisherman requires a knowledge of what is going on while the spoon drops. The trick here is to let the spoon fall freely, but still be able to detect

West Coast basser and angler's fishing buddy, Jim Maguire, wrestles a nice fish in clear water of San Diego lakes. Fish took a spoon Maguire was holding stationary, allowing spoon to unwind, flashing brightly.

the strike as the spoon falls back with controlled slack. There is no substitute for experience here. Spoon bites can be tricky, and total concentration is a must.

Rigging tricks can be a big help in vertical jigging. For example, almost all jigging spoons can be improved by simply removing the factory hook and replacing it with a soft bronze hook at least one size larger than the stock hook. This increases the hook gap and makes it easier to hook fish. Mustad No. 3551 treble hooks work well in the appropriate size.

Because bass will almost always be found in cover, expect to get hung up while you're vertical jigging. If this happens, don't get in a hurry; just follow this simple procedure to get unstuck. Position the boat directly over the snag and reel up snug with the rod tip about three feet off the surface of the water. Now gently jiggle the rod tip, using the weight of the spoon to work the hook point loose from the snag. This really works and, with a little practice, you become almost fearless when it comes to fishing spoons. If the cover you are fishing is really thick and you are constantly getting hung up, try replacing the treble hook with a single hook. You won't snag as often, but you will catch nearly as many bass.

Lead-body jigging spoons can be bent slightly to produce different actions. This is no place to overdo it, though — a spoon with too much bend usually is ruined, and the finish sometimes cracks. So be careful when bending.

Another factor which will alter the action is tying the line directly to the eye. Believe it or not, this will dampen the action considerably. To avoid this, use a plain wire snap. It will allow the spoon to fall freely and makes for quick lure changes. If the spoon is twisting your line, try tying a ball-bearing type swivel 12 to 18 inches above the spoon. In this location it won't kill the action.

The best rods for vertical jigging are the two-handed types like Browning GripSticks. These allow the angler to take up more of the slack on the hookset than will a shorter rod. These rods are seven feet long and a good swing will nearly always set the hook well, even in deep water. They also are better-suited to handling the heavier-weight spoons.

For most vertical jigging situations, light line is not a necessity. Usually 14- to 17-pound-test is fine. Only in very clear water will it be necessary to go to lighter line. The use of low-stretch line will make it easier to detect light bites and also to set the hook.

Jig 'n pig is a deadly combination on winter bass, and the size of the pork trailer dictates rate of descent. Drab, dull colors are the norm, pros say, although both prefer a little chartreuse in stained water. (Below) A calm fall day produced gentle strike for author, who says bass also may move the line a foot with a savage lure attack.

Jigging spoons are not the only baits for vertical fishing. The leadhead jig is very effective when presented in the same up-and-down manner. The jig also is another cold-water lure. "The main thing that triggers a bass into striking a jig is the rate the jig falls," explains Tommy Martin. "I feel like when the water is real cold and I want the jig to fall extremely slowly, and I don't want a lot of movement out of my jig, I'll go to pork for a trailer." The angler can control the rate of fall by using larger or smaller pork trailers. Use small trailers for a fast sink rate, and larger ones for a slower rate.

"The jig is my favorite lure," explains Martin. "I fish a Stanley Jig 100 percent of the time, and I do a lot of vertical fishing with the jig, especially in deep water." It is common to use large jigs for these type of presentations, he says. One-ounce jigs are almost a necessity in deep water and the extra weight makes it easier to maintain contact with the bait, and consequently easier to detect strikes. Because jigs represent crayfish, bass are used to having a good-sized object in their mouths when they attack one. Big bass like big meals, so be prepared. Jigs usually catch large bass.

For jig colors, Martins generally recommends these: brown in clear water or black/blue. For murky or muddy water, black and chartreuse, also black/green/chartreuse. Color will seldom be as important as how and where you present the jig. In nearly all jig-fishing situations, the basic colors will be adequate.

A good tactic to use during the fall and winter is to "run and gun," BUT fish methodically and carefully! In other words, try as many locations as possible during the fishing day, remembering that the fish are schooled-up tight. If you don't cover the spot you are fishing very thoroughly, you could miss a large school by just several feet. Unlike summertime, those bass will not move several feet to chase your lure. It requires placing the bait right on their heads.

Fish as many different locations as possible and your chances of finding the fish will increase accordingly. It is not uncommon to fish most of the day, only to finally find the fish in one spot about the size of the boat. Find them, and you can almost count on catching a limit of bass!

BECOME A PIER PRO

Sample Saltwater Angling With Feet On Firmament And You'll Have Come-Back-Again Fun!

By Ronnie Kovach

Anglers enjoy the twilight action and camaraderie on the end of the Belmont Pier in Long Beach, California. Regulars come as much for the socializing as they do the saltwater fishing.

That's one serious angler, watching his line intently as it swirls around pilings that are "home" to baitfish. And where bait go, so go predators.

You'll see a variety of tackle in use at virtually any pier. If the glamour fish aren't hitting, use a lighter outfit and have some fun on croaker.

PIERS ALONG the Atlantic, Gulf and Pacific coasts offer anglers from all walks of life a real opportunity to take a mixed bag of good-eating gamefish. Some prefer to concentrate on major gamefish species like bonito, stripers, tarpon and snook, while others are content to plunk for mackerel, perch and small bottomfish.

Whichever category suits you, there is a general "blueprint" that characterizes most of these structures. Understanding this blueprint and knowing the best times to work piers will greatly enhance the angler's potential for bringing home a sackful of fish.

TYPES OF PIERS

These long walkways may extend out anywhere from 10 yards to over a mile. Some piers are found in sheltered harbors and bays, while others lead directly into the ocean.

Different species will be attracted to a particular pier, depending on its location in relation to tidal flow and current.

For instance, piers that jut out from the beach in Florida or California are more prone to play host to pelagic gamefish. Some of these piers are long and straight, others are shorter and L- or T-shaped. Species like kingfish and barracuda on the Atlantic or bonito and striped bass in the Pacific gravitate to these structures because the subsurface structure teems with schools of bait, crabs, and shellfish. Larger pelagic species will follow the bait inshore, often herding them before engaging in massive feeding frenzies under the pier.

Other species such as halibut or flounder, perch, and croakers can be found off the shorter piers situated in quiet bays. These often are termed "resident" fish in the sense that they live around these structures all year long.

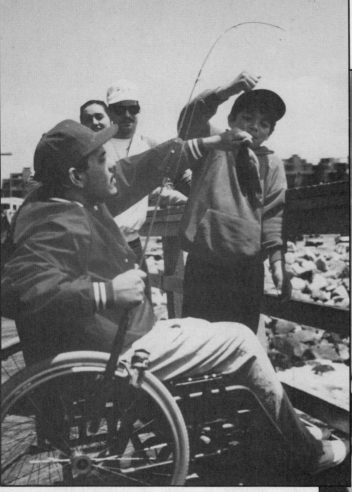

Opaleye, spotfin croaker, tom cod and other smaller fish remain around piers year-round, where they serve to attract larger gamefish. Lights will help lure baitfish, as with freshwater fishing, so use light to your advantage. Try your artificial there.

Anglers with physical disabilities are able to fish from most piers, as wheelchair ramps are standard.

WHERE TO FISH

Weekend anglers who approach a pier for the first time may be perplexed as to where to start fishing. On lengthy piers that face the open sea, the most common inclination is to walk to the end of the boardwalk and start there.

This isn't necessarily a bad choice — but a lot can depend upon the time of year. For example, certain migratory species such as bonito, stripers, and 'cuda will make routine feeding forays, moving from deep water to the end of the pier. But once water temperatures change and a particular seasonal movement of gamefish dwindles, so can the activity at this part of the pier.

Note, also, that these gamefish may traverse the entire

length of a pier, not just the deepwater end. The key will be the baitfish: If the bait moves toward shore, expect larger predators to follow.

However, with regard to access to deep water, almost all piers facing the open ocean can be potential hunting grounds for numerous kinds of sharks. These marine predators frequently will make daily migrations from deep to shallow water to feed. The ends of long piers are perfect locations to intercept this movement of sharks, as well as bat rays. Sharks and rays can prove to be sensational sport for the fisherman who wants the ultimate challenge working from the end of pier!

In backwaters, many anglers also will head for the end of

Some piers are huge, extending far out into bays or the ocean proper. Is it best to head right to the end? If you do, you're passing up a lot of productive water. Learn the species' behavior.

In some areas, sportfishing boats tie up to the pier where deckhands perform cleaning chores and hose down the vessel. Fish learn to expect the "freebies" and you can give them the steel surprise!

the shorter piers found here. Many of the bigger gamefish populating harbors and bays will be near the deepest and preferably moving water. Here, too, the ends of these smaller piers permit the angler to cast out toward the channels where many gamefish feed. This water beyond the pier often exhibits considerable current or tidal flow — another major attraction for bait and larger backwater species.

Moving away from the end of the pier, the fisherman can explore the middle sector. Here is where the piling structures may be most prominent. Shellfish such as mussels cling to the pilings, often in bulky masses. Smaller salt-water species such as perch, smelt, queenfish, herring, and mackerel will play hide-and-seek around these pilings. This effect seems to hold true, regardless of the length of the pier, whether in open water or on a sheltered bay. The smaller species will live among the pilings for sanctuary from large predators.

On the larger and longer piers, also consider working the surfline. Surprisingly, only a handful of pier veterans seem to fish the sandy beach that foams around the base of oceanfront piers.

In this surfline, a virtual smorgasbord of fish can be found, ranging from halibut and surf perch to stripers and sharks. Many of the more-accomplished pier fishermen try to present their baits or artificial lures directly parallel

Naturally, safety-conscious anglers must avoid overhead casting when on the pier; with practice, underhand cast provides almost the same result.

Pelicans close by are a good sign that these waters are "fishy." If you observe nature and learn where gamefish move in relation to pier, you increase your chances of success.

along the outside of the breakers. What you may find by casting into the surfline will depend upon the seasonal movement of a particular species.

There are subtler things to consider when scouting out a place to fish on the pier. Some piers in both harbors and in open sea have sportfishing boats that tie up alongside. Passengers are sometimes loaded onto the boats, walking down gangplanks from the pier's boardwalk. These fishing boats commonly attract both gamefish and pier dwellers. The deckhands may regularly empty bait tanks or clean the day's catch as the boat is tied to the pier. The fish will look forward to this daily routine of a "free handout." Don't hesitate to make a few casts around these vessels, particularly if bait tanks are being emptied or fish are being cleaned. Hook up!

Similarly, many piers have cleaning stations intermittently spaced along the boardwalk. Sharks, rays, perch, mackerel, and assorted smaller species will typically scavenge around the pilings below the cleaning tables for the "leftovers." Give 'em a try.

BEST TIMES

Successful pier fishermen may plan their trips to coincide with variables that affect the feeding patterns of pier species. Sharks and rays, for instance, are invariably nocturnal, whereas halibut caught from the piers seem to be primarily a daytime proposition.

But nighttime also is when both boater traffic and angling pressure is at a minimum. Certain gamefish like the different bass species will more readily strike bait or artificials in

Berkeley Pier near San Francisco provides boatless anglers a chance to reach offshore species. All manner of blue-water predators will follow baitfish in close to shore, and sharks and rays are common.

Some piers cater more to fishermen than others by providing permanent rod holders on the railings, fish cleaning stations, food and beverages nearby, and restrooms. Study state laws before heading out.

Retirees enjoy health benefits of sea air and physical exercise, not to mention good-tasting food that's good for you, to boot! Any tackle will do.

Most states limit the number of rods you can have in use at any one time, so check the regulations to avoid a problem. These boys are on seaward end of pier in Haulover, Florida.

the quiet of the night, rather than in the daylight hours.

Learn to utilize the lighting on a pier. As occurs with freshwater fishing, lights can attract a lot of bait. Larger gamefish, in turn, will slash into the illuminated water to harvest silhouetted prey.

There are seasonal phenomena that lure an angler to a favorite pier. Experienced pier pros watch for unexpected schools of squid or pelagic red crabs that may venture into local coastal waters. Similarly, Pacific pier experts take advantage of intensified feeding activity when the grunion make their annual spawning runs off the beaches.

By contrast, reports of a "red tide" condition usually signals a standstill in the marine fishery. This is a poor time to sample inshore fishing, particularly from a pier where the oxygen-depleted condition may be intensified.

BE MOBILE, ALERT AND CREATIVE!

Pier fishing can be a highly relaxing pastime. For some anglers, the mellowness of the environment and the camaraderie that develops among pier regulars is the main

When seasonal migration of gamefish occurs, ranks of pier veterans are swollen by influx of "weekenders." Good sportsmanship is the byword here, to avoid upset over inevitable crowding.

Halibut fishing often is best just outside the surfline, an area ignored by many pier anglers who feel the good fish are in deeper water. But in the crashing surf are found injured crabs, bait — and predators!

Piers along the Gulf Coast charge a nominal daily fee, collected at a set time each day. You usually can rent rods and reels, but must purchase terminal tackle items and bait. Ask locals for guidance — they'll help.

Men, women, children — all come to piers to challenge the fish swimming close in. There's mystery down there, too, since you don't know what'll take your bait until you get it in!

attraction to these structures.

However, for the diehard saltwater enthusiast, the pier can be an economical place to challenge a complex and intriguing fishery. From pelagic fish to smaller species for the table, to big-game-style strokin' for sharks and rays — piers offer it all. But success may require you to be mobile, alert and creative.

Don't get "hung up" on fishing only one spot. Move around, trying to intercept the different gamefish as they traverse the pier. If the trophy fish aren't biting, work a secondary lighter outfit for some of the less-prestigious pier residents like perch, smelt or mackerel.

Be aware of fluctuations in tidal situations. Some species are more prone to feed on incoming tides, others on the outgoing movement. Experience will help you to key in on particular species under optimal tidal conditions. Ask other anglers for guidance. With few exceptions, they'll be happy to share wisdom with you.

Finally, be creative with regard to methods. Don't hesitate to be imaginative and try something different in the way of a new lure or bait. Quite frequently, the fish found around the piers are subjected to a narrow menu of baits and lures. Give them something new and innovative to look at and you may be surprised at the results!

Fish that live under the pier year-round learn to orient on fish-cleaning stations, so there's a good spot to try some cut bait. Frozen shrimp nearly always produces interest on part of local fish schools.

Jigging artificial lures near the pier pilings might work in daylight or dark, as spoon's action and flash resembles an injured baitfish — easy prey for hungry predators. Become a line watcher and hook up!

SPINNERS & SPOONS FOR SUCCESSFUL TROUTIN'

These Are The Basic Lures Responsible For More Trout Than Any Other Bait. Try 'Em!

Author advises varying retrieve with spinner and spoons, and lady angler here returns lure with rod tip down low.

A higher rod tip changes angle lure swims through water, as does speed of retrieve. Count down your lures at first.

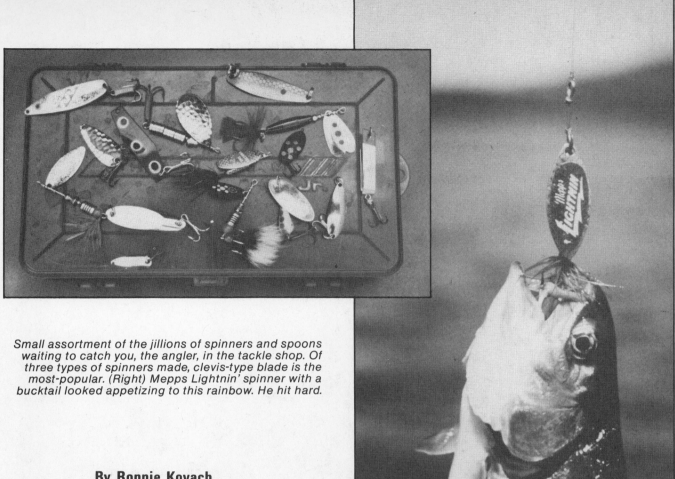

Small assortment of the jillions of spinners and spoons waiting to catch you, the angler, in the tackle shop. Of three types of spinners made, clevis-type blade is the most-popular. (Right) Mepps Lightnin' spinner with a bucktail looked appetizing to this rainbow. He hit hard.

By Ronnie Kovach

WITHOUT QUESTION, most trout caught in the United States are taken on bait. But more and larger fish are possible by using a select group of artificial lures called spoons and spinners.

The accomplished trouter can cover a lot of water using lures from either the bank or a boat. In contrast, the bait fisherman is typically relegated to soaking his offerings in a small area and hoping a fish finds him.

Larger trout seem to key in on the artificials. Spoons and spinners replicate the more prominent insects, amphibians, and baitfish that comprise the preferred menu for the bigger trout. They're usually larger than a gob of nightcrawlers or salmon eggs.

There are some generalized points that can be made to differentiate between these major styles of trout lures. Each design is distinct, requiring different presentations and precise selection.

Of all the lures used for trout fishing, the metal spoon has to be the most popular and versatile. Spoons come in an awesome array of colors, shapes and sizes. There are some

models, like the traditional red-and-white Daredevle, for instance, that are practically lifetime members of fishing's all-time "Deadly Dozen" list of freshwater lures. The uniquely designed Z-Ray enjoys more of a regional following among Western trouters — and each area produces local favorites. Most good tackle stores will stock a very comprehensive assortment of spoons to choose from, but to the recreational fisherman, selecting the right one can be mind-boggling. So what feaures do you look for in selecting which spoon to throw at your favorite trout lake? Let's start with size and weight.

The spoons for most trouting will range from miniature ultralight versions in 1/32-ounce, on up to about 1/2-ounce for casting or trolling for lunker-class fish. Manufacturers sometimes describe these supersmall spoons as "fly rod" models. In reality, few ever are used with traditional fly rods, per se. Most of these diminutive spoons are cast with ultralight rods and reels with 2- to 4-pound-test line. They are excellent in the backcountry lakes on small rainbows, brookies, and even goldens.

There are times when trout prefer the wobble-type spoons over the slimmer-profile, tighter-action spoons. If you don't get bit using one type, go to alternatives in style and color.

If your lure falls too quickly, add a hair hackle bucktail dressing of squirrel tail such as lure second from right. Blade color and finish will depend on clarity of water, sky.

Spoons of this size are difficult to cast, even with ultralight gear. Often the angler will trail these spoons behind a clear plastic float known as a bubble, or crimp a lead split-shot or two about 24 inches above the little lure for that extra casting weight.

The most popular size for spoons are ⅛- to ⅜-ounce. These will cast adequately with 4- to 6-pound-test line, and are good all-around choices for most generalized lake fishing and even for some of the larger streams. Heavier spoons, ½-ounce or more, are best-suited for big fish on large lakes worked slowly on the retrieve or trolled.

Trout spoons can be divided into three basic styles: wide-body, slim-profile, and flat wobblers. The first type is typically wide across the midsection. Sometimes the actual thickness of the metal is "fatter" than average with this type of lure. The wobble effect with this style of bait also is characteristically "wide" in action. That is, for its size, the spoon will produce a prominent, sweeping wobble on the retrieve.

There are times when trout are definitely "tuned-in" to this particular type of radical side-to-side movement. Spoons such as the popular Wob-L-Rite, Hot Shot, Little Cleo, and Daredevle head this type of wide-bodied spoon.

Like other gamefish, trout will at times "shut off" on one particular pattern (i.e., a lure, color, retrieve or any combination thereof) and "turn on" to another. With spoons, the fish may switch from a preference for wide-body spoons to a slim-profile model. The latter presents a very sleek, subtle silhouette in the water. Often anything more dramatic than this style bait will actually scare the fish. The action on a slim-profiled spoon is distinctively "tight," with minimal lateral wobble. Popular spoons like the Krocodile, Acme Fjord, Phoebe, and Mepps Syclops are prime examples of this slimmer spoon design.

The third type of spoon pattern moves away from the rounded, utensil-like shape that gives these lures their descriptive name. Instead, this group — the flat wobblers — have thinner, more angular forms. There is very little cupped effect in their surface area, as they're designed primarily to flutter seductively with a minimal amount of effort. Popular models used for troutin' are the Kastmaster, Z-Ray, and Super-Duper.

The lightest trout lures are hard to cast, especially if it's windy at all, but adding a plastic bubble float or split-shot ahead of the spinner about 18 inches will assist in getting lures out where the rainbows lurk! See text.

As a general rule, a spoon in a predominantly silver or nickel finish is your overall best choice in bright sunlight. Copper surfaces, or painted combinations of red and white, black and white, black and green, chartreuse, frog, or mixes with some orange or yellow spots, are good for cloudy, overcast days. Spoons either with solid or half-tone finishes in gold or bronze fall somewhere in-between as far as natural sky light conditions are concerned. I want to remind you that these are broad generalizations and it doesn't hurt to be somewhat unconventional if the traditional pattern seems ineffective on a particular day.

There also are a few other, rather exotic color schemes that are productive when spoon fishing for trout. I have found, for instance, that a black scale finish can be dynamite in the wee daylight hours around dawn and dusk. Apparently this dark pattern casts a more visible silhouette in the water against a dimly lit sky.

Natural trout-colored finishes on spoons also are effective at times, particularly in the rainbow or brown trout patterns. Similarly, other manufacturers use brilliant, prism-like, flect-o-lite finishes on the Super Duper, for instance,

to generate an exciting luster effect as the spoon is pulled through the water. One other interesting alternative is a natural pinkish salmon egg effect, found on the Seneca Little Cleo spoons, among others. This raised, egg-like surface gives the spoon the illusion of a cluster of salmon eggs drifting lazily by — a favorite natural food for hungry rainbows!

You will find trout spoons are made with smooth or hammered metal surfaces. The smooth finish will generate a subtle flash in the water. The hammered version reflects a tremendous amount of light, which bounces off the dimples or indentations on its surface. Sometimes trout want the more subdued, smooth-finish spoon; other times they home in on the more-vibrant hammered models. It is important to keep some spoons with each type of surface in your box, if only in simple nickel or gold versions.

The biggest mistake novice fishermen make in using a trout spoon is attaching it to a snap-swivel combination. Almost without fail, this will measurably reduce the necessary wobble that these lures are supposed to generate. Some spoons come with either a simple snap or a small split ring. In other cases, these lures are ready to go as is. Do not add

While natural baits account for more total poundage of fish caught, larger fish are taken on artificials. Too, for those who like to cast, you can stay busy all day.

anything else — just tie to either the snap or split ring, whichever is stocked with the lure.

As for retrieves, many anglers are clearly not imaginative enough when working a trout spoon. They simply throw it out as far as they can and begin a straight retrieve back once the spoon hits the water. There are a number of little tricks you can add to this presentation that may generate a few more hook-ups.

First, whether you are casting the spoon from the bank or from a boat, let it sink to varying depths. Don't just grind it back, wobbling a few inches beneath the surface. Trout will stratify along different thermoclines and strike zones on a given lake, and may move up or down in depth during the day. If you have sophisticated electronic fish-finding equipment on your boat, it will be easy to pinpoint precisely the depths the trout appear to be active. If you do not have these instruments or are walking the shoreline, you'll simply have to experiment by retrieving the spoon through different strata. So, let the spoon sink somewhat before you start reeling. Vary the sink from all the way to the bottom to a few feet below the surface. Count down your spoon so you can find trout after a hookup.

Be prepared for a strike while the lure is fluttering down on the fall. If you see a "tick" in the line or if the line seems to go unusually slack, quickly re-engage the reel, pick up the slack, and set the hook. These often are the telltale

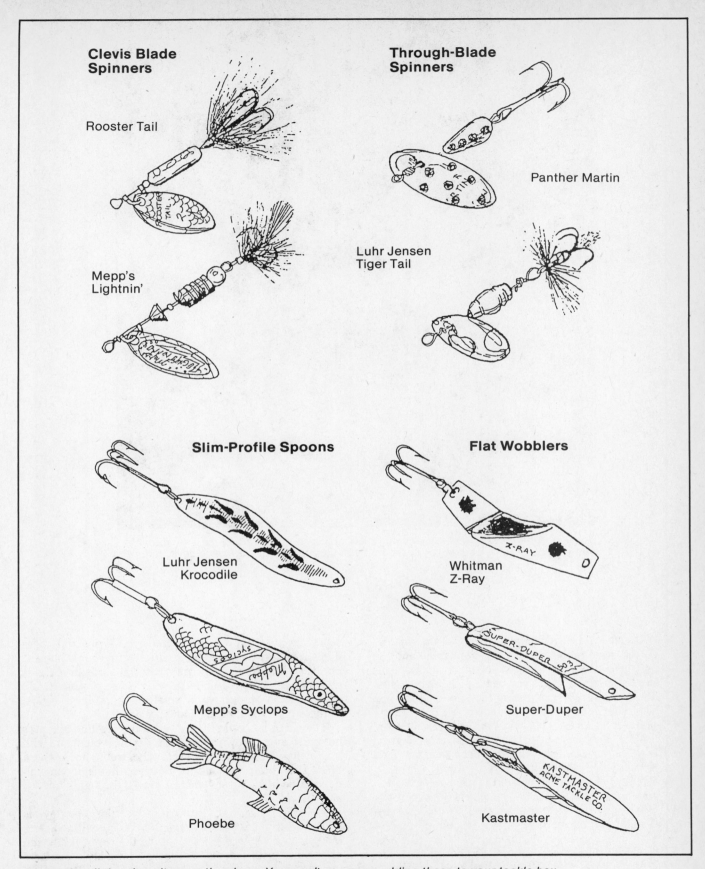

Clevis Blade Spinners

Rooster Tail

Mepp's Lightnin'

Through-Blade Spinners

Panther Martin

Luhr Jensen Tiger Tail

Slim-Profile Spoons

Luhr Jensen Krocodile

Mepp's Syclops

Phoebe

Flat Wobblers

Whitman Z-Ray

Super-Duper

Kastmaster

Among the all-time favorites are the above. You won't go wrong adding these to your tackle box.

If you're dunking bait, you're pretty much stuck in one spot, waiting for a trout to find you. But if you're casting, you can cover a bigger area of water and several depths.

signs of a trout that has inhaled the spoon "on the sink."

When the more-mundane straight grind fails, another simple retrieve also will generate some good strikes. This is called a "stop 'n go." Once you begin your retrieve, stop suddenly every so often, allowing the spoon to fall. Be especially ready for strikes on the sink. If you don't get bit after the spoon falls a few feet, start the retrieve again. Continue this stop 'n go action all the way back in. It is theorized that this presentation attracts the trout because it mimics a wounded baitfish struggling through the water.

Next to spoons, spinners account for the greatest number of trout caught on artificial lures. Spinners work primarily on sight and sound: The flash of the spinning blades, combined with the bright metallic body and colored-feather treble hook, make this lure tantalizing to a hungry trout. As the blade whirls through the water, the spinner generates a great amount of vibration that literally "calls in" fish.

A trout spinner thus functions primarily as a reaction bait. It is made to imitate a minnow or similar baitfish

scurrying to escape a large predator. Trout will react and strike at the spinner for a variety of reasons: hunger, curiosity, annoyance, or even territorial protection. Spinners can be effective under a wide range of conditions. They can be productive in small streams, large rivers, flatland reservoirs, or backcountry ponds.

There are a couple of spinner styles. In-line spinners comprise most thrown at trout. This is the typical lure with a straight wire shaft, cylindrical tube, treble hook, and a blade that rotates around the body. In-line spinners can have three blade arrangements: clevis, through-blade, or swivel.

The clevis design is by far the most popular. The clevis is a U-shaped metal bar to which the blade is affixed. The blade is thus allowed to spin around the wire shaft which runs through the clevis. Standard clevis-style spinners include the Mepps lines of baits, Luhr Jensen Bang Tail, Rooster Tail, and Shyster models.

Through-blade spinners do not utilize a clevis fitting.

Spoons — Actual Sizes

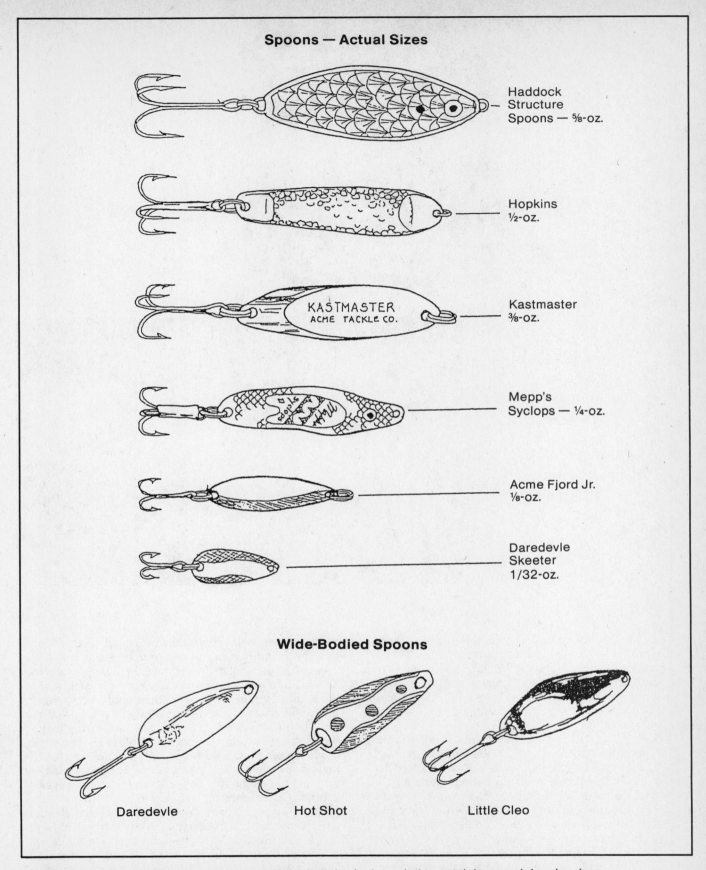

Haddock Structure Spoons — ⅝-oz.

Hopkins ½-oz.

Kastmaster ⅜-oz.

Mepp's Syclops — ¼-oz.

Acme Fjord Jr. ⅛-oz.

Daredevle Skeeter 1/32-oz.

Wide-Bodied Spoons

Daredevle   Hot Shot   Little Cleo

You can get a sense of the size of spoons and the fish they're intended to catch by examining drawings.

General rule calls for using silver or nickel blades in bright sunlight copper, gold or red-and-white when overcast or in murky water. New reflective blades are best in bright lighting situations, author's found.

No matter the spinner or spoon, don't attach a swivel ahead of the lure. This will deaden the action of the lure. Test each new purchase for optimum retrieve speed, then be ready to vary same to imitate dying bait.

Instead, the blade slides directly over the wire shaft, spinning freely. Spinners wth this blade configuration typically generate a lot of sonic vibration, because unlike the clevis style models, the blade meets greater resistance when pulled against the water. Common models of through-blade spinners are the Panther Martin and Luhr Jensen Tiger Tail.

The simplest of all and the least-used spinner is the swivel model characterized by the old-fashioned Colorado spinner. This lure is made by joining two swivels together with a ring in the middle where the small blade also is attached. The blade wobbles rather than rotates along the swivels, generating a very slow, subtle flash.

As for blade size, a rough rule of thumb is that a larger blade will make the lure sink slower as it displaces more water. The blade will spin best using a slow retrieve. Hence, a spinner with a bigger blade would be an excellent choice when fishing slowly for surface-feeding trout.

Conversely, a narrower, thinner blade spins faster and yields greater flash. It will sink faster and would be a good pick for fishing deeper in lakes or in larger river pools.

As with your spoons, you always should try to vary your presentation with spinners. In any body of water, retrieve the spinner through various depths until you locate the trout. But how do you make repeated casts to that particular stratum once you find where the fish are feeding? Same as with spooning: "count down" to a given depth.

Make your first cast and let the spinner sink to the bottom while counting how many seconds it takes. Retrieve it from as near the bottom as you can. On subsequent casts, subtract two seconds on each new toss, working from bottom to top. Once you find the fish, simply remember how far you counted down when you got bit. This will allow you to make repeated casts to the same approximate depth.

You also can intentionally slow the sinking of most in-line spinners by adding a feathered treble hook. "Feathers" — often squirrel tails — create a lot of drag and resistance in the water. If larger spinners with bare treble hooks sink

Angler (below) is light and mobile, not loaded down with terminal tackle rig, bait bucket or box, etc. A few small spinners or spoons in your palm-sized tackle box and you can move on. (Right) Revolving blade of spinner acts to "call" fish by making vibration and noisy commotion.

too fast and you're getting hung up, add some feathers. Any tackle shop has these hairy dressings.

As with spoons, most recreational trout fishermen also make the mistake of casting the spinner out and retrieving it almost the instant it hits the water. Does this resemble a scared or wounded baitfish? For that matter, how many baitfish have you seen cruising along in a steady, straight line? Baitfish move erratically, fluttering, darting, and always franctic about hungry predators.

Try to imitate this natural action by mixing in a few "creative" movements to your spinner retrieve. For example, try the stop 'n go technique mentioned earlier. As with the spoon, pause once in awhile to let the spinner seductively fall, then start reeling again. Next, twitch the rod tip occasionally to make the spinner jump or dart about. Another possibility is to crank the lure very quickly for a few feet, then slow it down, only to speed it up again.

As for the spinner blade colors, the same holds true as with spoons: On clear days, nickel blades are your best bet; on cloudy ones or in dirty water typical of early season runoffs, switch to bronze, brass, gold, or copper blades that the trout can see more easily. Blades with fluorescent colors are sometimes effective under darker conditions, as are those with reflective prism finishes under clear skies. A black blade with some contrasting white, red, yellow, or orange spots will sometimes produce outstanding results

when traditional metallic colors aren't working. This holds true in both clear and stained water.

With regard to the spinner's primary body color, consider the natural forage baits available in the water you're fishing. For example, white or yellow patterns seem to always work on lakes where threadfin shad make up a major portion of the baitfish population. Similarly, in streams there are many small aquatic and terrestrial creatures tumbling around in the water. These include worms, newts, hellgrammites, grasshoppers, and waterbugs. Darker-pattern spinners in black, brown, frog, and crawdad-orange shades would be solid choices here.

Whether you prefer spinners or spoons for trout, learn the proper "feel" of the lure. Make a few warm-up casts with a new purchase to determine the right speed of the retrieve so the spoon wobbles correctly or the spinner blade spins properly. If the lure seems "dead" in the water, increase the speed of the retrieve to generate more action. If the lure starts to plane the surface, slow down a smidgen. Each spoon or spinner will have its own particular "speed threshold," so to speak.

Above all, be imaginative and creative when it comes to both the selection and the retrieve of these key trout lures. Always try to give the trout a little something different to look at when you use spoons or spinners, and be prepared for action!

CHAPTER 20

ACTION AWAITS ON WHITE BASS

Nomadic Schools Chase Shad And Provide Top Sport During Springtime Spawning Runs

By Larry Larsen

When it's hot and humid, bank anglers can forget about white bass — they're down deep somewhere.

Small crankbaits attract their share of white bass from mid-depths. If now spawning, don't expect a vicious hit; it's then more like a crappie. Mouths are soft, so don't hit 'em too hard.

IF TANGLING WITH 30 OR 40 fish averaging over a pound apiece causes a stirring of your angling juices, then the white bass is for you. Although many waters are pressured for their largemouth and hybrid striper fisheries, the fiesty whites are overlooked.

Whites are caught year-around, but when they concentrate in tailrace areas below dams and in tributaries of lakes during the spawn, they're much easier to locate. It can get wild and crazy when millions of white bass feel the urge between late February and late April, depending on the weather.

Moderate rainfall and warm weather are key elements in spawning movement, as increased water flows and warmer temperatures can send the females upstream. Torrential rainfall can delay the initial run, or even ruin the fishing. Swollen streams play havoc with anglers attempting to get in on the action. Late winter and spring droughts can extend the spawning run over a longer period, but the larger females may make only a token appearance.

Timing is all-important for the white bass fisherman, since peak concentrations may appear suddenly and be over in a week or two. There actually are two white bass runs "scheduled" each spring. First is when the small males make their early spring appearance at the spawning grounds. The true run happens about a month later, when egg-laden females weighing up to five pounds swim upstream to a watery rendezvous with the males. They continue to feed voraciously during this spawning run.

Tailrace below a dam can offer hot action during the spawn, or earlier when smaller males arrive. Taking 50 fish in a day is not unusual.

Largest females will tip scales at about five pounds, but they fight as if they weighed several more pounds, author says. They feed voraciously throughout spawning run. See text.

Springtime whites can put a lot of excitement in the angler's life. Folks casting from the bank just below spillways may catch 40 to 50 on a good day. For three or four weeks, it may be difficult to cast out a lure and not catch some white bass. 'Most everyone can catch a mess of these fish.

Spillway angling is also dependent on the weather. As water conditions change, fishing techniques vary below these dams, and the better white bass anglers keep up with changing patterns. Muddy runoff from heavy rains results in cool and murky spillway current. Schools of whites then may go deep, near the bottom.

Tandem crappie jigs are favorites under such conditions for both the hungry bank and boat anglers. The small leadheads should be rigged with a bullet-type slip sinker just above the tandem rig — the added weight enables the offerings to drop to the fish quickly, and provides extra casting distance that's handy for bank fishermen.

Tail-spinner lures are productive, cast easily, sink fast and provide additional flash, which is often important in murky water. Heavy, compact flutter spoons called "slabs" also can score impressive stringers of the deep fish, particularly the larger ones. White plastic grubs can be extremely effective when allowed to settle slowly behind a minimum of one-quarter ounce of weight. These lures, which closely resemble the small minnow forage that white bass chase, also will result in a bonus black bass or striper upon occasion, so be prepared for the surprise!

Trolling small jigs through open waters is one way to locate a school of white bass, and then you can set to work trying to boat every one you hook. There's not danger of overfishing the white bass.

One advantage to the murky, cool water is that white bass often will hit all day long. They seldom let the high, bright sun phase them. Their feeding binge at depths sometimes is hard to turn off!

Although bank anglers can clean up on the fish below dam spillways in the spring, boats are an even better bet for full fish boxes. It's generally easier to get at them, and there's less competition than being shore-bound.

It's impossible to fish-out a lake's white bass population; at least, that's what our fisheries people think. Their research over several years has proven that even when 20 percent of a given lake's population has been caught, the white bass fishery remains unharmed. Couple this with the fact that white bass seldom live longer than three years and

you have justificaion for very liberal bag limits existing on the prolific white bass.

SCHOOLING PRINCIPALS

Once the whites begin schooling and feeding near the surface in the later phases of the spring run, a topwater rig can be deadly. Commonly used is a topwater plug with a trailing jig some 18 inches below. This is more effective as the water clears and warms. Minnows and small white or yellow crankbaits also are effective clear-water baits.

Nice stringers of white bass have been taken from schools chasing reservoir shad on the surface during summer and fall, but springtime can be an excellent time to take the large whites in deep water. In larger impoundments, they

Large white bass like this pair are found beneath schools of smaller whites, especially when up on top busting their favorite dinner, shad. Getting your lure down to the larger fish sometimes is hard.

typically congregate in the reservoir arms leading to a flowing stream or river during spring. This occurs prior to their actual spawning activities and runs up into the tributaries.

Speed and depth control are the important factors when white bass are "schooled up" in 15 to 20 feet of water. The lure must be presented at that exact depth for any hope of action, and a too-fast speed will pull spoons and spinners up and out of this fish-catching range. Heavier spoons get right down on them; lightweight spoons are more difficult to work at the right depth. A snap swivel should be tied on in front of the spoon to prevent line twist problems.

After the pre-spawn "grouping," where small bunches join together to form huge schools, the actual spawning runs to the tributaries occur. These fish seek out rivers and streams with good current and gravel or sand bottoms. Thousands of whites will migrate into these small tributaries to drop their eggs over vegetation and bottom structure. Thus, some of the best white bass action can be had in rivers flowing into the impoundments.

Schooling whites frequent the deeper pools and quiet waters below gravel or sand bars. Casting slightly upstream of such holes and retrieving slowly should result in plenty of hits and additional tugging on the wading fisherman's

Author recommends use of net, especially if gunning for larger white bass, even if you're expert on lip-landing largemouths. The flesh of the white's mouth is soft and you will lose many without the net.

belt stringer. Speed of the retrieve is critical — experiment until a productive one is found. Most that you hook in a swift current will give you a battle you won't soon forget. Often the water is clear enough to see their movement — and them to see yours — so be careful and quiet if you're wading. They are vulnerable during the spawning period and spook easily.

White bass usually strike very softly, much as would a crappie. They simply grab the lure gently and stop it. You need to watch your rod tip for even a slight twitch. But at other times, they'll sock a lure harder than many freshwater fish. When they're spawning full swing, they'll usually hit the lure hard! Sometimes, they're so aggressive that it's hard to keep the lure out of the white bass' mouth!

I feel a small landing net is essential. Whites have fairly soft mouths and a hook pulls out easily. Regardless of your expertise in lip-landing largemouth, use the net for whites.

DEEP-WATER THOUGHTS

After spawning, white bass will go back to the depths, only occasionally appearing on the surface to bust schools of shad. If you do spot a school of whites tearing up the shad on top, motor over quickly before the action subsides. You'll have a ball!

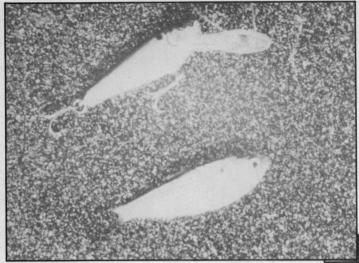

When white bass are busting shad on top, sling a Rebel Pop-R into the melee and prepare to wage war! You must be quick to capitalize on sighting.

Small shad are what roving white bass schools are seeking in the murky depths, so a deep-diving crankbait of appropriate size and color will work.

The length of time that a white bass school will feed on surface shad schools can vary from a minute to 30 or 45 minutes. The action usually is fast and furious, and the fisherman who takes his time putting fish on a stringer won't catch as many as another who's dropping his fish into a live well. If whites are on top, forget about stringing fish!

In summer and early fall, late afternoons and early mornings generally are best for feeding activity. Since the nomadic whites usually are moving, it's hard to predict exactly when they'll be feeding in your area. But if you notice them feeding in one area one day, they'll probably be back in the same area the following day — unless a severe weather condition alters their course, that is.

Like other fish, white bass school up in similar sizes, but you can increase the quality of your bag by trying two things. First, let your lure fall through the frenzy (if possible), then retrieve it along beneath the activity. You'll get the larger whites this way and, at times, some nice large-mouth bass that are hanging around.

The second thing to try is to cast to the rear or sides of the school for the occasional lunker white. These larger fish want their share, but don't want to get lost in the middle of the feeding school. If the school goes down, you'll have to go down after them with a tail-spinner bait or something heavy. Many times you can scrape a couple up off the bottom after a school has returned to the depths.

Night angling during the hot summer months can be productive, especially if you use shad minnows for bait. Either hang a couple of lanterns over the side of your boat to get the insect/minnow/fish cycle going, or fish from a lighted fishing dock if one is available on your lake. The light attracts large schools of minnows, which in turn attract the white bass.

The white bass is fun to catch, but at times he can be, well, almost impossible. The fish is constantly on the move, searching for or following his favorite meal, the

Daiwa has introduced its Samurai System of matched rods and reels for white bass and other freshwater species. Extra casting distance is welcome, as whites spook easily.

In summer, a couple of Coleman lanterns — which now burn unleaded fuel, same as car — get the insect/baitfish/white bass cycle going after dark. Prepare to clean plenty.

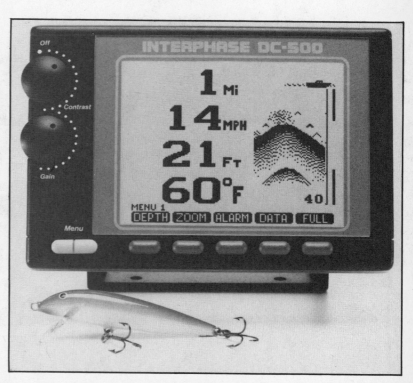

To enjoy success on schools of white bass, particularly in the summertime when fish go down deep to find cooler water, you must have fishfinder/depth finder like this Interphase DC-500 unit.

Mann's Bait Company Stretch 1-Minus models are rattling, float-at-rest baits that resemble forage fish. A good topwater tosser for feeding fish or suitable for downrigger trolling.

Trolling motors get a workout when searching for schools of nomadic white bass. They just won't stay in one place!

Eagle Ultra I.D. and Ultra I.D. Plus are mid-priced liquid cyrstal graphs that feature on-screen menus without any knobs, switches or gauges. The built-in fish alarm could reveal the presence of white bass school while under way.

shad. Whites hunt in schools and will herd the shad into a tight circle before cutting into them. This is easily spotted on top, but they are very hard to find and catch.

When you do find them, they're a great fish for breaking in new fishermen. Catching a large school of whites when they are up top busting shad will give a newcomer the fishing fever for life. Even though most of the whites you tangle with will be less than three pounds, they'll scrap like a four- or five-pounder of another species. They'll slug it out below the surface and have more endurance than most other freshwater fish.

Whites usually are on the move during winter, and it's difficult to pinpoint their location. They'll migrate up and down the reservoir in search of a traveling school of shad.

Due to these migratory habits, white bass may be found roaming over very large areas of a reservoir.

EFFECTIVE TROLLING PASSES

When whites are nomadic, trolling may be required to eliminate unproductive water and locate schools in the shortest period of time. You often can pick up white bass by trolling the riprap along the dam. They usually move along paths like river beds, submerged roadbeds and dam faces.

In the cooler months when whites are scarce, start by trolling the dam area in 15 to 30 feet of water. If no luck, move to the old river bed in open water and troll its length at similar depths, if available. Fish around and over any sub-

Hardest part about catching larger whites is getting your bait down to 'em — smaller fish up higher won't let the bait get through without hit!

Tributaries of reservoirs are good places to connect with spawning white bass. This angler has a stringer full of the tasty fish. Try them!

merged islands or humps. Troll submerged roadbeds that define a particular path. Feeder streams and rivers also are a good area to search as shad will move up and down them in their continuous search for food.

On a windy day, get out in the windswept areas — when safe to do so, of course. The wind and wave action will pile up the baitfish on shallow, wind-blown points and exposed banks. With chop decreasing light penetration, you can fish shallower for the nomadic whites shadowing the shad.

While finding whites in cool weather by trolling is effective, locating schools by using a depth finder or LCD in open water also works. Small blips near the surface indicate a school of baitfish, and a school of whites is nearby, possibly.

Blips or lines near the bottom can mean a large school of white bass, so it's a good idea to always keep your eye on the instrument as you traverse the lake. You won't usually find many white bass near shore unless it's very windy, so concentrate your efforts in deep water.

Deep-water movements are dictated by food and weather conditions. A shoreline plugger really has no chance for whites during winter months. Don't waste your time in the shallows.

But some good news: You don't need to fish early and late in winter. White bass seem to strike best in the afternoons during cool weather, but the mid-mornings also can be good. So sleep in — then go get top sport on the nomadic whites!

CHAPTER 21

TAG & RELEASE GOES HAWAIIAN

And Proves Size Isn't Everything When It Comes To Marlin Contests!

In the past years, HIBT was fondly called "Fithian's Fishing Follies" for the carnival-like atmosphere generated by Peter Fithian (fourth from right). He attracted many movie stars like Arte Johnson (left).

After loading operation that rivals a Marine Corps amphibious landing for sheer precision, the fishing gets under way with a cannon blast and radio signal broadcast to fleet of local boats chartered for the event. Teams put baits in water at harbor entrance.

Besides the reward of hugging a lovely lass selected as Miss Billfish, anglers who bring in ahi (yellow-fin tuna) also collect points. Don George of the Waikiki Yacht Club on nearby Oahu got 100 points.

By Jack Lewis

WHAT KIND of fishing tournament can you win by catching, tagging and releasing your finny quarry? What kind of contest is it when a marlin weighing only 160 pounds can win over one weighing 569½ pounds?

That contest is the Hawaiian International Billfish Tournament, held late each summer off Kona, Hawaii. And the disparities mentioned above all come under the heading of conservation.

Let's look at the 1989 competition to get an idea of just what happens in this granddaddy tournament and the whys and wherefors.

On the first day of fishing, John Henderson of the Golden Anniversary team of the International Game Fish Association caught the 569½-pound female black marlin — a rarity in Hawaii, where the Pacific blue marlin dominates the scene. That gave his team 770 points for the tournament: The fish's weight, plus 100 extra points for being the biggest fish of the day and an-added 100 points because the marlin weighed over 500 pounds. Henderson, a New Zealander, caught the fish on 80-pound test line. Had he

made his catch on 50-pound test, he would have been awarded an additional 33⅓ percent of the fish's weight in extra points.

An additional 100 points goes to the team that boasts the biggest fish of the tournament, too, and the team that boats a fish that has been tagged and released earlier gets either 200 points or the weight of the fish, whichever is greater.

Oddly, tag-and-release is what the Hawaiian International Billfish Tournament — locally known as HIBT — has come to be all about. One of the more recent rules allows 200 points for any marlin that is caught, then tagged and released. Many of these fish have sonar devices attached by the boat's skippers so that scientists of the Pacific Gamefish Research Foundation can track their habits and migration patterns.

It was the tag-and-release program that won the 1989 tournament for the team representing the American Samoa Gamefishing Association. The biggest fish of the tournament, the 569½-pounder, had been caught on the first day. On the second day, the Samoans caught a male Pacific blue that weighed only 160 pounds. It qualified, since any marlin weighing more than 100 pounds is in the running and counts for points. Because the fish was taken on 50-pound test line, added points gave the Samoans a total of 213 for the day.

In the following four days of fishing, the Samoans caught four more marlin, all of them small. Thinking in terms of tactics instead of poundage, each of these four was tagged and released, bringing an automatic award of 200 points per fish. In the end, the Samoans had amassed 1,013 points; good enough to win the tournament title!

The tag-and-release program was instituted several years back by scientists who explained how important the program could be in terms of preserving fishing in the area. During the 1989 contest, for example, 60 marlin were caught by 37 teams. Of the total take, 37 marlin were released to fight an angler another day!

In the more than three decades of its existence, the annual tournament has gone from a frank attempt to draw more tourists to Kona to a full-blown campaign to learn more about the habits of the Pacific blue and to preserve its future in the local waters.

From the beginning in 1959, Peter Fithian, chairman of the Hawaiian International Billfish Tournament Association, has ramrodded the annual tournament. That first year, there were only 24 teams entered — and most of them were from local fishing clubs. In 1988, teams totalled 76, coming from 23 countries. There could be many more, except that the event has become an invitational contest necessitated by logistics. When the tournament started, there were only half a dozen charter boats in Kona waters; today there are more than 150, but not all of them take part in the tournament. Some have to be left for casual fishing tourists.

The Kona pier is not large, and the daily boarding of the boats is conducted with the precision of a military operation. With only five boarding areas, all of the teams can be boarded and on their way to the fishing grounds in less than 20 minutes. There are rules for this procedure as there are for almost any contingency that may come up, ranging from mooring and maneuvering to delivery of the catch at the end of a day.

Dating back to the early days — before it became what might be termed an international institution — the tournament involved a good deal of showmanship. The annual parade, held the day before actual fishing gets under way, is a local event that draws tourists as well as locals from all of the islands. In the early days, it served to attract press attention to the tournament, but today it introduces the teams to the public. Each team is carried on a float of some sort, waving to the crowd and sporting their national colors. The parade has become an institution in its own right, local residents contend.

There used to be teams from Hollywood, such stars as the late Lee Marvin, Jonathan Winters, Arte Johnson, William Conrad and a host of others taking part. The late Richard Boone, then a resident of Hawaii, had his own boat and even sponsored a trophy to the best charter boat skipper picked each year.

They tell tales of how Boone, recently arrived from Hollywood to take up residence, expressed an interest in getting involved in the tournament. Peter Fithian, who plays by the rules he helped create, explained to the film

Jim Carven caught this 539½-pound Pacific blue in the sapphire waters just off Kailua-Kona, and poses with fish that will be dissected by scientists of Pacific Gamefish Research Foundation. They hope to preserve the species.

star that everyone started at the bottom among the volunteers. For a couple of years, Boone could be seen on the pier early in the dawn hours, helping to fuel charter boats prior to on-loading fishermen.

While the whole series of tournaments may have started with an idea by Peter Fithian, hundreds of volunteers are involved each year and a number of sponsors are involved. Continental Airlines and Hawaiian Airlines, for example, fly in press representatives, as well as contestants; Crazy Shirts, a Kona concern, furnishes appropriately marked T-shirts for teams, volunteers and press groups; the County of Hawaii donates funds to help publicize the event and support the press contingent; Azabu, an Island hotel, which serves as tournament headquarters, virtually turns over its facilities to the fishing visitors. Even a taxidermist from far-off Florida, J.T. Reese, is a sponsor of the annual event.

In the 30-plus-year history of the tournament, there have been only three repeat winners: In 1967 and again in 1968, the tournament was won by Florida's West Palm

Australian Peter Goadby inspects hook and leader from tournament catch for conformance with rules. He's seen — and decried — the demise of several gamefish species, wants to aviod that with marlin.

Contemplative trio of the late Lee Marvin, Jonathan Winters and the late Richard Boone share an aside during long-ago HIBT. Boone started at the bottom of the ladder when he volunteered to help with HIBT, and Marvin was addicted marlin fisherman.

Beach Fishing Club. Such a double-up didn't happen again until 1977/8, when the Las Vegas Sport Fishing Club took the title in successive years.

The last such double entry was the Laguna Niguel Billfish Club of California. The team won the title in 1985, then in 1986, Gil Kraemer caught the first — an only — "grander" taken in all those years. His catch tipped the official HIBT scales at 1062½ pounds. The mounted marlin now occupies a wall in the lobby of the King Kamehameha Hotel to let visitors know that such world record fish do exist in local waters.

There may be some sort of jinx attached to such successes, however. In the years since this giant was landed by Kraemer, no member of his team has taken another marlin of any size during the tournament! Similar histories seem to have been the case with the other double winners.

Participation in the HIBT is not cheap. Transportation, entry fees, charter boat rental, room and board and incidentals can run several thousand dollars per contestant. For such an expenditure, you might expect a giant gold-plated trophy, but that's not the case.

The winners in the various categories of the annual event are awarded wooden trophies carved from native Hawaiian koa wood; attractive, but not overly expensive.

Funds derived from the annual tournament are funneled to the Pacific Gamefish Research Foundation, which maintains laboratories and a staff on the Kona waterfront.

Australian Peter Goadby, a recognized authority on billfish and the senior judge of the Hawaiian International Billfish Tournament, has expressed the reasons for the foundation.

"In our lifetime, we all have experience of what has been the sad and frightening story of the Atlantic bluefin, the Pacific bluefin and the Indian Ocean Southern bluefin. These all are living cases of what happens with our over exploitation, poor data and mistaken interpretation that fish stocks can cope, of competition between countries, of political decisions, of stock in trouble and the trouble not recognized.

"The history of the brief span of the Atlantic broadbill

recreational fishery is even shorter in its establishment, decline and demise. Most of us in our billfish fisheries have seen the decline in strike rate, in day-to-day action on boats — or tag-and-release — despite improved knowledge, equipment on boats, tackle and technique.

"The future dictates further improvement in all these factors for the recreational fishing industry to survive, an industry shown in many areas and recognized by some governments to be worth more recreationally — in tourist dollars, as in the case of Kona — than commercially."

All of this has led to some interesting thoughts on bait recommendations by Kona's professional charter boat skippers. While they can hardly refuse to support a client who wants to use live bait, the majority of these skippers now equip their boats with artificial baits, if they are supplying the tackle.

Phil Parker is a retired charter boat skipper and a long-time tournament volunteer. While he doesn't advocate one type of bait over the other publicly, he obviously has some feelings on the matter.

"If live bait is used, it has to be rigged so that it can swim about and draw in a marlin. Once the marlin takes the live fish, it holds it cross-ways in its bill until it is certain the smaller fish is dead. Then it turns it 90 degrees and gulps it down.

"Once the bait has been gulped, the angler must set the hook. The hook invariably is set in the fish's stomach lining and this creates pain. It also brings on some violent action by the fish in most cases."

"If the fish thus hooked breaks the line to escape, it may well die later on as a result of infection in the stomach; a waste.

"With an artificial bait, makers design them so that they are tapered. The marlin will take it in its mouth and start to squeeze it, suddenly realizing that it is not real. As the device starts to slide out of the marlin's mouth because of the tapered design, the fisherman must set his hook. But the hook must necessarily be planted in the small but soft part of the fish's mouth, just behind the extended bill.

"This also can cause a good deal of action on the part of the fish, but should the line be broken in the battle to bring it to gaff, the fish will simply swim away, perhaps to be caught another day."

The biggest fish of the 1989 tournament was found to be carrying a broken line and a hook from an earlier unsuccessful hook-up.

The largest fish ever taken in the tournament — the grander landed by Gil Kraemer — was caught on an artificial lure called the Doornob that was created by one of his team members.

The rules for the HIBT cover several pages of small type, but those covering the tag-and-release facet and the resultant 200 points are explicit. For instance, "An angler who elects to tag and release a billfish must so declare that intention to the boat captain prior to the time the swivel touches the rod tip or the leader is taken in hand."

In addition, "The swivel must touch the rod tip or the leader taken in hand and the fish tagged and released. The hook or hooks must be disengaged from the fish or the leader cut and retained for the judges after a fish is tagged.

"All dead fish or any deemed by the crew to be dead or injured sufficiently to cause death must be boated and brought to the pier and treated as a weighed fish."

The sharks, incidentally, have a say in who the winners may be. Any fish that is damaged — partially eaten, to be precise — by a shark is disqualified from being counted for competitive points.

Each day, all boats leave a starting line at the sound of an

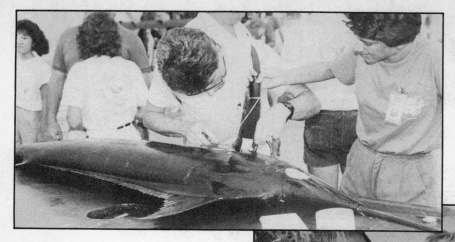

Pacific Gamefish Research Foundation scientists remove skin covering fins, seeking answers to mystery of marlin "lighting up" phenomenon in which the fish changes color in attack bait.

Parade has become something of a Kona institution in its own right, and it is how contestants are introduced to public and visiting press. Rising Sun team of Japanese anglers had to qualify for HIBT, then be invited.

on-shore cannon. All fish must be hooked by the closing signal each day, which is announced to all boats by radio. If a marlin is hooked-up at closing time, the angler is allowed to continue to play the fish until boated. Only fish caught on rod and reel, trolling or drift fishing, qualify for points. Handlines are permitted only for catching baitfish and live bait may not be passed between boats, competing or otherwise. Outriggers, downriggers, kites and birds are permitted, provided the actual fishing line is attached to the snap or other release device, either directly or with some other material. The leader or double line may not be connected to the release mechanism either directly or with the use of a connecting device.

There are stiff rules as to the type of hook arrangements that will be allowed, as well as type and length of leaders. Each of the contestants is briefed thoroughly on what will and will not be allowed and an infraction is viewed sternly. In fact, the rules state that "any person, including charter boat captains, guilty of an infraction of the rules may be disqualified from participation in future Hawaiian International Billfish Association tournaments."

In the early days of the tournament, it was known by some as Fithian's Fishing Follies because of the carnival-like atmosphere that prevailed: the annual parade, the participation of movie stars who didn't know all that much about fishing and other means of gaining notoriety for a tiny, off-the-track fishing village.

Today, Kona is a thriving city that is growing by leaps and bounds as people discover its constant sunshine, calm swimming beaches and fishing opportunities. And, like the city, the annual fishing tournament has grown in stature and purpose. Its support of the Pacific Gamefish Research Foundation is proof that these fishermen and the tournament's sponsors want the marlin to continue to be an attraction.

But it is not without its problems. With the growing community of homes, new businesses and throngs of tourists, traffic is one of them.

Most of the streets still are narrow; there are no freeways on the island and, while this helps to maintain the small-town atmosphere, it can lead to frustrations.

As Hal Wood, longtime volunteer reported, one native of Kona looked sadly at all the tall hotel buildings, at the smothering traffic that crawled along Alii Drive — the city's main thoroughfare — and shook his head.

"Look da traffic," he said. "All da fault of Peter Fithian. If he hadn't stahted da kine billfish tourney, we'd bin still da same like 50 years ago."

When told of the comment, Peter Fithian nodded his head, perhaps a bit sad in his own right. Unlike his critic, he realizes there's probably no real solution for the elusive and sometimes unwanted entity called progress.

CHAPTER 22

WEBSTER'S WAYS FOR WALLEYE

Photos by Anne & Robin Wood

Learn How To Score, When To Fish, What Tackle To Use, Baits And More!

By Bill Wood

Author hoists hefty stringer of Canadian walleye taken along southwest shore of Queen Island at Lake of the Woods. Fish averaged from one to a hefty four pounds.

Resort owner Bill Webster favors 18-foot Alumarine boats fitted with 20hp Mercury outboards controlled from stern, as author demonstrates near one of many islands dotting Lake of the Woods (left). Back-trolling is super method.

Few meals equal a shore lunch of panfried walleye fillets dipped in milk and instant mashed potatoes. Great grub!

ANNE'S ROD bent suddenly and she hollered, "Stop the boat! I'm hung up again! It feels like a log." She started reeling in line as I eased the 20hp Mercury into forward.

"Stop! It's a fish...it's a fish! I've got a walleye! It's a big walleye!" she screamed as she held tension on the light graphite spinning outfit. After a few minutes of giving and taking line, the 27-inch Lake of the Woods walleye was thrashing alongside the boat. After missing twice, I got the net under her prize just as it threw the #4 Mepps Aglia spinner.

I was somewhat chagrined. I had just spent four days patiently hunting walleye by the book. Tackle selection, bait, underwater structure, water temperature and feeding times all were carefully considered. My tactics produced a lot of small walleye, several yellow perch and a few small-mouth bass. Every day I spent hours out flailing the water. Then my wife, Anne, jumped in the boat for her first evening troll around the island and wham! She landed the biggest fish of the trip — thirty yards in front of our cabin, no less!

Our June walleye expedition started on a cool, clear Saturday morning in Kenora, Ontario, Canada. A light breeze was blowing across Lake of the Woods from the west. The weather forecast was for more of the same all week. The solunar tables forecast a peak fishing week.

While Anne and our daughter, Robin, slept in our room at Inn of the Woods, I wandered outside and stared at the lake. Cloud-like schools of baitfish drifted around moss-covered boulders. Slender ribbon leeches undulated lazily five or six feet below the surface. Boatloads of fishermen roared across the lake en route to some secret honey hole.

We were to be picked up at noon at Devil's Gap Marina by fishing resort owner and guide, Bill Webster. It was our second visit to Webster's Northcliff Island Resort. I was anxious to get out on the water and apply a winter's worth of walleye study.

As I paced the hotel dock, it dawned on me that I could be fishing instead of wishing. So I unpacked an ultralight outfit, tied on a Mepps spinner and began casting around the dock. In about 45 minutes I caught and released a half-dozen juvenile Northern pike. The time passed quickly. I

A yellow Rapala Shad Rap proved irresistible to this junior-sized walleye during one of author's casting sessions to break monotony of back-trolling. When one angler got bit, others switched to productive bait and took fish.

hardly noticed the clusters of men and women preparing boats, tackle and coolers for a day on the lake.

One friendly gent, Mark Dugan, came over and commented that I had stumbled onto one of Kenora's little secrets. Inn of the Woods is a round, six-storey tower that stands in the lake on concrete stilts. The dock is a shady haven for Northern pike that spawn under the hotel and live in the adjacent bay. Dugan, executive director of Ontario Sunset Country tourism agency, said that walleye, smallmouth bass and pike are taken regularly from the dock.

Catching a few Northern pike was a great way to start a fishing trip. However, our goal was finding and catching walleye. I asked Dugan about the walleye fishing. He was enthusiastic over good reports that had come in during the past few days. "We had a long, cold winter and the ice has been off the lake for only about a month," Dugan said. "Fishing will be dynamite."

Like most area residents, Dugan referred to walleye as pickerel. Pickerel and walleyed pike are common local names for walleye in some parts of the U.S. and Canada.

Walleye actually are members of the perch family. The

Call 'em pickerel, walleyed pike or just plain walleye, you've got to match your arrival time with proper water temperature and stage of spawning cycle for best results. Author boned-up all winter in anticipation of this trip.

name association with pike probably is because they inhabit many of the same areas.

I got more good news from a couple of local fishermen and one of the employees at the Kenora Canadian Tire Marina: Many anglers had brought in good catches during the past couple of days. The weather had cleared and the water temperature was in the 55- to 65-degree range. The walleye had apparently recovered from spawning and were starting to cluster in their traditional feeding areas.

The clerk in the marina tackle shop asked where we planned to fish and recommended a chart to use during the trip. The large-scale chart published by the Canadian Hydrographic Service provided detailed navigation and underwater contour data.

As with other species of fish, walleye habits are linked closely to changes in water temperature. They congregate near spawning grounds when the ice melts and water temperatures climb to the low 40s. Fishing can be extremely good during this period — if you are able to locate warm gravel and sandy shallows where they breed.

Spawning begins when the water temperature reaches 45 to 50 degrees Fahrenheit. Following the spawn, the males

On keepers the author figured to enjoy at mealtime, he inserted stringer through the fish's bottom lip. This keeps them healthy during a long trip, and makes it possible to release smaller fish you replace on the stringer.

may remain around the spawning area for a few days. Females move to deeper water to recuperate. Fishing normally is poor during both the spawn and post-spawn periods.

Most successful fishing trips are a mixture of educated guessing and luck. This time we had hoped to narrow the odds by learning everything we could about walleye habits and fishing patterns at Lake of the Woods. To hopefully stack the odds in our favor, we included solunar tables in the plan. Our goal was to hit Lake of the Woods during the peak spring period following the post-spawn doldrums.

According to experts, we needed to plan our trip for a week when water temperatures would be in the 55- to 70-degree range. Making that kind of prediction for northwest Ontario is a challenge. Not gifted with clairvoyance, we decided to try another approach: We found a week in mid-June when the solunar tables predicted peak fishing. Everyone checked their work and school schedules. We had a match! The next step was contacting our friend and walleye mentor, Bill Webster. Luck provided an available cabin and good weather.

Bill Webster owns and operates Northcliff Island Resort,

Filleting lessons are part of the service offered by Northcliff Island Resort owner, Bill Webster.

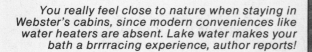

You really feel close to nature when staying in Webster's cabins, since modern conveniences like water heaters are absent. Lake water makes your bath a brrrracing experience, author reports!

located about 15 miles southwest of Kenora. Northcliff is one of 10,000 islands which dot Lake of the Woods. The 1,697-square-mile mesotrophic lake straddles the border between Ontario and Minnesota. The island appears on the lake chart as an unnamed triangle about one mile north of Crescent Island.

Northcliff is a dream under construction. Bill bought the 15-acre island while serving as a pilot in the Canadian armed forces. Since his retirement from the military, he has designed and built three extremely comfortable, two-bedroom log cabins which offer simple amenities. Warmth,

dryness, firm beds and propane-fueled stove and refrigerator are the only concessions to civilization.

The beauty of the resort is that everything fits together and complements the natural setting of the island and lake. Gaudy cabins and electricity would destroy the wilderness feeling you get listening to the love calls of courting loons and watching bald eagles glide from their perches in tall pines. Pure, cool water is taken straight from the lake with only a little straining to remove suspended pollen. Bathing is a cold and exhilarating adventure.

We had ideal conditions for this walleye trip. The pre-

Note the lightweight gear favored by Bill Webster: 6- to 8-pound-test line, lightweight spinning tackle and #4 Mepps Aglia spinner provide top sport and catch more fish. True, you snag more often, but that's life!

vious spring we hadn't caught many fish. Hopefully, we learned some of the things we should and shouldn't do. Bill cautioned us that he would not accept excuses this time. He also reminded us that heavy tackle is not needed to catch walleye.

Tackle is critically important when trying to outwit walleye. We are saltwater and Southern reservoir anglers, accustomed to using stout tackle. Medium and heavy tackle is fine for aggressive fish, but walleye are subtle. Largemouth bass are timid in the winter and spring when water temperatures are below 60 degrees. However, compared to walleye, winter bass are ferocious.

Fishing equipment suitable for line above 10-pound-test is out. Tackle shops in walleye country recommend light or medium spinning outfits. Four to 10-pound-test line is sufficient for most types of walleye fishing. Looking around the docks in Kenora, I found a mixture of spinning and spincasting anglers. A few people were using ultralight equipment. Very few local fishermen use the high-tech baitcasting outfits that are popular with the American bassin' crowd.

Anne used her small Cardinal 753 spinning reel loaded with 8-pound-test Bagley Silver Thread on a light-action Berkeley Stinger 5½-foot graphite rod. Robin preferred her Zebco 20/10 spincasting reel and 4½-foot Shakespeare rod. My choice was a Shimano 10 ultralight spinning reel with 6-pound-test Silver Thread on a 5½-foot Berkeley Lightning Rod, a birthday present from my two favorite fishing buddies. We caught walleye on all three outfits.

Light equipment and line enable you to use a wide range of baits. Most importantly, they are essential for feeling a walleye's extremely light bite. It is so light and tentative that I can't even describe it as a hit or strike. It feels more like a cautious slurp than a bite. Imagine tasting a spoon of hot soup broth and you'll get the picture.

Like other types of fishing, selecting artificial baits for walleye can be an expensive and frustrating experience. Bill Webster is the original north country miser and provides first-rate advice for his guests. His annual Northcliff Island Information Sheet cautions newcomers not to buy tons of lures.

Bill fishes almost exclusively with artificial lures and believes firmly in #3 and #4 Mepps type spinners. His favorite is a brass Mepps #3 Aglia. During one of our many fishing and coaching trips, he told me that if he had to

An occasional smallmouth or small Northern pike will come over the side on casting venture, but Bill Webster keeps only enough to eat. He manages to fish frequently, when he's not adding to his construction project!

pick one lure for a survival kit, it would be a #3 Aglia.

I am as addicted to trying new lures as catching fish. Like many anglers, I spend a lot of time agonizing over new tackle. Books, magazines and tackle catalogs are stacked all over the house. Each one contains some pearl of fishing wisdom and enticement to buy some new color and shape of lure. Lures hanging in the jaws of fish on TV shows become essential for the tackle box. Each fishing trip means several visits to tackle shops. The search for the perfect bait continues to the marina. Every local favorite has to be checked out.

Preparing for this trip was no exception. I read several recent articles about deep-running crankbaits, jigging spoons, leadhead jigs and the traditional live-bait rigs. So the tackle boxes were stocked with several sizes and colors of each. We had baits for morning, mid-day, afternoon, evening and night.

Bill's fishing style is simple and effective. He has a favorite rod and Mitchell 300 spinning reel loaded with 6- or 8-pound-test line. He carries an assortment of spinners in a weathered plastic, pocket-size tackle box. Solunar tables showing the best days and times to fish according to moon and tide data don't mean much to him. He fishes in the late evening after finishing his chores. His favorite tactic is slowly back-trolling spinners along the 15- to 30-foot dropoffs that surround nearby islands. He picks fishing locations by weather conditions and information contained on his hydrographic charts. He has fished with customers using various electronic fish finders but doesn't own one. Bill just back-trolls spinners and catches walleye.

Back-trolling is the most popular method for hunting walleye at Lake of the Woods. It is extremely productive and allows you to socialize while you cover a lot of water. Most of the boats are controlled from the stern and the driver is in a better position to steer the craft slowly backward along shorelines and around underwater obstacles. Back-trolling also causes the lines to run forward along the bow and prevents accidental tangling in the propeller.

The most common boat and motor combinations are 16- to 18-foot aluminum V-hulls with 20 to 40hp motors. Bill Webster maintains a fleet of 16½-foot Alumarine boats with 20hp outboards. Other camps at the lake use similar craft. The boats are excellent for all types of fishing. They also are extremely seaworthy and can get you back to camp safely when the wind kicks the lake into a frenzy.

Following local custom, we spent most of our time back-

If you get tired of back-trolling, you can disembark on any island and cast a spell, as author does here.

A 16- to 18-foot boat is spacious enough for three anglers. Anytime you're on the water, though, you must keep an eye on changeable weather.

trolling. It is a bit tricky at first for the driver. You have to watch all of the lines, steer and control the throttle simultaneously. Most of the walleye are on or near the bottom. This means trolling deep and snagging a lot of rocks. The skipper stays busy controlling the boat while fish are landed or lures are freed from snags. A snag and fish on at the same time with a stiff breeze blowing the boat around can cause a scene reminiscent of the Keystone Cops.

When we back-trolled, each of us would use a different type of bait. When a fish hit, we would all switch to the successful bait until it proved unproductive. During one of these trial-and-error periods, I snapped on a No. 8 yellow Rapala Shad Rap that got good reviews in one of the magazines. We were on the southwest side of Queen Island working a weedy ledge that varied in depth from 10 to 15 feet. It was about 6:30 p.m., two days after the full moon, prime fishing time according to the solunar tables.

Within 10 minutes, two healthy keepers were on the stringer. Anne switched to a matching Shad Rap. In an hour we landed about two dozen walleye, several smallmouth bass and a couple of yellow perch. Nine walleye,

weighing from one to four pounds, went on the stringer for a late evening fish fry celebration. Few fish can compare to walleye fillets dipped in milk, instant mashed potatoes and slowly panfried.

If you are accustomed to casting or jigging, trolling can become boring. Another method for catching walleye is to troll until you locate a group of fish, then drift back over the area and work it by casting and jigging. We tried this several times in protected coves at Queen and Crescent Islands, and found that it really works. It also provides a pleasant change of pace. After an hour or so of back-trolling, we found it relaxing to let the boat drift and either cast or jig. This also enabled us to try a variety of other lures.

As with other types of fishing, walleye are sensitive to presentation and prefer certain colors. During this trip, fluorescent yellow, green and chartreuse were the most effective, regardless of time of day or location. Plain brass, silver and red and white produced fish, but not as consistently.

The real key to outwitting the fish seemed to be presen-

Anne Wood lets a 27-inch walleye test the drag on her lightweight spinning reel. She caught the largest fish of the vacation close to the dock on her first outing.

Ultralight tackle made catching small and medium-sized walleye a real thrill. Weather was comfortable enough to permit shorts and tee shirts during mid-day sessions.

tation. Slow, methodical back-trolling, smooth rhythmical jigging and moderately slow, straight-line retrieves on deep-diving crankbaits were the most effective. The slow speed and consistent rhythm made it much easier to feel a fish's light, curious tap.

We caught several fish by working leadhead jigs tipped with either live leeches or plastic grubs along underwater points and dropoffs marked on the charts. Like most game-fish, walleye feed near particular types of structure. The charts of Lake of the Woods are extremely accurate. Water levels vary with the season, but a check with the marina will help you adjust depth data. Points, ledges, dropoffs and saddles between underwater rock formations are clearly marked and reliable. Weed beds are easily located by trolling, jigging or casting crankbaits.

Electronic depth finders might speed up the search for fish, but we managed well without them. Another group staying at the island used a portable LCD device. Their total catch was about the same as ours using the Bill Webster system.

Whenever I see pictures of a good catch, my first ques-

tion is: "Where did you fish?" My second question is, "How did you catch them?" We learned that to catch walleye on a productive lake the first step is timing your fishing with peak feeding periods. Second, concentrate your efforts on areas with underwater structure that attracts baitfish. Third, vary your live or artificial bait selection until you find the right combination. Finally, use light tackle and fish slowly, patiently concentrating on the feel of the line.

Our adventure in Canada's Lake of the Woods wilderness area ended much too soon. We accomplished our goal and were going home with the authorized limit of frozen walleye. It was a fantastic learning experience. We would miss the feisty beavers toiling on their lodges. Mornings would not be the same without sharing experiences with Bill Webster over cups of freshly brewed coffee. Most of all, we would miss the pair of common loons that allowed us to visit their nest and see a single glistening brown egg in a secluded cove we named Nursery Bay. Maybe next year the new loon will welcome us back!

CHAPTER 23

CATFISHING THE COLORADO

Or, When In Moab, Do As The Moabians Do
— Or Don't — And You'll Take Some Good Grub!

By Russ Thurman

Author slings unripened beef liver and stinkbait rig toward middle of scenic Colorado River.

It took quite a while for "educated" catfish to learn what it was supposed to do, as determined by numerous "expert" sources author encountered in Moab (left). Even then, it was only after "modifying" this advice that author Thurman scored on Utah cats. (Above) Dipping fingers into gooey, odiferous Mr. Catfish commercial stinkbait built character!

RED CANYON WALLS towered on both sides of the Colorado River as I made another cast. Catfishing the Colorado is, well, tough work. There's *so* much to put up with — a quiet, gentle-moving river, a soft westerly breeze and magnificent scenery. With such distractions, it's almost tough to concentrate on hauling in catfish!

It was early July and I was fishing just outside of Moab, Utah, in the heart of Canyonlands National Park. It's there that nature's stone monuments, carved by erosion during centuries, guide the Colorado River south toward Arizona. I was catfishing because I wanted to fish the fabulous river, and with rare exceptions fishing the Colorado near Moab means fishing for whiskerfish.

Now, this whiskery stinger isn't exactly on the top of my "must-catch" list. I've never been overwhelmed with desire for a trophy cat mount. But I wanted to fish the Colorado, so when in Moab, do as the Moabians do!

First I needed some expert advice on how to catch this often-maligned — but great eating — gamefish.

"Ain't nothin' to it. Get a hook, stick on some stinky meat, throw it in, wait awhile and haul in the catfish," opined Mr. Expert, leaning against the fishing tackle section of a Moab hardware store. "Here, let me show ya." He dug into a battered wallet for a photograph of himself and another angler holding a batch of catfish. "That's me

'n Harry. Nighttime's the best for catching catfish. Get a couple of lawn chairs and some smelly bait and you can't keep 'em off the bank."

"It doesn't sound very challenging," I offered.

"Who cares?" he asked, hunching his shoulders and opening his arms wide.

I finished selecting my tackle and headed for the check-out counter, pausing only briefly as I passed the section where lawn chairs were on display.

"If you're talking *serious* catfishing, you're going to need a boat with some electronics. You can't just go throw a line in the river."

Expert Number Two poured forth his wisdom in serious tones as a waitress poured another cup of coffee as I clumped my elbows on the lunch counter of a local cafe.

"What about laser-guided fish hooks?" I asked, hoping to lighten the discussion. He ignored the comment.

"Catfishing is a serious sport," he said. "Of course, once you locate them, catching them is no great feat. They'll bite on 'most anything.

"But first you gotta find them and that's not easy. Yep, you'll need a boat."

All I wanted to do was fish the Colorado River. Maybe I'll just spend the day whitewater rafting.

There probably are thousands of ways to catch the many species and subspecies of North American catfish. They

Star of the show, and talk of the town, was three-pound Channel cat author displays. While quantity of fish may have been lower than locals' nighttime catches, size was larger. Record is 55 pounds for species.

Chunk of beef liver appears below rod tip as angler retrieves line. Setting was peaceful and magnificent.

are found in rivers, lakes, reservoirs and even the ocean. Would you believe walking catfish? Yep — in Africa and Southern Asia. They can live on land for extended periods.

North American catfish can grow to remarkable sizes, with the blue catfish topping the scales up to 150 pounds. The blue catfish prefers deep water and feeds off the bottom of rivers. Flathead catfish, probably the tastiest cat in North American waters, averages five pounds but can reach 100. The Channel catfish, our Colorado River species, usually is found in deep, cool water. It weighs in at two to four pounds, with the largest tipping the scales at 55 pounds. The small Stonecat (about a pound) likes swift-flowing

rivers with rocky bottoms, and the Sea cat, up to five pounds, can be found in both salt and fresh water.

While my experts had differing advice on how to catch catfish, they all agreed on one thing: Catfish are good eating. Whether panfried, deepfried, broiled, barbecued, smoke cooked or cooked over an open flame on a stick, catfish is rated as one of the most delicious gamefish. What it lacks in prestige and respect it more than makes up for at the dinner table. And I wanted to find out firsthand!

Catfish, regardless of the species, generally like rivers where there's a slow-moving current. Deep pools are favorite hideouts, although cats often move to shallow water to

Is there any doubt that 10-year-old Tim Showder is hooked on fishing, thanks to a 10-inch Channel cat.

Many youngsters get their first exposure to delights of fishing when a chunky catfish inhales a baited hook.

feed. Bottoms with large rocks, firm sand, small stones or logs all are ideal habitat for catfish.

Along the Colorado River there are countless rocky overhangs, many at the bottom and to the side of whitewater rapids. These are excellent feeding grounds for whiskers. The pools beneath stony overhangs are deep and provide — especially those on the south side of the river — cooler water, while eddies created by the whitewater push plenty of food into the pools. Most of these pools can be fished only from a boat, since the shoreline is well-guarded with rock formations. Brush-crowded shorelines also protect some excellent fishing spots although, in some of these areas, hardy fishermen have cut trails to the river.

The "stinky meat" my first expert had advised as bait was right on. Catfish use their whiskers (barbels) to find food and they aren't picky. While their eyesight is less than 20/20, their sense of smell is acute.

My experts provided this list of catfish baits: insects; worms; chicken; lamb; liver from rabbits, chickens, and beef; gizzards; congealed blood; hot dogs (cooked or raw); fish eggs; cheese and even bar soap ("Yeah, just cut off a chunk and hook it on.") In Utah, it is unlawful to fish with corn, hominy, any live fish or parts of fish.

The first word in "stinky meat" is important. The worse

Trotlining is illegal in Utah, with anglers limited to two hooks on a single line. Author wanted his two baits up off the bottom, and thus attached sinker at end of line.

Uncle Josh's Mr. Catfish cheese bait is designed to appeal to cat's excellent sense of smell — and almost ruined the author's in the process of baiting up! Man, that's ripe!

it smells, the better. Most serious catfishermen will leave their bait jars of liver, cheese, or meats in the sun for a few days "to ripen." If you can't bear the idea of opening your customized ripe bait, there are a number of manufactured stinkbaits. I bought Uncle Josh's Mister Catfish Cheese bait. I also bought a tub of frozen beef liver; however, I opted not to ripen my liver, so to speak.

So, armed with my stinkbaits and borrowed tackle from my Pa, I headed for the river at 7 p.m. to do some night angling for Colorado catfish. My brother, Robert, once lived in Moab and still visits there often, so I respected his opinion as to where to catch catfish.

We had travelled less than two miles up the river, parked the car in a clearing, and casually hiked to a spot on the river with thick brush to our backs and the river and its breathtaking monuments to the front. At last I was going to fish the Colorado!

There still was plenty of daylight to prepare my cat-catching rig. At the end of my 10-pound mono I tied a size 7 common snap swivel. I use a Palomar knot on all my hook-

ups, this after trying most other knots, with lost fish as my reward. The Palomar, while not fancy, works. I attached a half-ounce bell sinker to the snap swivel. (Although most of the advice I'd gotten called for weight to be above the hooks so the bait would settle on the bottom, I wanted the bait to be suspended just above the bottom.)

Holding the sinker in my fingers, I measured off two feet of line and attached another snap swivel. I rigged a size 6 soft bait treble hook to 12 inches of extra 10-pound line, tied a loop at the other end and hooked it to the snap swivel. The treble hook would hold my Uncle Josh's Mister Catfish.

I measured off another two feet and attached another snap swivel, and then a size 4 snelled hook — just right for the beef liver. In Utah, only two hooks may be used when fishing the Colorado and trotlining or set-line fishing are not permitted on the river.

Baiting-up was an experience. The liver was easy to cut and hook, but Mister Catfish was an eye opener — or, rather, a sinus opener! Uncle Josh has indeed produced a

Many successful catfishermen prefer to "enhance aromatic appeal" of their stinkbaits by leaving them to begin decomposing in container left in warm sun. Author didn't.

A tantalizing chunk of fresh beef liver is trimmed on piece of driftwood prior to attachment to bait-holder hook in methods described in text. He favors Palomar knot.

stinkbait — no false advertising here! I apprehensively dug my fingers into the dough-like concoction and rolled it into a ball around the treble hook.

Before I could cast, I had to get the remaining sticky goo off my fingers. Here's where a larger towel than the one I carry is vital. My small towel soon became saturated with leftover Mister Catfish; sand then became my washcloth.

I finally was ready to fish the Colorado. Even with the close brush I still managed a 150-foot cast, not quite in the middle of the river, but far enough. I had cast slightly up-river and the current pulled the sinker downriver until it settled at an angle just below our location.

I propped the rod on a forked stick and settled back to chat with my brother. Heck, that's what Mr. Expert Number One and Harry had done and look at all the catfish they'd caught! All the same, I kept an eye on my rod tip, which was dipping slowly in rhythm with the current. I'd decided to try several of Mr. Expert's suggestions — just let the bait sit, the catfish will swallow it and "then just haul 'em in." My rod tip jumped several times, but I waited. The rod jerked again, but I left it on the forked stick. I wasn't used to this type of fishing. I was more wired for trout and bass where a hit meant set the hook, but I was testing advice.

After a time, I reeled in my rig and all the bait was gone. Time to face Mister Catfish again. Same cast, same spot, same technique, same empty hooks. Round three with Mister Catfish. Same results.

Round four. This time I stood, deciding I needed to bring more "fishing" into this fishing of the Colorado River. Shortly after the sinker settled, I got a tap, and I did my "turn them inside out" hook-setting jerk, reeled the line tight, and waited. Another tap, much stronger this time and I tried to sling the fish into New Mexico. I reeled the line tight and waited. Nothing. I then reeled in two empty hooks.

It was becoming painfully clear to me that these catfish had not read the chapter on how they were supposed to swim up to my bait, grab a mouthful of hook and then wait to be hauled in.

Rod is bent almost as much as stickups protruding from shoreline as author battles his first catfish. Fish sought to escape by severing line in rocky structure.

Author now has credentials of "Mr. Expert" and can freely dispense wisdom from counterstools of cafe. Inexplicably, fish grows larger with each retelling.

Round five. I was now into my full-fledged, serious fishing stance. I'd even pulled a length of line away from the rod, holding it in my left hand so I could feel the slightest hit. I waited. It was dark now. The sun's golden spotlight had danced across the red rock formations in a breathtaking display. Down the river, heading our way, I could hear the guide on the tourist boat describing the river's magic at night. I waited. Tap! I jerked. This time the line moved downriver. I reeled in a brawling foot-long catfish. It had been worth rounds one through five. The treble hook was embedded in his upper mouth. This was it for the night.

Two days later I returned to the same spot at 5:30 in the morning. I'd learned catfish are a lot tougher to catch than I'd been told, and Mister Catfish builds character. I used

the same rig — the top hook was baited with beef liver, still fresh, the lower hook balled with Mister Catfish.

For three hours I fished as if it was the highest-paid fishing tournament in history. The results: one cat that went 12 inches. Even with all my concentration on fishing, I still was able to enjoy the beauty of the river, the cliffs slowly being lit by the dawn and the pure, unpolluted quiet. At 8:30 a.m., I started getting my gear together to leave. Most of the river was reflecting full sunshine and Mr. Experts had said you catfish at night.

So I baited-up for that last cast. Same spot, same pattern. Tap, jerk, reel, wait. Tap, jerk, reel, but this time I lost line to the drag. I caught sight of my line where it entered the shimmering water. It was moving toward the bank

You can opt for store-bought baits like these shown at right, or do your own thing. Catfish will even eat soap!

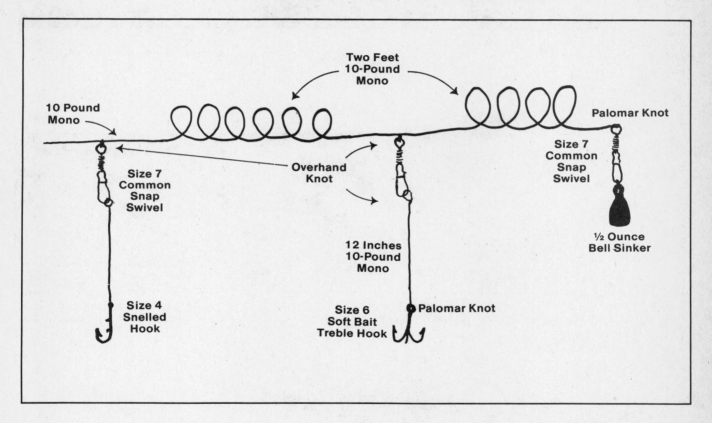

10 Pound Mono

Two Feet 10-Pound Mono

Palomar Knot

Size 7 Common Snap Swivel

Size 7 Common Snap Swivel

Overhand Knot

½ Ounce Bell Sinker

12 Inches 10-Pound Mono

Size 4 Snelled Hook

Size 6 Soft Bait Treble Hook

Palomar Knot

downstream. I lost more drag. Carefully I lifted the rod and then eased it forward while reeling. The line moved toward the middle of the river, bending my stout rod. Then abruptly, the line headed toward the bank again.

I moved slowly downriver about 10 feet, all the time reeling in line. I was concerned the cat, which I knew had to be two to three pounds, was heading for rocks or other submerged structure to try to break the line. I raised the rod again and took in more line. For several minutes the catfish made the run, back and forth from the center of the river to the bank. I wasn't in a hurry or concerned about losing the fish — they have extremely tough skin and mouth structure. Once hooked, they don't often get away. I was more concerned with the line being scraped and broken.

I finally reeled the cat into shallow water and pulled it

ashore. The size 4 hook was barely in its lip, the liver still attached. At 20 inches and 3¼ pounds, the Channel catfish was the talk of several "Expert" hangouts in Moab — places where *I* go now.

If you're going to fish the Colorado River, be prepared for several things. One, you'll be fishing for catfish — not the prettiest gamefish, but it sure is good eating. Two, the scenery is magnificent. Three, some of the most fun I had in my quest to fish the Colorado was receiving advice from the locals. Do the same; you'll meet some great people.

Most of all, remember catfishing can be terrific. They don't just wait to be hauled in, at least not the ones I caught, you don't need a boat or a long-distance drive, and you can catch a respectable catfish in full daylight.

Oh yes, lawn chairs are optional.

HOW TO SKIN AND FILLET CATFISH

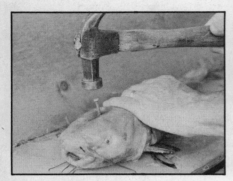

Excedrin headache #1, catfish style, gets the skinning procedure started.

Takes a sharp knife to cut leathery skin just behind fish's gill plate.

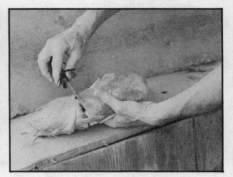

Cut continues over backbone and to pectoral fin on other side of fish.

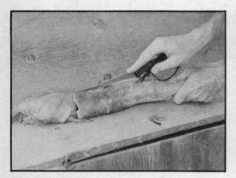

Slit skin along side of spine from head to tail, as author demonstrates.

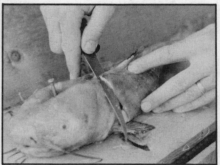

Gently saw the sharp knife blade under skin at juncture of two cuts.

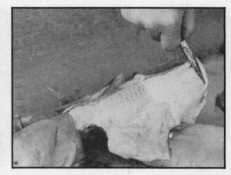

Using needlenose pliers, pull skin in continuous motion from head to tail.

Catching and landing catfish can be exciting, but then comes the real pleasure: the eating. Catfish, although often belittled for their looks and lack of glamour as a gamefish, are, without dispute, one of the tastiest of all fish.

To preserve the flavor, fish should be cleaned of entrails as soon as possible. Once done, you're ready for the next step in preparing catfish for the dinner table: skinning and filleting.

The tools you'll need are: a sharp fillet knife, pliers, paper or cloth towels, and a hammer and nail. A pair of Kevlar gloves like those made by DuPont also will prove, ahem, handy. They will not only protect your hands from sharp bones or a slip of the knife, but also give you a sure grip on slippery catfish.

Start with a lengthwise cut on the underside of the fish from the vent to the tail. Also insure the throat connection has been cut. Once done, you should have an open fish from the throat to the tail.

Next, make cuts on both sides of the fish from just behind the pectoral fins to the top of its head. Be careful of the catfish's "horns," the sharp pectoral fins.

Since catfish are extremely tough to hold in place, a nail through its head will make your job a lot easier and safer. With the fish lying on a board, or if in the field a log or stump, drive a nail through its head. Don't drive the nail too far, since this makes removing it later a messy job.

With the fish firmly in place, cut the skin from the

Catfish skin is remarkably tough and it holds together during its removal.

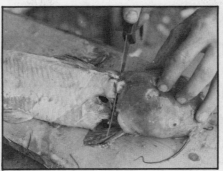

Off with his head! You may need an assist from a heavy hammer blow here.

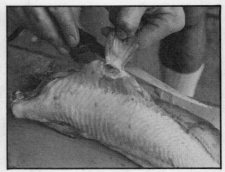

Pectoral fins get the slice next. If you need to resharpen blade, do so.

The fillet procedure begins the cut alongside backbone. Watch dorsal fin.

Slice the flesh away from rib bones by starting at tail as shown here.

A pair of toothsome fillets make up for cat's shortcomings as a gamefish.

top of its head along both sides of the dorsal fin to the tail. Using a knife, separate the flesh and skin at the cut behind the fish's head. Once you have about a half-inch of loose skin, grasp it with a pair of pliers (I prefer long-nosed type) and firmly pull the skin away from the flesh. Do not jerk; use a firm steady pull to prevent tearing the skin.

It also is helpful to pull the skin back, not up, so keep the pliers close to the fish and pull toward the tail. Steady the fish with your free hand.

Once the skin has been removed from both sides, cut the fish's head off. Care should be taken here. The backbone at the break point is extremely sharp and can cause injury. First, cut across the back of the head as far as you can, then push the knife down until spine snaps. For large cats, you may

have to use a larger knife and perhaps a hammer to sever the backbone.

Cut the tail off at the point where the flesh ends. Next, slice off the dorsal and pectoral fins. Now you're ready to fillet your catfish.

Start with a cut the full length of the backbone of the fish, insuring the cut is down to the bone. Then beginning at the tail, make a flat cut as close to the skeleton as possible, and, using a sawing cut, slice forward, keeping the filleting knife against the backbone while lifting the flesh away. Repeat filleting on the other side. Trim away any fatty flesh.

There you have it, two catfish fillets. Guess what's for dinner!?! — *Russ Thurman*

Author Jason Alley fights a leaping silver salmon, one of dozens caught during two fishable days. Variety of techniques worked — fast retrieve, slow retrieve, bounce on bottom, fish up high, etc.

CHAPTER 24

GO NORTH FOR SILVER FEVER

The Silver Salmon Are Energetic Acrobats In The Aleutian Island Chain of Alaska!

By Jason Alley

Photos By John Alley

MY ANTICIPATION was high as Benny Kerns, an expert Alaskan guide, maneuvered our Zodiac inflatable boat swiftly toward the river's inlet. "This is a hot spot," he snapped with confidence. "If you boys don't catch anything here, then something is definitely wrong." For the first time in two days there was sunshine, its rays chasing the foul weather which had been our constant enemy.

Kerns cut the 35 horsepower motor and drifted toward shore. Picking up the new Shimano rod, I sent a ⅞-ounce silver and pink Pixie lure sailing into the blue sky heading into the murky green waters of Alaska's Dog Salmon River.

I had just begun the Pixie's retrieve when a tug resembling a small strike halted the lure. My response was automatic, setting the hook with superior force. A sudden splashing frenzy erupted on the surface, the violent churning, boiling water taking me by surprise and the leaping antics of this powerful foe, reminiscent of a majestic jumping marlin, left me breathless.

A short time later, a beautiful 12-pound silver salmon was in my net. This is why I had journeyed into this rugged frontier. I had just caught my first case of "Silver Fever."

My interest in fishing the Alaskan waters for silver salmon was spurred by my dad, John Alley. Two years earlier he had hunted caribou in the vast wilderness of the Alaska Peninsula. Dad's world-record-class caribou not only left him with fond memories, but also an urge to fish the rivers teeming with silver salmon.

His hunting guide was Benny Kerns of Alaska Wilderness Outfitters. Kerns and partners Ron Taylor and Les Crane own and operate a first-rate, big-game hunting and fishing camp on the famed Alaska Peninsula in the heart of some of the finest moose, caribou and brown bear country known to man. Their camp on the Dog Salmon River lies about 90 miles southeast of the town of King Salmon in the middle of the Aleutian Island chain. It is located 25 miles from the Bering Sea and, oddly, 25 miles from the Pacific Ocean.

Our adventure began the first week of September with airline flights from Seattle to Anchorage to King Salmon. There we caught a chartered bush plane to the Dog Salmon River and the Wilderness Outfitters' camp, accessible only by air. There was steady rain during our flight, a prelude to the next nine days. Landing on the river, we taxied to a dock beside a makeshift landing strip and were greeted by Benny Kerns.

Our gear was loaded onto the Tundra Mover, a tracked vehicle resembling a small tank that maneuvers easily on

This 16-pound coho, bright as newly minted silver to show it was straight from the sea, was largest caught on salmon expedition. John Alley took fish on ultralight tackle!

What memories are made of — a hooky-snouted spawner that's already started to turn dark. While quality of the meat may have deteriorated, fighting ability sure didn't.

the rolling, soft tundra. At camp we met Les Crane, his wife, Bessie, and their dog, Bo. Home for our stay would be a 30- by 40-foot rustic cabin built in the 1950s. Considering the remoteness, the cabin was quite comfortable. It slept seven, had electric lights powered by a generator, a heating and cooking stove, and even a shower. New quarters are under construction.

The view from camp beat anything I'd ever seen. The Aleutian Island chain was formed by a huge circle of volcanoes that rim the entire Pacific Ocean. A mountain to the south is Old Smokey (Mount Chiginagak), with an elevation of 6,925 feet. Smoke still billows from the side of the mountain. Mountains gird a vast tundra basin, miles of flats that are dotted with small lakes. Nearly all are populated with Northern pike. We fished for pike, but really came seeking salmon.

There are several native villages here. Inhabitants of Pilot Point (population 67) and Ugashik (a bustling village of 10) live off the land, fish and hunting. Most also are commerical fishermen.

It's a vast, remote area that can be both beautiful and harsh. The weather can be miserable. For us, only three of our nine days were fishable. High winds and rain kept us indoors, and mudslides in the mountains made rivers unfishable. Tremendous wind storms gusted up to 90 mph. No one can guarantee the weather in the Aleutians. That's why most hunting and fishing trips are long ones — to allow for bad weather.

"We are close to the birthplace of the major storms that go down through Canada and into the lower 48 states," explained Benny Kerns. "We have the Pacific's warm air moving up one side of the Aleutian mountain range to meet colder air from the Arctic. Pacific storms generally are warmer, with temperatures in the fall hitting about 45 to 50

Design of Shimano's Aero Spinning reel on left contrasts markedly with traditional spinning reel. Lip shape and method of laying line on reel are secrets to long casts anglers needed on Alaska's wide Dog Salmon River.

Fish in the 10-pound range were an every-cast result, especially when using Pixie spoons in flourescent pink and orange with silver bodies.

degrees. Storms from the Northwest off the Bering Sea can be 10 degrees colder. As the season goes on, that gap widens. Sometimes in winter it's 40 degrees and then drops to 25 below zero. It's even been down to 30 to 40 below."

All that may tempt you to scratch the Aleutians from your list of places to fish, but despite the weather, the place is exciting. It's true wilderness, in itself a challenge. Besides, that's where you find silver salmon.

Coho salmon *(Oncorhynchus kisutch)* are commonly called silver salmon. They are found in the central and western areas of Alaska. The coho is the second-largest species of salmon behind the giant king salmon, and can weigh up to 36 pounds and measure 35 inches in length. However, the average full-sized adult will be about 10 pounds and roughly 28 to 30 inches long. Characteristics include small freckles on the back and upper tail lobe, silver body, and maroon sides when spawning. Males

develop a hooked snout with large teeth.

Coho enter spawning rivers from August through November, usually when the water is at its highest. Adults school in large pools, ponds or lakes for weeks, then move into shallow tributaries with clean gravel areas to spawn. An adult female may lay from 2,400 to 4,500 eggs from late September through January. When hatched, fry school in shallows along shorelines, then establish individual territories. Juveniles will grow rapidly during the early summer months, then winter in deeper pools. After two to three winters in fresh water, they migrate to sea in early spring as smolt.

While an adult king salmon is prized for its size, silvers are the spectacular fighters and most acrobatic of all Pacific salmon. Their antics when hooked have been compared to the bonito and bonefish. Silvers also are a table delicacy.

Silvers can be taken with salmon egg clusters, spoons,

Guide Benny Kerns prepares to gently release one of salmon taken during a pair of fishable days, with volcanic mountains as a snow-capped backdrop.

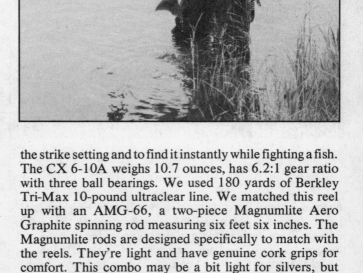

Because anglers planned to release most fish caught — the limit is five fish per day with five in possession — barbs were bent back on hooks. Thus, you had to keep the pressure on a hooked fish, right up to landing it on bank.

spinners and streamer flies. The Alaskan limit for silver salmon is five per day, with five in possession and no size limit.

The rain continued outside our cabin on the first morning, but we were busy unpacking and preparing tackle. We both had new 1990 Speed Master CX Aero Spinning systems from Shimano. The CX Aero reels have two friction-reducing features for long-distance casting: the AeroWrap and Aero Spool.

When fishing line comes off a normal spool, it flies in big, air-catching, distance-robbing loops. The AeroWrap and Aero Spool eliminate this.

The reels also have an all-new gearing system that eliminates uneven winding and line overlap. Instead of using a traditional circular gear to drive the spool, these CX Aero Reels have worm gears like those used in baitcasting reels. With the two-speed oscillating movement, the spool moves at a fast speed outward and at a slower speed inward. This causes line to wind onto the spool in a unique pattern — the line doesn't rub against the line next to it or cut into layers of line beneath. The spool's longer and shallower design also enables the line to glide over the spool's narrow lip, barely touching it, while flying off the spool in smaller, more tightly controlled loops, diminishing air resistance.

The reels are made of an exclusive compound developed by Shimano engineers that is as light as graphite and even more resistant to torque and stress. The reels have a fighting star drag system which is featured on the CX 6-10A, one of the reels we used. This enables the angler to lock in

the strike setting and to find it instantly while fighting a fish. The CX 6-10A weighs 10.7 ounces, has 6.2:1 gear ratio with three ball bearings. We used 180 yards of Berkley Tri-Max 10-pound ultraclear line. We matched this reel up with an AMG-66, a two-piece Magnumlite Aero Graphite spinning rod measuring six feet six inches. The Magnumlite rods are designed specifically to match with the reels. They're light and have genuine cork grips for comfort. This combo may be a bit light for silvers, but worked great on smaller streams, rivers and lakes for pike.

Our other outfit, a bit heavier, consisted of a CX 8-12A reel, weighing 10.3 ounces with the 6.2:1 gear ratio and three ball bearings. We used Berkley Tri-Max 14-pound ultraclear line on the reel. The rod, an AMG 70, is seven feet in length. Both combinations are excellent in handling and feel, and superb in casting ability.

The lure we used most was the Pixie Egg Spoon by Blue Fox Tackle Company of Cambridge, Minnesota. This is without question the most popular lure in Alaska for all types of salmon and trout; it has been labeled the Number One lure in Alaska. The Pixie utilizes a unique synthetic

Silver salmon are the most-acrobatic of all, guide told salmon anglers, and here proved his point. That's a happy Benny Kerns with throbbing rod.

Negotiating the slushy Alaskan tundra on foot is laborious at best, so the tank-like vehicles were especially welcome to anglers who fished small lakes for husky Northern pike.

egg sack insert, which provides color attraction and aids in visibility in the often-murky water. The Pixie ranges from ¼- to ⅞-ounce. We had the most success with the ⅞-ounce fluorescent pink, with bright orange a close runner-up. When the water was calmer, we used ½-ounce spoons in the same colors.

Other lures we used included ones made by the Triple Teazer Company out of Kent, Washington, which were excellent for pike and good on trout, and medium-sized silver Kastmaster lures from Acme Tackle Company. These, also, are proven performers.

While we prepared our gear, we also learned about the area and the coho from Benny Kerns. He's been guiding in Alaska for six years, and is an expert on the big game and fish of the area.

"Normally the silver salmon start running up these rivers the latter part of August, and they can run through the middle of October," he explained. "As they move up-river, they start changing color and in the texture of their meat, because they're getting ready to spawn. If you catch a bright silver-colored salmon, it's fresh from the ocean.

Once they start turning pink and gradually bright red, they're getting closer to their spawning dates. The closer to spawning, the less desirable their meat. But they're still catchable and give you a fight!"

Kerns also is a noted oarsman, a reputation gained guiding boats on the Dog Salmon River and other waterways throughout the Alaskan Peninsula. His partner, Les Crane, also is a registered Alaskan guide, a former Alaskan wildlife official, and a master gunsmith and craftsman. He's 73 and has been an Alaska resident for more than 20 years. He provides a wealth of information to those hunting and fishing the Alaskan territory. The third member of the group is bush pilot Ron Taylor. For eight years, Ron has been flying hunters and fishermen in and out of the Alaskan Peninsula.

The equipment used by the Alaskan Wilderness Outfitters includes two 15-foot, air-transportable Zodiac inflatable boats with 35 hp Johnson outboards. These are for fishing lakes and rivers. A 10-foot, aluminum flat-bottom boat with a 15 hp motor can be toted to remote lakes using one of three tracked tundra vehicles. While they travel only 5 mph, the vehicles are vital — it's extremely difficult to walk on the slushy tundra.

Late the first afternoon the rain subsided, but the river was unfishable — they wouldn't be able to see even our brightest lures. Fortunately, we were able to fish a couple of lakes for Northern pike, landing two three-pounders. We took the pike on Kastmaster lures, but they also hit spoons and plugs. Steel leader is essential when fishing for

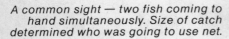

The half-ounce and ⅞-ounce Pixie spoons were heap big medicine for fast-running Dog Salmon River. With stiff wind blowing, long rods put heavy lures in big-fish range.

A common sight — two fish coming to hand simultaneously. Size of catch determined who was going to use net.

pike. Dad had one Kastmaster consumed by a Northern pike in the 20-pound range, only to have the fish snip the 14-pound line with its sharp teeth.

The Northern pike *(Esox lucius linnaeus)* has an elongated body and head, with a broad, flat snout shaped somewhat like a duck bill. The mouth is armed with sharp teeth that are constantly being replaced — especially after eating lures!

Bad weather continued to hound us for the first few days. We tried fishing the river, but it was just too muddy. The weather was getting everyone down.

The murky waters began to clear as the worst of the wind and rain subsided. We were ready! As we started down river in our Zodiac, the water was calm and smooth as glass. The day was filled with welcome blue skies with puffy white clouds, highlighting a spectacular view of the Aleutian mountain range.

Kerns guided the boat to where the Dog Salmon intersected a tributary, a spot known as Two Rivers. As he beached the Zodiac, silvers began jumping. My second cast was a hit and I landed the first of five fish in six casts — the action was intense! Kerns was getting his share of the silver action. When Dad quit snapping photos and got to

fishing, it was common for both of us to be hooked up simultaneously.

This was a time of quickly learning how to fish for silvers. While there are many different techniques, my system was based on some basics: cast to the middle, keep the line taut and retrieve with medium to fast cranks, dragging the lure along the bottom of the river.

Dad, however, prefers to keep the lure off the bottom. He begins the retrieve as soon as the lure hits the water. He pulls back on the rod, then winds in the line while moving the rod forward, pulls back, winds. This pulls the lure along, keeping it spinning. Kerns used a slow, steady wind. He lets the lure sit on the bottom and then uses a slow, steady wind to pull the lure in. This keeps the lure floating in the water fairly deep. We all caught fish, so experiment with these techniques, or perhaps others, to attract silvers.

Because the water wasn't clear, we used brightly colored lures the fish could see easily. Orange or fluorescent pink were our hottest colors. Silver seemed what the fish liked best as background. Lures in the ⅞-ounce class proved best. The larger lure was really needed because of the high winds and swift current. The heavier weight permitted us to cast farther, getting our lures to the middle of the river

When weather finally cleared enough to permit fishing, anglers headed to several lakes near comfortable base camp. Kastmasters and Triple Teazer lures were especially good on prehistoric-looking Northern pike.

where there was often a trench. With a little experimentation, I was able to keep the lure moving along the bottom.

Getting silvers to notice your lure is one thing, hooking them is another. While we did have some silvers snatch the lure and run with it, most of those I caught gave no more than a nibble. They were attacking the lure, but not the way a bonito attacks: wham and run. Silvers attack the lure because it irritates them. It's spawning time and they're not feeding, just annoyed by the lure. Many times they jumped the lure. In fact, I landed my biggest silver by hooking him in the dorsal fin. It took a long time to land him because I had to reel him in sideways. I released — its unlawful to keep foul-hooked fish.

I also experimented a lot with the best drag to use and how to land a fighting silver. One of the nice features of our Shimano reels was the drag system. Once set, it was easy to increase or decrease without losing concentration on fighting the fish. And do silvers fight! I'd cast, keeping my Pixie moving along the bottom. Bump. I'd jerk, set the hook and the fish would be off and running. They're real jumpers, leaving the water time after time. What energy! They also roll during the fight, often wrapping so much line around themselves that they close off their mouth and gill plates.

Often I'd tighten the drag to slow a running silver, then I'd battle to regain the line I'd lost. I'd pull up and then wind down, then pull up, wind down, and then he'd be off again and I'd lose line even against the tighter drag. I'd start all over again — pull up, wind down, pull up, wind down. It was exhilarating!

I also hooked into fish we called sleepers. They'd make you feel you were hooked on the bottom. I'd be dragging along the rocks and I'd get a small bump and I'd jerk, wind down and the line would get taut, but wouldn't move away so I'd think I was hung up on weeds. I'd start winding in my line, which felt like I was dragging a big batch of weeds. Oftentimes I had 10 feet of line left when, boom! The silver would explode into a fight!

While we enjoyed eating salmon during our stay and brought some back home, most of the silvers we caught were released. We bent the barbs back on our hooks so they could be easily removed from the fish's mouth. This, of course, added to the challenge of landing a fighting silver. The line had to be kept taut and the retrieve had to be as steady as possible. We also tried not to handle the fish much before releasing them, in order to reduce the trauma. We also released the fish gently, rather than just tossing them back into the river. We held the fish upright and with a free hand forced water through their gills in order to increase the amount of oxygen the fish was receiving. Within a short time the fish was swimming away.

One of the most unusual catches of the trip belonged to my Dad. It happened the day he'd spent taking pictures while Kerns and I were landing silvers. When he couldn't keep away from fishing any longer, he grabbed, much to our surprise, an ultralight rod with a Shimano GT 1200 reel loaded with eight-pound-test line. He fixed a ¼-ounce Pixie lure to the line and started casting. We, of course, couldn't help but make fun of his lightweight gear. "You'll see, you'll see," was all he said. We continued our fishing until we heard him shout, "Hook-up! Hook-up!" He then reeled in a two-pound juvenile coho. We kidded him no end.

He tried to ignore it, casting once again. This time it looked like he'd snagged some brush, but then the brush, or something, began to move. Suddenly, Dad's small reel began to empty at a vigorous rate. He clamped down on the fighting drag carefully, knowing he had only eight-pound test to work with. Then, there was a large dorsal fin slicing through the water with ease, ripping out 100 yards of line.

"The closest I could figure was I had no more than 20 yards left on the spool," Dad later recalled. "I tried desperately to gain what I had lost, but when I would gain 20 feet of line, I'd lose 25. I cringed at every leap and splash my adversary would make."

The tug-o-war went on for 20 minutes as Dad moved up and down the shoreline, holding the horseshoe-bent rod high over his head. He finally maneuvered the fish closer to my position and I netted the fighting silver. Even then the fish wasn't through. With one final burst of energy, he nearly ripped the net out of my hands.

He was a beautiful fish, his bright silver color shining like diamonds in the sunlight. He'd not been out of the saltwater long. At 30 inches and 16 pounds, he was the largest fish of our entire trip, ironically caught on the lightest line and smallest lure. Of course, after all the ribbing we'd given Dad earlier, he now spent a good deal of time talking about this fine catch. We didn't have much to say in return!

One of the treats we had during our stay was the fine meals prepared by Bessie, the camp cook. She was kind enough to share her special recipe for salmon.

She starts by frying round pieces of salmon in butter on one side until dark brown. Then she flips them over and adds her special sauce of melted butter, brown sugar and teriyaki marinade sauce. She continues frying until the salmon are done. They taste outstanding.

Another recipe from Kerns also was tasty. He starts by chopping the salmon fillet into chunks about two inches square. He prepares a bag of brown sugar and Bisquick, coating the chunks well and then frying them in butter. Once they are brown on both sides, he pours the remains of the bag onto the chunks to form a glaze. Delicious!

In planning your trip to Alaska, here are some tips to make your stay easier. Once of the most important pieces of gear to take is hip boots or waders. They are essential for both hunting and fishing in Alaska, since you can get soaked walking across the tundra. Rain gear is vital, too. You don't go outside in the wilderness without rain gear.

While weather may have given anglers heartburn — hence the bottle of Tums on the filleting board — the recipes for salmon from Bessie and Benny Kerns didn't. See text.

Warm clothing includes turtlenecks and, of course, long-sleeve shirts. Polypropylene and wool are the most desirable fabrics for warmth and comfort. Insect repellent is needed to ward off the hordes of biters.

The cost for a non-resident fishing license is $20 for a 14-day permit, which is the one most often used since short fishing trips aren't really taken in Alaska.

Each fisherman should have two rods and reels because of the unpredictability of what can happen in the rugged wilderness. We lost parts to one reel and broke one rod. Also, bring plenty of film for your camera. For picture-taking buffs, Dad recommends a 28 to 35mm wide-angle lens for fishing photos.

The fish boxes we used in camp were provided by the Alaska Wilderness Outfitters (Alaskan Wilderness Outfitters, Attn: Benny Kerns, P.O. Box 295, Homer, Alaska, 99603). They were quite handy in transporting the 10 salmon we brought back to the Lower 48. The limit you can take home is five fish per person.

For those fishing in Alaska, it's important to remember airlines generally won't take fish boxes if they weigh over 70 pounds, unless they're counted as excess baggage. Depending on the airline, there may be a $35 extra charge for the fish box.

Due to the extensive amount of air travel one goes through in flying to and from Alaska, and in our case the Alaskan Peninsula, the Anchorage airport offers overnight cold storage for fish boxes. The fee of $6 is really a good deal for Alaska fishermen.

After nine great days, our plane lifted Dad and I off the Dog Salmon River for our trip home. It was raining, but it didn't put a damper on my thoughts. Yes, the weather had been tough; yes, it had been a challenge; but I loved it. I shall never forget any of it, especially our fishing frenzy that took place that fateful day in September, nor the friendship received from Kerns, Les and Bessie. It certainly was a once in a lifetime experience, resulting in a severe case of Silver Fever I'll always remember!